WALKING IN MALLORCA

June Parker

Walking enthusiast and lover of the challenge and spirit of all wild places. (1927–1998)

In the early 1980s June Parker, together with her second husband, Alan, made the first of her many visits to Mallorca. An experienced mountaineer and hillwalker in Britain and Europe, she was entranced by the island's rugged beauty, but bemoaned the lack of a comprehensive walking book.

Challenged by her friends to write one, by 1986 June had produced her classic guide. With Alan's unstinting support, she had succeeded by virtue of a typical combination of self-belief, dedication and dogged determination to overcome all obstacles. Her egalitarian philosophy underpinned her belief that the world's wild, remote and beautiful areas should be open to all.

Clive Griffiths and Jane Ridings

Paddy Dillon

Paddy Dillon is a prolific outdoor writer with over 30 books to his name, more than a dozen booklets and brochures, and he also writes for a number of outdoor magazines and other publications.

Paddy lives on the fringe of the English Lake District and has walked, and written about walking, in every county in England, Scotland, Ireland and Wales. He has walked in many parts of Europe, as well as Nepal, Tibet, Africa and North America.

For this new edition of the guide Paddy walked all of June Parker's routes, amending them and the accompanying maps as necessary where conditions had changed over time.

He has continued to collect information keep this guidebook up-to-date, as well as writing a guidebook to the GR221 trail through the mountains of Mallorca for Cicerone.

WALKING IN MALLORCA

by

June Parker

(Updated by Paddy Dillon)

2 POLICE SQUARE, MILNTHORPE, CUMBRIA LA7 7PY
www.cicerone.co.uk

© Alan Parker (updated by Paddy Dillon)
Fourth edition 2006
ISBN-10: 1 85284 488 4
ISBN-13: 978 1 85284 488 2
Reprinted 2010 (with updates)
First edition 1986, second edition 1991, third edition 1997

Printed by KHL Printing, Singapore

A catalogue record for this book is available from the British Library.
All photographs are by Paddy Dillon unless otherwise stated.

Acknowledgements (1st–3rd editions)

June and Alan Parker would like to thank all the friends who have helped in trying out new walk descriptions or in making suggestions about itineraries. We would specially like to thank Mary Clarke and the late George Clarke, Stan and Jan Crawford, Jim and Ann Fielding, Brenda and Joe Lockey, Juan Noguera, Charles Rhodes and group, David and Lily Rowe, Ernie Shepherd and friends, Stan and Margaret Thompson and Menna and George Vincent. Thanks too to all the walkers, too numerous to mention individually, who have written with comments on the book and the walks. We would like also to thank Ronald Bagshaw, Jim and Sue Bannister, Ken and Chris Bricknell, Derek Fieldhouse, Graham Hearl, David Ormerod, Oliver St John and Richard Strutt. Special thanks to Geoff Haworth for introducing us to Morey, and to Tim Pickles for his walk on the Dragonera Island skyline.

Advice to Readers

Readers are advised that, while every effort is made by our authors to ensure the accuracy of guidebooks as they go to print, changes can occur during the lifetime of an edition. Please check Updates on this book's page on the Cicerone website (**www.cicerone.co.uk**) before planning your trip. We would also advise that you check information about such things as transport, accommodation and shops locally. Even rights of way can be altered over time. We are always grateful for information about any discrepancies between a guidebook and the facts on the ground, sent by email to info@cicerone.co.uk or by post to Cicerone, 2 Police Square, Milnthorpe LA7 7PY, United Kingdom.

Front cover: Above the Cúber reservoir from Puig de sa Font near Morro d'Almallutx (Walk 8b) (photo: Alan Parker)

CONTENTS

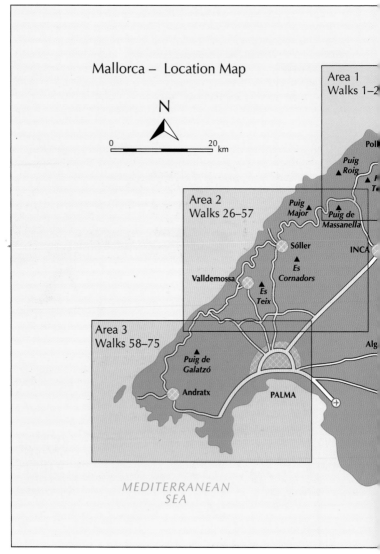

Mallorca – Location Map

N

0   20 km

Area 1
Walks 1–2

Poll

Puig
▲ Roig

▲ H
Te

Area 2
Walks 26–57

Puig ▲
Major   ▲
   Puig de
   Massanella

● Sóller

▲
Es
Cornadors

INCA

Valldemossa ●

▲
Es
Teix

Area 3
Walks 58–75

▲
Puig de
Galatzó

● Andratx

Alg

PALMA

⊕

MEDITERRANEAN
SEA

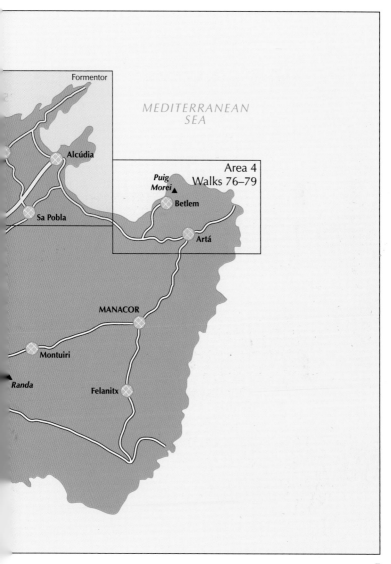

Formentor

MEDITERRANEAN
SEA

Alcúdia

Area 4
Walks 76–79

Puig
Morei ▲

Betlem

Sa Pobla

Artá

MANACOR

Montuiri

Randa

Felanitx

Map Key

═══ Ma-10 ═══	major roads
══════════	minor roads
──────────	walking route (various colours)
··············	alternative route (various colours)
Ⓢ	start point (various colours)
····················	track (not used on walks)
─ ─ ─ ─ ─	seasonal river
■	habitation
▲	summits
◦	*font* or water tank
ᴾ	large car park
●	lighthouse or tower
▨▨▨	town
▬	sea or reservoir
㉕	walk number
⟶	direction of route
⟶	direction arrow

Contour colour key

	500–600m		1200–1300m
	400–500m		1100–1200m
	300–400m		1000–1100m
	200–300m		900–1000m
	100–200m		800–900m
	0–100m		700–800m
	sea level		600–700m

LIST OF SKETCH MAPS

ROUTES LIST

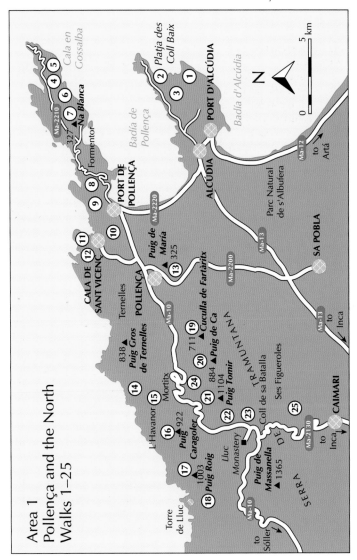

Area 1
Pollença and the North
Walks 1–25

Area 2 The Central Mountains

A horse enjoys a rest below the rugged peaks near the Coll de l'Ofre (Walk 33)

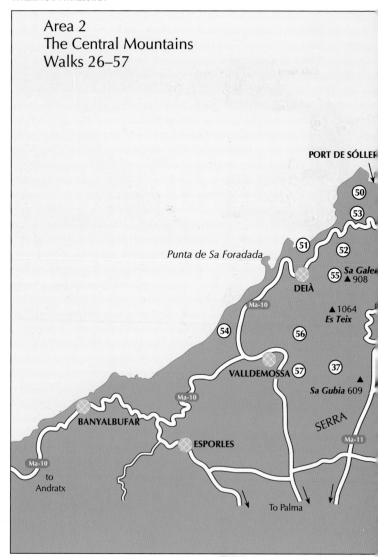

Area 2
The Central Mountains
Walks 26–57

PORT DE SÓLLER

50

53

Punta de Sa Foradada

51

52

55 *Sa Galer*
▲ 908

DEIÀ

Ma-10

▲ 1064
Es Teix

54

56

VALLDEMOSSA 57

37

Sa Gubia 609

BANYALBUFAR

SERRA

Ma-10

Ma-11

ESPORLES

Ma-10

to
Andratx

To Palma

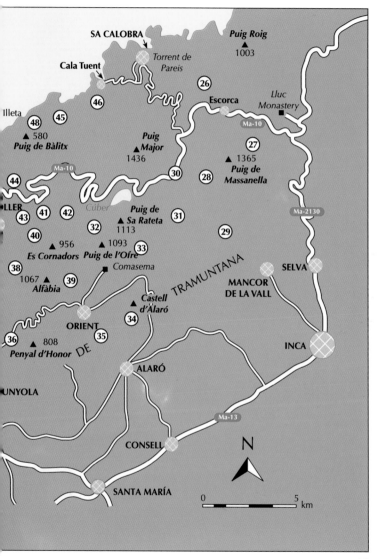

Area 3 Andratx and the South

The southern half of Sa Dragonera as seen from a mirador near Sant Elm (Walk 70b)

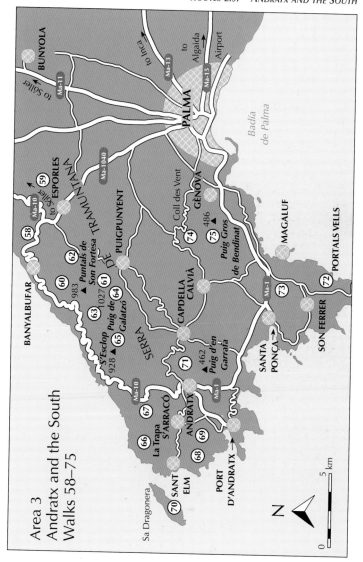

Area 3
Andratx and the South
Walks 58–75

Area 4 Serra de Llevant and Randa

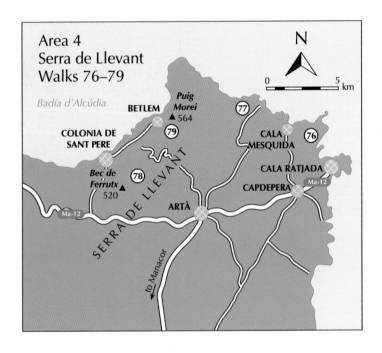

Mountains and Tops over 1000m

Mountains	Tops	Height	Comments
1 Puig Major	Puig Major	1436m	Inside military zone; no access.
	Penya de Migdia	1398m	Outside military zone.
	West top of Migdia	1356m	
	Puig de ses Vinyes	1108m	Overlooking Gorg Blau reservoir.
	Serra de Torrelles	1079m	Above the C-710 / Ma-10 road tunnel.
2 Puig de Massanella	Puig de Massanella	1365m	An enormous massif of long ridges
	Twin tops to South	1348m	separated by valleys leading up to the
	Unnamed top to West	1259m	high gaps of Coll des Prat and
	Sa Trona	1061m	Coll de sa Línia.
	Puig de ses Bassetes	1212m	
	Puig d'en Galileu	1182m	
	Sa Mola	1169m	
	Es Frontó (E)	1063m	
	Es Frontó (W)	1006m	
3 Tossals Verds	Puig de Tossals Verds	1118m	South of the Gorg Blau and east of the
	South top	1099m	Cúber reservoirs.
	Puig de sa Font	1071m	
	West top	1028m	
	Morro d'Almallutx	1064m	
4 Puig Tomir	Puig Tomir	1104m	At the head of the Pollença valley.
	Southwest top	1083m	
5 Puig de l'Ofre	Puig de l'Ofre	1093m	
6 Puig de Sa Rateta	Puig de Sa Rateta	1113m	On the same ridge as Puig de l'Ofre
	Na Franquesa	1067m	
7 Alfàbia	Alfàbia	1067m	In the middle of the long ridge.
	Palou	1053m	Northeast of Alfàbia.
	'Antennae' top	1025m	The one with the antennae.
	Sementer Gran	1013m	At the north end of the ridge.
	S'Aritja	1005m	Southwest of Alfàbia.
	Puig des Coll des Jou	1052m	Off-set from the ridge.
8 Es Teix	Es Teix	1064m	Between Valldemossa and Deià. No
	Teixoch	1065m	access from Coll de Sóller.
	Puig des Vent	1005m	
9 Puig de n'Ali	Puig de n'Ali	1038m	East of Coll de sa Línia.
10 Puig de Galatzó	Puig de Galatzó	1027m	Highest peak in southwest Mallorca
11 Puig Roig	Puig Roig	1003m	Most northerly peak in Mallorca.
12 Es Cornadors	Es Cornadors	1009m	Demoted to 956m on latest maps.

*The heights are taken from the latest MTN25 series. The criteria for separate mountain status (the 12 mountains listed in **bold** on the left) are a separation of 1km or more, and a re-ascent of 100m or more.*

Looking along the crest and across the gap from El Fumat to Roca Blanca (Walk 4)

PREFACE TO THE FOURTH EDITION

Walking in Mallorca quickly established itself as a classic guidebook, serving walkers well for 20 years as they explored the rich and varied landscapes of Mallorca. Things have changed in that time, and access has been lost on some of the original routes. Updated editions took account of changes, but eventually the time came for a complete overhaul of the guidebook.

This fourth edition is presented to walkers in full colour, with plenty of wonderful pictures, all the routes walked and checked again, and all the maps redrawn. The book remains essentially that of the late June Parker, with the original text altered to take account of changes in the landscape, or clarified where necessary to assist walkers with route finding. Since June first described her routes, some have been signposted and are well trodden, while others remain quiet and less frequented. Some tracks have become roads, and some new paths have been opened. Where routes have been lost, this is regrettable, but in many instances it has been possible to find alternatives.

While updating this edition it has been my pleasure to walk in June's footsteps and to be guided by her writing and maps. I am indebted to the late Alan Parker, June's husband, for making available a wealth of maps and background reading, much of it annotated in June's own hand. Those wriggling pencil lines and scribbled notes in the margins gave an insight into the painstaking creation of the guidebook, as well as offering further guidance to my own footsteps.

I also gratefully acknowledge the help and assistance given to me by Jaume Tort, whose knowledge and enthusiasm for walking in Mallorca is second to none. Jaume provided much helpful information of the sort that only a local mountain guide could supply, enabling me to circumvent access problems and bring new walking trails to the attention of readers. Some of Jaume's pictures grace the pages of this edition and he checked that my use of Mallorquí place names and additional language notes were sound.

Paddy Dillon, 2006

Walkers cross over the first 'window' on the ridge of the Serra de Cavall Bernat (Walk 9) (photo: Jaume Tort)

INTRODUCTION

GENERAL BACKGROUND

The Balearic Islands, or Illes Balears, lie in the Mediterranean, between Barcelona on the coast of mainland Spain and Algiers on the North African coast. This favoured position is responsible for the sunny, temperate climate attractive to both sun-lovers and walkers, and it is worth pointing out right from the start that temperatures in July and August, which may be ideal for sunbathing, are far too hot for any serious walking by most people. These months are best avoided, and the recommended 'season' for walkers is from the beginning of September to the end of May.

Mallorca is the largest of the islands and has long been well known as a paradise for sun-worshippers. That it is also a paradise for discerning walkers has now been discovered by those who enjoy the attractive and varied scenery, the equable climate, and opportunities for walking in quiet places where other people rarely go. Add to this the extensive Mediterranean flora, the spring migration of birds and the potential for photography, and it is hard to understand why Mallorca was neglected as a walking area for so long. That this is no longer the case is witnessed by the increasing number of walkers on popular routes. However, it is still possible to walk in quiet areas, especially in winter.

The main mountain chain in Mallorca is the Serra de Tramuntana, which lies along the northern coast and reaches heights of over 1000m in many places, culminating in Puig Major

at 1436m. The Serra de Llevant in the east, although only topping the 500m contour, also offers walks of surprising length and quality, having the same sort of high mountain characteristics as the Serra de Tramuntana. Many of the mountain tops are almost bare of vegetation and the hard, rough limestone gives excellent walking and scrambling, with loose rock being extremely rare. There is a varied flora, including dense evergreen forests, maquis and garriga in the arid zones, sub-alpine flora on the approach to the peaks, and an enormous number of beautiful flowering shrubs that give an extra dimension to many walks.

The small size of the island means that almost every walk is enhanced by views of the coastline and the sea. The sea varies in colour from the palest greens and blues to incredible dark ultramarine and purple, often with small bays of white sand between steep cliffs that plunge dramatically into the water. In fact the coastal walks vie in attraction with the inland mountains, and although they may not reach any great height, often go through very wild and uninhabited country.

Many of the walks in this guidebook go through pathless and rough areas where some experience of route finding is needed. Some make use of excellent tracks and paths that are very easy to follow, most of which are a legacy of the past, having been made by those who worked in the now defunct rural industries of snow collecting and charcoal manufacture. Some of these paths are

Package tours include accommodation at one of the resorts, such as Magaluf

neglected, overgrown and difficult to find, but some have been repaired and waymarked.

Maps are not entirely reliable in the matter of footpaths, and while some routes have been signposted and maintained by the Department de Natura i Medi Ambient and local councils, many are marked only by small cairns or paint marks. Care is required if using maps to plan your own walks – steep cliffs or very complex ground can be encountered and maps give little or no indication of this.

SCOPE OF THIS GUIDE

This book is written for the experienced mountain walker who is used to walking in mountains like the British ones in all seasons. It is not comprehensive, but provides a selection of walks of all degrees of difficulty, and should enable those limited to a short holiday to make the best use of their time.

Circular walks have been described whenever possible, but sometimes it is necessary to return the same way to the starting point.

Most of the walks depend on the use of a hired car, but Mallorca does have an excellent public transport system too. Some walks can be done directly from Cala de Sant Vicenç, Pollença, Port de Pollença, Sóller, Port de Sóller, Valldemossa, Esporles, Banyalbufar, Andratx and even Palma.

ACCOMMODATION AND TRAVEL

Although the development of the tourist industry in recent years has led to the spread of large concrete jungles, these are in the main confined to the coast around the bay of Palma, from Peguera to S'Arenal. There is no need to stay in this area, as there is plenty of accommodation throughout Mallorca in places that remain comparatively unspoilt.

The resorts that are the best centres for walking are described later (see Choice of Base). There are certain advantages to staying in Palma, the capital, including an excellent network of roads in every direction, and an equally excellent public transport system, provided you are based near the centre.

One advantage of the tourist development of the island is that a number of tour operators offer package holidays throughout the year, with the effect of keeping prices down to a reasonable level. By far the cheapest way to get there is to take advantage of any special offers that include the use of a car at a reduced rate. These offers may only apply to the winter, but then that is the best time to go for a walking holiday.

It is of course possible to book a 'flight only' deal and find your own accommodation independently. On the whole it works out more expensive to book into a hotel this way, but less expensive to take an apartment. There are an enormous number of apartment blocks, and some smaller ones often belonging to small bars and restaurants. It is easier to arrange this sort of holiday on a second visit when you know your way around, and also if you can speak the language.

English is always spoken in larger hotels, but by no means always in smaller places where cheaper

Palma is the major city on Mallorca and the most important public transport hub

accommodation is more likely to be found. Remember that many hotels close in winter, although those that do open are rarely full. The exception to this is Christmas, New Year and Easter, when booking ahead is always advisable.

Those who are able to take advantage of a long-stay winter holiday can obtain extremely good rates for stays of up to four months. The best of these offers are usually from November to March, if you can get away for that length of time. There is a regular ferry service from Barcelona to Palma, which may be worth considering for a long winter stay, but the costs of two ferries plus overnight stays on route make this quite an expensive option.

There is no useful campsite on Mallorca, though there is a basic site in the mountains at Lluc. Those wishing to camp or bivvy in the mountains should ask permission at the nearest farm. In many areas there is a prohibition against lighting fires because of the risk of dry vegetation catching fire. Many walks can be done easily from a base in a small town or village, and longer two- or three-day backpacking walks can easily be devised.

A popular annual event is organised by walking clubs on the island, in which a large number of walkers set out on a three-day walk through the Serra de Tramuntana. The route is different each year, but always very tough, and only a small number complete the whole course.

Note For more information on accommodation and travel, see Appendix 2, which is an alphabetical reference section giving details of accommodation, public transport, car hire, and so on.

CHOICE OF BASE

The best resorts for walkers are Cala de Sant Vicenç and Port de Pollença in the northeast, Sóller and Port de Sóller on the north coast, and Port d'Andratx in the southwest. Newly established refuges are also becoming popular with walkers.

Cala de Sant Vicenç is a small, quiet resort with sandy beaches, and a spectacular view of the steep cliffs of the Serra del Cavall Bernat across the sparkling green-blue sea. It is surrounded by pine woods and good for quiet walks, orchids and birdwatching.

Several walks start from here, and it is no great distance to drive to the starting points for other walks. There is a bus service, although this is very limited in winter.

The Oriola is a quiet, family-run hotel on the edge of the village, offering a home-cooked set meal in the evening and an attractive lounge with a library of English books. Juan Noguera is very knowledgable about walking, wild orchids and birdwatching and speaks excellent English. Open March to end of October, ☎ 971–531998.

Port de Pollença lies on the coast in a sheltered position. It has a narrow strip of sand, a large marina, and much development has taken place here in recent years, so those who remember it as a small fishing village will doubtless be horrified by all the changes. However, it has not been ruined in the same way that some of the resorts on the south and east coasts have, and it remains an attractive place to stay.

Cala de Sant Vicenç is a pleasant little resort in the northeast of Mallorca

Nothing can spoil the splendid backdrop of the Serra del Cavall Bernat and the quiet bay with its shallow water and sandy beaches.

There are numerous hotels and apartments, a better bus service than Cala de Sant Vicenç, and plenty of shops and supermarkets, so it is a good choice if there are children or non-walkers in your party. We recommend the Hotel Daina, ☎ 971–866250, and friends speak highly of the Flora Aparthotel, ☎ 971–866176.

Sóller lies on the north side of the island between the mountains and the sea. It is an excellent centre for walks and has good public transport, with the train to Palma, a tram to the port, buses to Deià and Valldemossa, and the summer bus service that runs over the mountains to Pollença.

There is a good old-established hotel near the station, the Hotel el Guia, which can be personally recommended, and is open from April to October, ☎ 971–630227.

Port de Sóller has many more hotels and apartments clustered round the attractive circular harbour. It is linked to Sóller with frequent tram and bus services and is a good place for the independent walker. Not many tour operators seem to offer holidays here, especially in the winter.

The Hotel Es Port, ☎ 971–631650, makes an excellent base and is open Feb–Nov. Los Geranios, ☎ 971–631440, is open all year. There are also numerous apartments around the port.

Banyalbufar is a small village about halfway between Sóller and Andratx. It

Puig Major, seen here under snow cover, is the highest peak in Mallorca at 1436m (photo: Jaume Tort)

is set on a steep, terraced slope between mountains and sea and is a good centre for walking in the southern Serra de Tramuntana.

The Hotel Mar i Vent is family run, with excellent cooking, and can be personally recommended. It is open all year except for December and January, ☎ 971–618000. Two others open in summer are the Hostal Baronia and the Hotel Sa Coma.

Port d'Andratx at the extreme west of the Serra de Tramuntana is another picturesque harbour with a marina. It is a good place for walking and there are a number of modest hotels here – the Hotel Brismar on the seafront can be personally recommended, ☎ 971–671600.

Like Pollença in the north, Andratx has been saved from development by its distance from the sea. It is a charming old town, dating from the 13th century, with a weekly market on Wednesdays.

CLIMATE AND WEATHER

The climate of Mallorca is typically Mediterranean – winters are mild, summers are hot and dry and there is plenty of sunshine all year round. The relative humidity is near constant throughout the year at around 70%, and this, together with sea breezes, makes even the hottest summer day pleasant and enjoyable, provided you are not walking uphill. There are almost 300 sunny days during the year, and even in the winter months there is an average of five hours of sunshine each day.

When rain falls, it often does so in sharp, heavy showers that soon

29

clear up, except for occasional days of torrential rain that occur in the late autumn and early spring. There can be different weather conditions in different parts of the island. Naturally the rainfall is greatest over the high mountains, varying from 1000mm per year near Puig Major to less than 400mm on the south coast. On bad days it is usually possible to find a sunny or sheltered place to walk by avoiding the high tops.

Recent bad storms include November 2001 and January 2003, when trees were toppled and some remain lodged across paths. A small tornado felled woods and snapped trees in half around Valldemossa in September 2004.

Snow is quite common on the mountain tops – so common in fact that it was formerly collected during the winter months to make ice for use in the summer. At sea level it is very rare, and there was great excitement when several inches fell in January 1985 – local people said it was the first time this had happened since 1956. The snowfall in the mountains was tremendous and much damage was done to trees, with many roads blocked for days by snow and fallen trees.

When the roads were cleared, people from Palma drove up to the mountains to make snowballs and load snow onto the tops of their cars. Snow fell across the whole island, even around Palma and on the beaches, in January 2005.

The central plain, protected by the Serra de Tramuntana to the north, enjoys an almost sub-tropical climate. In winter the average temperature here is 10°C, whereas it is 6°C on the northern coast.

The following table gives a rough indication of what to expect, but remember that these are averages and apply to Palma. For example, in February 1990 there were 25 days of perfect 'summer' weather, and most days the lunchtime temperature was 18–21°C, then it shot up to 28°C and plummeted to 5°C two days later.

Temperature (°C) and number of rainy and sunny days per month

	Jan	Feb	Mar	Apr	May	Jun	Jul	Aug	Sep	Oct	Nov	Dec
Max. temperature	14	15	17	19	22	26	29	29	27	23	18	15
Min. temperature	6	6	8	10	13	17	19	20	18	14	10	8
Av. temperature	9	8	11	13	17	21	26	24	22	18	14	12
Rainy days	8	6	6	7	4	2	2	1	5	8	8	9
Sunny days	23	22	25	23	27	28	29	30	25	23	22	22

This section is necessarily very brief and the emphasis is on scenery. Those interested in geology should read one of the field guides listed in the Appendix 4, Further Reading.

BRIEF GEOLOGICAL HISTORY

The Illes Balears lie on a submarine sill extending northeastwards from Cap Nao on mainland Spain and are an extension of a chain of mountains known as the Baetic Cordillera. These mountains are part of the Western Mediterranean block, pushed up in a major mountain-building episode at the end of the Carboniferous period, the Hercynian orogeny. It is thought that a ripple fold in a northeast–southwest direction was then thrown up by pressure from the northern landmass, and that this fold underlies the main mountain chain of Mallorca, the Serra de Tramuntana.

Subsequent earth movements raised and lowered this block a number of times, with various land bridges uniting it temporarily with Europe and Africa. It is these land bridges that partly account for the variety of flora and fauna on the islands.

Major events in the Mesozoic period were the laying down of thick deposits of Triassic clays and marls, followed by Jurassic and Cretaceous limestones, when all southern Europe, the Mediterranean and North Africa was a synclinal basin under a sea known to geologists as the Tethys. Even during

The central plain, or Es Pla, is well cultivated, and covered in old windpumps (photo: Jaume Tort)

these times there were periods of uplift, when the high land in the north was above water, and during the Cretaceous period there was probably a land bridge with Catalonia.

In the Eocene period massive earth movements caused folding of vast areas of southern Europe and North Africa, and it was at this time that both Alpine and Himalayan folding and uplift occurred. In Mallorca the pressure against the Hercynian block was responsible for further folding on the same axis as the original ripple fold. This, and later folding and faulting along the same axis, gave rise to steep scarp slopes facing northwest with gentler slopes on the southeast side.

A series of lakes was formed at the foot of these slopes when surface water was trapped above impermeable Jurassic rocks – alluvial deposits dated at 50 million years, or late Eocene, are evidence of this.

A land bridge is believed to have existed in the lower Oligocene, then in the Miocene there was a further submergence, with deep-sea deposits being laid down over a wide area. At the end of the Miocene further elevation brought the mountain chain up to its present height. The islands did not achieve their present form until the Quaternary.

SURFACE FEATURES TODAY

Although large areas of the exposed rocks on Mallorca are limestones of various ages, and Triassic clays and marls, mention must be made of other rocks that will be observed from time to time when walking in the mountains.

There are a number of minor igneous intrusions of a dark doleritic rock, probably of Triassic age, seen for example in the Ternelles valley. In the northeast there are extensive areas of very coarse conglomerate in which rounded pebbles, boulders and angular fragments are well cemented together, giving a 'pudding-stone' appearance. This will be seen on Walk 11, Puig de l'Aguila. Here there is an outcrop of an attractive pink, white and black rock, not a true marble, but the result of pressure and percolating solutions acting on the limestone.

Outcrops of cross-bedded sandstones can also be seen, for example in the picnic area of the pine woods at Cala de Sant Vicenç.

There are three distinct areas of Mallorca that can be considered as structural–morphological units: these are the main mountain chain of the Serra de Tramuntana, the central plain, and the mountains of the east, the Serra de Llevant.

The Serra de Tramuntana

The Serra de Tramuntana is a chain of mountains some 80km long that lies in a northeast–southwest direction along the line of the original ripple fold, with 12 peaks and 36 tops over 1000m in height.

There are many ridges showing the same directional trend as the whole chain – the Serra del Cavall Bernat (Walk 9) is one of these. The steep northwest scarp slopes are a striking feature, particularly the coastal scarp that makes much of the shoreline inaccessible. This feature is well seen on the circuit of

Puig Roig (Walk 17). As pointed out at the end of General Background earlier in this introduction, these scarps are not always marked on maps and this should be borne in mind when planning independent walks.

Many of the rocks at the surface high up in the mountains are deep-sea calcareous, dating from the Miocene. These are hard, medium-grey rocks, often sculpted into fantastic pinnacles and with conspicuous 'flutings' caused by rainwater erosion. This phenomenon can be seen when driving along the Ma-10 from Pollença to Lluc, where it has developed on massive conglomerates.

There are many areas of typical 'karst', or limestone pavement, where percolating water has enlarged the joints of the rock into deep fissures called 'grikes'. The ridges between, known as 'clints', can be knife-sharp, and negotiating this sort of terrain calls for great care from walkers. By far the most badly dissected limestone we have ever seen is on Puig Gros de Ternelles between the summit and Coll de Tirapau – it is so bad that this walk is no longer recommended. Walk 16 and Walk 17 both traverse areas of impressive rock scenery near Lluc and are recommended.

There is one major watercourse on the island, the Torrent de Pareis (Walk 26), which has worn through great thicknesses of rock to expose earlier Jurassic strata of a very dense, hard limestone, sometimes dolomitic.

Simplified Geological History

Era	Epoch	Events	MYA
Quaternary	Holocene	Covers human settlement over the past 10,000 years.	
	Pleistocene	Mallorca separated from Menorca. Ibiza separated from Formentera. Period of last ice ages. Fluctuating sea levels.	2
	Pliocene	Land bridge between Mallorca and Ibiza broken.	7
	Miocene	Elevation and uplift to present height.	
		Coral reefs established in shallow seas.	19
Tertiary	Oligocene	Partial submergence, but with land bridges.	38
	Eocene	Major folding and earth movements.	
	Palaeocene		63
Mesozoic	Cretaceous	Land bridge to Catalonia formed.	
		Deep-sea limestones deposited.	136
	Jurassic	Deep-sea limestones deposited.	190
	Triassic	Thick deposits of clays and marls.	225
Palaeozoic	Permian	Ripple folding in NE–SW direction.	280
	Carboniferous	Hercynian mountain-building period.	345
	Devonian	Earliest rock formations in Mallorca.	410

MYA = millions of years ago

The Central Plain

The central plain, or Es Pla, consists of Miocene and late Plio-Pleistocene deposits that are poorly exposed. Large areas are completely flat and covered with a layer of *terra rossa*, a red and very fertile soil consisting of the insoluble residue left behind after the solution of limestone by ground water. The red colour is due to the accumulation of iron oxides. When recently ploughed this earth is bright red and makes a striking contrast to the pale blossom of the almond trees or the dark green of the carobs.

Elsewhere there is an undulating relief, and along the southern border of the Serra de Tramuntana is a belt of low hills derived by erosion from the main range. Occasional inliers of folded Triassic and Jurassic rocks rise up prominently from the central plain, such as at Randa on Walk 80.

One of the best ways to view the central plain is by taking the SFM train from Palma to Sa Pobla.

The Serra de Llevant

The Serra de Llevant is a lower range of hills, only just exceeding 500m in height, running from the Artà peninsula towards Manacor and Felanitx. The folding here is considered to be more recent than that of the Serra de Tramuntana. Triassic and Jurassic strata are overlain by Cretaceous and the mid-grey Miocene limestones. There are extensive areas of karst, and some large Jurassic cave systems near the coast, including the Coves del Drac, des Hams and d'Artà, all open as show caves.

Peonies are among the many flowering species that delight visitors in spring (photo: Jaume Tort)

The pleasure of walking on Mallorca is greatly enhanced by the rich variety of plant and animal life. Wherever you go you cannot fail to notice the immense range of flowers and shrubs, and how different the vegetation is from that seen in Britain.

Ornithologists have been visiting the island for many years, mainly in spring and autumn to catch the migrants, but there is plenty all year round to interest the walker with a casual interest in birdwatching.

The information here is necessarily brief and the reader is referred to Appendix 4 for further reading.

FLORA

Four varieties of native trees are found in the woodlands of Mallorca: **pine**, **oak**, **olive** and **dwarf fan palm**. Others, such as **black poplar**, **London plane**, **ash**, **elm**, **hawthorn** and **blackthorn**, will be observed on the banks of streams.

A striking feature of the forests is how green they are in winter, not only because of the preponderance of evergreens, but because the autumn rains wash off the summer dust that gives a drab, grey appearance to the trees. Both the pines and the oaks are perfectly adapted to the long, hot and dry summers, the pines having leaves reduced to narrow, grooved cylinders, and the oaks having thick, leathery leaves with a waxy coating, so that both types of tree cut down on loss of moisture by transpiration.

The **Aleppo pine**, *Pinus halepensis*, grows from sea level up to 1000m and is abundant everywhere. It can be 20m high with a straight trunk, but is frequently bent and twisted in windy situations. It often grows in fairly open stands, but is sometimes found in mixed woodlands with evergreen oaks. Two other pines are seen, but not commonly – the **stone pine** or **umbrella pine**, *Pinus pinea*, recognisable by its umbrella shape, and *Pinus halepensis var. ceciliae*, recognised by its upwardly growing branches.

Of the five different evergreen oaks the most common is the **holm oak**, *Quercus ilex*. It has been much used in the past for making charcoal, but is still abundant. Other varieties are the **kermes oak**, **cork oak**, **Lusitanian oak** and *Quercus rotundifolia*. (Antony Bonner's *Plants of the Balearic Isles* gives full details of how to recognise and where to see them, see Appendix 4 for details.)

It is not known whether the **olive**, *Olea europea*, existed wild on the island before it was domesticated. The sub-species Oleaster does exist and it is believed that the cultivated olive was developed from this in Syria. Another sub-species, *var. sylvestris*, grows on the island.

The cultivated olive grows up to 10m in height and has distinctive silver-grey foliage. Olive trees are seen everywhere, on the central plain and on terraces cut into the mountain slopes, where they will be noticed on many of the walks. Some of the trees are very old,

1000 years or more, and their gnarled and twisted trunks are very striking.

The beautiful **carob tree** is very common. It has thick, shiny leaves, the new growth being lighter green than the old, so that it often has a two-tone appearance. The fruits are conspicuous, being large pods that are green at first but become brown on ripening and eventually almost black. They have a high sugar content and are used to feed cattle, although they also make an acceptable snack food for walkers.

The **dwarf fan palm**, *Chamaerops humilis*, is most distinctive, with its sharp, lance-like leaves arranged in fans. It occurs in only three localities in Mallorca, but is abundant in these areas, which are the northeast around Pollença and Alcúdia, the Artà peninsula, and the southwest near Andratx.

Although trees are few in variety, there is such a wealth of flowering shrubs that it is impossible to list them all here. Of the more outstanding ones that are to be seen on the walks in this book, the most common is the **lentisk** or **mastic tree**, *Pistacia lentiscus*, a dark, spreading, evergreen shrub that grows from 1–3m high and has a resinous smell. It grows in all situations, from sea level to high in the mountains, and is said to ward off thirst on hot days if a sprig is kept between the lips. The leaves have 3–6 pairs of dark green leaflets with blunt tips, and the flowers that occur in the leaf axils are either reddish or brown, followed by fruits that are first red and then black.

Very noticeable too are the beautiful deep-blue flowers of the **common rosemary**, *Rosmarinus officinalis*, a dense, aromatic shrub that seems to bloom somewhere all the year round. The deepest blue flowers have been noticed on Formentor and the Serra de Sant Vicenç, with swarms of bees humming around each plant.

In March and April yellow **brooms** burst into flower, making golden splashes of colour across the hillsides. First seen is *Genista lucida* in March, localised around Artà and the southwest, then the thorny broom, *Calicotome spinosa*, in April, easily recognised by its trifoliate leaves and long, sharp spines.

Hypericum balearicum, an endemic **St John's wort**, is another common shrub found on mountain slopes, in woodlands and by the roadside. The yellow flowers may be seen sporadically all year, but it is at its best in spring. The leaves are deep green, narrow and crinkled. There is another endemic St John's wort, *Hypericum cambessedesii*, which grows in the beds of mountain streams. It has the same flowers as balearicum, but the leaves are long and flat and of a beautiful pale, almost luminescent, green.

Asphodels are everywhere, growing along roadsides and on barren wasteland from the seaside to the mountain tops. The tall spikes of white flowers with a reddish-brown vein on each petal are very conspicuous. In spite of its name, *Asphodelus microcarpus*, it may grow to as much as 2m high. It is not eaten by animals and its presence is a sign of neglected and overgrazed ground. There is a smaller variety, *Asphodelus fistulosus*, which is less common. The flowers may be pink, but it is most easily identified by its leaves, which are round in cross-section, while those of *microcarpus* are V shaped.

The arbutus, or strawberry tree, produces round, red, sweet, edible fruit in winter

One of the most attractive groups of shrubs are **rock roses,** regularly found in oak woods as well as in more open spaces. Most common is *Cistus albidus*, or grey-leaved cistus, which has velvety leaves and large pink flowers with a crumpled appearance. It flowers from April to June and is very aromatic. *Cistus monspeliensis*, or narrow-leaved cistus, with smaller, white flowers, is also common and starts to flower in March. Less common is sage-leaved cistus, *Cistus salvifolius*, with large white flowers.

The **strawberry tree**, *Arbutus unedo*, is not in fact a tree, but a striking, tree-like shrub, with big shiny leaves, and fruits that turn orange and then deep red in October and November. The fruits, which are edible, soft and sweet, ripen at the same time as the white flowers of the following year's crop are in bloom.

Tree heather, *Erica arborea*, grows up to 3m high and is dense but feathery looking, with hundreds of tiny white or pale-pink flowers in terminal heads. *Erica multiflora* grows around 1m high and is pink.

Some of the **euphorbias** are very striking, especially the tree spurge, *Euphorbia dendroides*, which forms hemispherical bushes with bright-yellow glands surrounding the flowers. *Euphorbia characias* is smaller, but very attractive, with reddish-brown glands. Anthony Bonner (see Appendix 4, Further Reading) says there are about 20 different species in the Illes Balears, but only these two are easy to identify.

Walkers will notice two '**hedgehog**' or '**pincushion**' plants, with sharp spines that are an adaptation to wind as well as a protection against being eaten by grazing animals. These are *Teucrium subspinosum* and *Astralagus balearicus* and they are very difficult to tell apart when not in flower (in fact in Mallorquí they are both called *coixinets de monja* or 'nuns' sewing cushions').

Smilax aspera, or **European sarsaparilla**, is a climbing plant with hooked spines on the stems, growing up through shrubs and hedges to 1–2m high. The leaves vary enormously in size according to the conditions, being very large in cool, shady places and small and narrow in sunny ones. *Smilax balearica* is an endemic variety growing in the mountains. It has minimal leaves and is extremely prickly, and is a nuisance to walkers as it often fills crevices in otherwise bare limestone. Its

A few crocus minimus *appear to be rooted in bare limestone near Lluc Monastery (Walk 22)*

backward-curving thorns are notorious for lacerating flesh and clothes, and are a good reason for not wearing shorts on some of the rougher walks. The *Mallorquí* name is *aritja*, and there are thousands on the aptly named Pla des Aritges, crossed while following the Camí de s'Arxiduc (Walk 55 and Walk 56).

One of the commonest mountain plants is *Ampelodesmus mauritanica*, a pampas-like grass. It is easier to use the short *Mallorquí* name, **càrritx**, for this grass, which forms enormous clumps covering large areas, and from a distance sometimes gives the illusion of being close-cropped turf. The tall, narrow leaves curve over to reach the ground, and it is very easy to step on them with one foot and trip over them with the other. You soon learn to lift your feet high when walking a narrow path between clumps of *càrritx*!

So far we have concentrated on trees and shrubs, and some other plants that make their presence obvious to the walker, but there are also a number of smaller, less conspicuous plants that are well worth seeking out.

As early as December the tiny **Crocus minimus** shows its lilac-pink flowers before its leaves on many an otherwise barren mountainside. The very common, but delightful and delicate little **Cyclamen balearicum** can be found in flower in March, if you look under the sheltering leaves of other shrubs on the mountains and in the woods. Its leaves, not unlike those of houseplant cyclamens, are a mottled greyish-green and can be seen everywhere.

Another common plant with similar leaves is *Arisarum vulgare*, or **friar's cowl**, which flowers in winter. Also similar in leaf shape are **Arum italicum**,

Arum pictum and *Dracunculus muscivorus*. The latter is particularly striking, with a spotted, reddish-purple 'spadix' (a fleshy spike bearing flowers) and 'spathe' (a large bract enclosing the flower head) and strangely incised leaves.

There is not enough space here to describe plants of other habitats, such as the coast and sand dunes, cliff-faces and marshlands. For these the reader is referred to the books listed in Appendix 4.

Before moving on to the birds of Mallorca, however, there are two striking plants that deserve a mention, although they are not native. One is the **prickly pear**, sometimes used as a dense, protective hedge, and whose fruits are edible. The other is **Agave americana**, a plant with huge, leathery leaves as long as 2m. After about 10 years it sends up an enormous tree-like flower spike, up to 10m tall, after which it dies.

Finally, Mallorca is a wonderful place for **orchids**, flourishing in the pine woods near the sea, inland in the mountains, and even thrusting up through tarmac at the side of the road.

BIRDS

Please bear in mind that this section is written for walkers rather than birdwatching experts, who are referred to the books listed in Appendix 4. However, even those with a minimal interest in birds are likely to find this interest stimulated by the sheer number and variety of birds to be seen on nearly every walk – binoculars and an identification book are a must.

Some of the walks described coincide with good birding areas, such as around Na Blanca (Walk 7) and Vall de Bóquer (Walk 8). There is an excellent chance of spotting birds on many of the other walks too – in fact the only birds missed would be ducks and waders, many of which can be seen at the Parc Natural de s'Albufera in northeast Mallorca (see below), and a visit to this area is highly recommended.

The best time for birdwatchers to visit is during the peak migration season in April and May, with the last half of September and the first half of October as a second choice.

There is an important birdwatching and conservation organisation, the Grup Balear d'Ornitologia i Defensa de la Natura, or GOB, based in Palma, which is very active. Amongst other things they have acquired land at Sa Trapa for conservation, cooperated on the black vulture re-establishment programme (see below), and produce an annual review and other publications. (Incidentally, the filming of nesting birds is subject to Spanish law – anyone planning to do this should seek advice from GOB, ☎ 971–496060, or see their website at **www.gobmallorca.com**.)

Although GOB is well supported locally, many other local people are more interested in shooting birds for the pot, both in and out of the official season, which is from the end of August to the end of January. Thrushes are regarded as a serious pest in the olive groves and the traditional practice of caça a coll, or 'thrush netting', is still allowed, and these birds may be seen hanging up in bunches on market stalls. (In addition, a plateful of robins has been sighted in a domestic refrigerator, for example.) However, many birds are protected by law, and if any illegal shooting is observed it should be reported to GOB, together with evidence such as photographs or details of car number plates.

All **eagles**, **vultures**, **harriers**, **owls** and **flamingoes** are protected, and author Eddie Watkinson (see Appendix 4) describes how, with the help of GOB, two men were heavily fined for shooting a flamingo.

Of all the birds of Mallorca, the **hoopoe** always arouses great interest, even after many sightings. It is extremely striking, with barred black and white wings and tail and erectile crest, but quite common in many localities, and often flushed out of hedges as you drive along.

Most exciting of all the birds on the island, though, are the large birds of prey, especially the **black vulture**, which may be seen soaring over the Serra de Tramuntana or along the rugged coast between Sóller and Pollença (see below).

Besides the resident black vulture, other raptors to be seen in winter are **red kites**, **peregrines**, **kestrels** and **booted eagles**, and more rarely the **golden eagle** and **short-toed eagle**. Marsh **harriers** are resident and breed on the larger marshes, while **hen harriers** and **Montagu's harriers** are occasional visitors. **Ospreys** are frequently seen on the marshes, and sometimes inland at the Gorg Blau and Cúber reservoirs.

One of the most interesting birds is **Eleanora's falcon**, which breeds in large colonies on the coastal cliffs all the way from Formentor in the northeast to Dragonera in the southwest. They arrive in late April, but do not breed until later in the summer, then the young birds

feed on tired migrants, an activity that may be observed during September and October in the nesting areas.

Other birds of the mountains include the fairly common **crag martin**, which can be seen on many walks, as well as other places including the marshes, where flocks of about a thousand may be catching insects on mild winter days. **Alpine accentors** occur in small flocks in the northern mountains, but personally we have only seen them singly (one accepted some of our lunch high up on Massanella on a cold New Year's Day).

The **blue rock thrush** is resident in fair numbers, but not easily seen, in spite of its bright, metallic-blue plumage – it tends to disappear behind rocks or bushes as soon as sighted. **Pallid swifts** breed on the cliffs, and small colonies of **alpine swifts** may be seen in a few places, such as the Artà peninsula or near Puig Major.

In woodlands the most common winter residents are **blackcaps**, **black redstarts**, **crossbills** and **goldfinches**. **White wagtails**, **meadow pipits**, **serins** and **greenfinches**, **linnets** and **great tits** are also common, and **robins** and **chaffinches** abundant. **Firecrests** are found at altitudes of 800m, and **rock doves** are fairly common, nesting on cliffs such as those around Formentor, as well as in the woods.

The many areas of maquis and scrubland are the preferred habitat of a large number of birds, including many warblers – the **Sardinian warbler** is a very common resident, as is the **fantailed warbler**. **Marmora's warbler** is resident but somewhat elusive – it may be seen in the Vall de Bóquer on Walk 8, and Walk 7 to

Na Blanca passes nesting sites near Cases Velles.

During the winter there is a great influx of birds from further north in Europe, including **starlings**, **thrushes**, **finches**, **waders** and **wildfowl**. **Goldcrests** are numerous and may even outnumber the resident firecrests.

OTHER WILDLIFE

July and August are the poorest months for wildlife, apart from **grasshoppers** and **cicadas**, but walkers will want to avoid these two months anyway. Even in mid-winter there are numerous butterflies and moths, and they are abundant the rest of the year (author James Parrack mentions that 32 species of butterflies and 250 of the larger moths have been observed, see Appendix 4).

Red admirals may be seen in winter, **clouded yellow** and **painted ladies** more commonly in spring. Some exotic species, such as the **two-tailed pasha**, arrive in May from North Africa, and the **Mediterranean skipper** is found from May onwards (see Pine Processionary Caterpillars, below).

Other invertebrates include shell-bearing molluscs, with gastropods or **snails** being of particular interest. In the mountains, snails form the basic diet of the blue rock thrush, and it has been noticed that the colours of their shells vary in different areas and from season to season. This colour variation is probably of survival value, depending on the colour of the background vegetation.

A large number of frogs live in the marshes and up to an altitude of 800m in the mountains, and many breed by the outlet from the Cúber reservoir. Most of the frogs are an endemic form of the **marsh frog**, *Rana ridibunda*, but there is also a **green tree frog**. Three species of toad are found on the island: the **green toad**, the **natterjack** and the **midwife toad**. They mostly hibernate in winter, but on mild days can be heard croaking at the Gorg Blau or below the dam at Cúber.

There are four species of snake: the **grass snake**, **viperine snake**, **ladder snake** and **cowl snake**, none of which is capable of causing fatalities. The only snake I've ever actually seen was high up on the south ridge of Puig Roig. It was no more than two feet long, and slithered away into a rock crevice so fast I could not recall its appearance afterwards. It should have been hibernating, but must have come out to enjoy the hot sun.

Two species of broad-toed lizard or gecko are found: the **wall gecko** lives mainly in lowland areas, but it is the **disc-fingered gecko** that is more common in the mountains. The latter is the bolder of the two, but they both disappear quickly when approached. Both are eaten by hoopoes, and both hibernate, but also come out of hibernation on sunny winter days.

There are few large mammals on Mallorca. This is because of two natural calamities that occurred after the severance of the island from the mainland some 800,000 years ago. The first of these was a rising of the water level, with widespread flooding, and the second was climatic changes associated with mainland glaciations during the Quaternary period. After this, the final doom to a number of species was brought about by man, not only as a hunter, but as a

Lagoons and reed beds make up the extensive reserve of Parc Natural de s'Albufera

destroyer of the forests through charcoal burning and cultivation.

The **wild boar** and the **red fox** probably survived until this century, and the **pine marten** and **genet** still survive, along with true **wild cats**, **feral cats** and **weasels**. Pine martens are still trapped or shot (we once saw one hanging by its neck from the branch of a tree). Of the smaller mammals, **shrews**, **hedgehogs**, **bats**, **rabbits**, the **brown hare** and various **rodents** are quite common. Rabbits provide food for man as well as birds of prey, which also do well off smaller rodents (although extra food is being provided to aid the survival of the black vulture). **Feral goats** are the animals most frequently met on mountain walks, and the tracks they make through the prickly scrub and the *càrritx* are often a help to the walker. They are also frequently hunted as 'big game'.

From some of the cliff walks it is worth looking out to sea for whales and dolphins. There are occasional sightings of **sperm whales** and **killer whales**, but

mostly it is the **common dolphin**, and sometimes the **bottle-nosed** and **Risso's**, that are seen. **Pilot whales** are rare, and **rorquals** more likely – on rare occasions they have been beached after heavy storms.

THE PARC NATURAL DE S'ALBUFERA

The Parc Natural de s'Albufera is the largest wetland area in the Illes Balears and one of the most important in Spain. It is on the northeast coast of Mallorca between Alcúdia and Can Picafort and covers an area of over 1700 hectares.

In the 1960s the northern part came into the hands of property developers, and at one time it was thought this might be the fate of the whole area. However, in 1985 the Govern de les Illes Balears purchased a large area, and it is now a well-managed nature reserve with a reception centre, eight hides and an observation tower. More than 300 species of birds have been observed, most of them marsh birds, but also woodland species, and others among the dunes and trees bordering the canals. It is well worth spending time here, and there are many paths and tracks providing quite long walks.

A circular walk can be made by returning along the coast, which is bordered by pine woods at Es Comú. The reserve can be reached by bus from Port de Pollença, Alcúdia or Can Picafort – ask for the Esperanza, which is a hotel near the entrance. If driving, watch carefully for the very sudden and narrow turn signposted near a roundabout. There is a small car park and toilets near the reception centre, and free leaflet maps are available in English.

Cars are not admitted to the park, nor are dogs. Access for cyclists is more restricted than for walkers, and all visitors need a permit, obtainable free from the reception centre (groups must apply in advance). The park is open from 09.00 to 18.00 from April to September, then 09.00 to 17.00 from October to March. Interesting interpretative displays can be studied in a building called Can Bateman. (971–892250 for further details, or visit the park website at **www.mallorcaweb.net/salbufera/index.html**.

THE BLACK VULTURE RECUPERATION PROGRAMME

Since the beginning of the century Mallorca's resident population of black vultures has seriously declined. In recent years attempts have been made to reverse this decline, and already some success has been achieved.

The first and simplest method has been to put out food for the vultures high up in the mountains – since tractors replaced horses and mules there is less carrion, which would have been a natural source of food in the past. The second method has been the introduction of immature and injured birds recovered on the mainland – 12 of these were introduced between 1984 and 1987.

The third method has been to release into the wild chicks hatched in captivity, through the technique known as 'hacking'. Fledgling chicks are put into an artificial nest with a tame vulture that cannot fly, and are fed under cover of darkness so that they do not become accustomed to human beings. The chicks teach themselves to fly, and already a number have successfully integrated with the local population.

These birds live, breed and feed in the high mountains. They are wonderful and exciting to watch, but it is essential they are not disturbed, and for this reason walkers in the area between Puig Roig and Ternelles should take special care to keep to footpaths, avoid undue noise, and preferably limit numbers in walking parties to less than six. The area of L'Havanor is particularly sensitive, and access is discouraged during the long breeding season from January through to July. The Black Vulture Conservation Foundation is based at Son Pons, Campanet, tel 971–516620, **http://bvcf.joopbox.com**.

PINE PROCESSIONARY CATERPILLARS

A number of curious features will be noticed when walking through pine woods, including strange, grey, nest-like objects hanging from branches from January until March, and brown plastic boxes, with bags attached, suspended from branches throughout the year. The fact is that the pine woods of Mallorca are under serious threat by attacks from 'processionary' caterpillars. The caterpillars get their name from their habit of walking in single file when searching for food, and can form chains many metres long. They have voracious appetites and devour the leaves of pine trees (and other trees) and eventually the trees die.

They secrete fine silk threads, used for returning to their nests, which are the strange grey objects seen hanging in the trees.

Various attempts have been made, at enormous cost, to eradicate the caterpillars. At one time cartridges were issued free to encourage people to shoot the nests out of the trees, but this was stopped when it was found that the free cartridges were being used in normal hunting pursuits.

Cutting off and burning branches with nests on has been tried, but is only effective if the burning is done on concrete, as the caterpillars can burrow into the ground and chrysalids can survive there for a year, to emerge as moths.

Large areas have been treated with insecticides, but the best results are being obtained with biological control, using traps containing pheromones – these are the brown boxes with bags seen hanging from the trees in many woods. The pheromones attract the female moths (capable of laying up to 200 eggs), which get trapped in the lure and die, and no damage is done to other flora and fauna.

Mallorca is crisscrossed by old mule tracks, though mules are now rarely seen

MAN AND THE LANDSCAPE

There is evidence that Mallorca was inhabited more than 6000 years ago, when man made use of natural caves. In the 1960s bones of extinct antelopes mingled with human remains were found in the Cova de Muleta near Sóller, and these human remains were dated at 3985BC ±109 years. The cave is in a Jurassic limestone outcrop and consists of two levels connected by a vertical chimney, forming a natural animal trap. Another major site, even older, is that of Son Matge, near Valldemossa. This is dated at about 4730BC, and had been used as a corral for animals, then as a habitation, a burial site and a workshop.

These caves are not easily accessible, but in the village of Cala de Sant Vicenç there are some caves that are partly natural and partly manmade. The former are probably dwelling caves, and the latter – long, rectangular rooms – probably burial chambers. These caves are to be found at the western edge of the village in a small park full of flowering shrubs, and their date is probably about 2000 years later than that of the Cova de Muleta.

In 1979 a very important find was made on the Serra de la Punta, which separates the Sant Vicenç valley from the main road between Pollença and Port de Pollença. Local climbers found the entrance to a large cave that had been used as a burial chamber. It was carefully excavated, the objects found sent to various museums on the mainland for evaluation, and some of these have now found their way back to the museum in Pollença.

The most interesting finds at Serra de la Punta were the remains of two wooden, bull-like creatures with hollow bodies, which have been carbon dated at 320BC and are assumed to have contained human ashes (reconstructions can be seen at the museum).

Some time during the 2000 years before the Romans arrived, the Balearic people progressed from living in caves to building stone dwellings – megalithic structures containing towers or *talaiots*. Although not a great deal is known about these times, there are a number of sites where these megalithic structures can be seen. Near Artà there is the Talaiot de Ses Paisses, but the largest and best documented is that of Capocorb Vell, near Llucmajor. This is maintained as a national monument by the Institute of Catalan Studies and is well worth a visit. It contains 28 dwellings and five *talaiots* – two square and three circular. One of the square *talaiots* has an opening at ground level from which a low tunnel descends in a spiral to a small room partly roofed by olive-wood branches (to go in here means hands and knees and a headtorch). The function of this room was probably religious. This village has been dated at about 1000BC and was thought to be occupied well into Roman times.

Mallorca has no mineral resources, so the finding of ingots and bronze artefacts, such as the bronze button

45

Jaume I of Aragon, 'the Conqueror', siezed Mallorca from the Moors in 1229

at Serra de la Punta, shows that there must have been trading with merchants from the civilisations of the eastern Mediterranean. There would have been settlements on or near the sites of most of the present ports. The Carthaginians provided garrisons to protect their trading posts, recruiting from among the local warriors, who were armed with leather slings. (The name of the islands, the Illes Balears, comes from the Greek verb *ballein*, meaning 'to throw'. The leather slings fired stones the size of tennis balls, which were carried in a leather pouch. Legend has it that boys were trained in this art by having to shoot down their daily food from where it had been placed high up in the trees.)

The Romans invaded the island in 123BC, building the cities of Palma and Alcúdia (then known as Pollentia). The remains of the Roman town at Alcúdia include the theatre on the road to Port d'Alcúdia, and other buildings near the Tucan crossroads. In the Pollença area there is a 'Roman' bridge on the north side of the town, which is actually much later in date. The remains of a Roman aqueduct, which was thought to take water all the way to Alcúdia, are seen in the Ternelles valley.

The fact that there are so few Roman remains on the island is partly due to the depredations of the Vandals after the Romans abandoned it. During this time the main settlements began to develop a few kilometres inland from the ports, which is why today the towns of Pollença, Alcúdia, Sóller and Andratx each has its own separate port.

Watch towers were built between 1550 and 1650 on headlands and hills so that warning of approaching invaders and pirates could be given. These watch towers, or *talaias*, are seen on many walks. They are usually circular and can often be climbed to a viewing platform at the top. One of the best preserved and restored is that of the Talaia d'Albercutx, on the Formentor peninsula.

After the rout of the Vandals in North Africa by the Byzantine general Belisarius, the Illes Balears were incorporated into what is now Tunisia. Mallorca again became a trading post protected by military strongholds, this time of the Byzantine Empire.

This period was followed by very unsettled times and constant strife between the Moors and the Christians, beginning with Arab raids in AD707. (This is still re-enacted today in various folk festivals, such as that held in Pollença every 2 August.) Arab influence on the development of agriculture during times of peace is still to be seen in the countryside. They introduced the *norias*, or waterwheels, used to pump water from underground reservoirs and wells, and the *seguias*, or open water channels, used to irrigate the fields. They also began the terracing of the steep hillsides with massive drystone walls, or *margers*, that enabled cultivation of otherwise impossible places. Place names on maps are another legacy of the Arabs – *bini* means 'the house of', as in Binisalem and Biniaraix. In Palma the arches of the Almudaina palace and the Arab baths are still to be seen, and there is a Moorish influence on many country houses.

The modern history of Mallorca dates from 1229, when Jaume I of Aragon (known as 'the Conqueror') led an expedition of 150 ships and 16,000 men to reclaim the island. The landing was made at Santa Ponça, after storms diverted the Aragonese from the original plan of landing at Port de Pollença. After several months the reconquest was complete and a new state proclaimed in March 1230.

Although a modern style of government was introduced, this was not the end of Mallorca's troubles, but the beginning of new ones. When Jaume I died in 1276 he left the estates of Aragon, Catalonia and Valencia to his eldest son, Pere III, and the Illes Balears, Rousillon and Montpellier to his younger son, Jaume II. Pere III's son and successor, Alfons III, then invaded Mallorca and proclaimed himself king – the Castell d'Alaró (Walk 34) was one of the last strongholds to hold out against him. Alfons committed such terrible atrocities during this siege that he was excommunicated, and eventually Jaume II returned to the throne and proved an excellent ruler.

During Jaume's reign Palma cathedral and Castell de Bellver were built, and he patronised the great scholar Ramon Llull, who founded a hermitage at Randa and wrote his major works there. Jaume encouraged the development of trade and agriculture by granting charters to 11 market towns, and his son Sanç continued his father's enlightened policies, although bad health obliged him to spend much time away from state affairs.

Under Pere IV the Aragonese again invaded the island, at Peguera in 1343. Sanç's nephew and heir, Jaume III, tried to regain possession, but was killed in battle in 1349, bringing to an end

the reign of the independent kings of Mallorca, which became part of Aragon. (In 1716 Mallorca lost the title of kingdom and became a province of Spain.)

From 1349 until the present Mallorca has had a chequered history, with invasions, rebellions, and natural disasters such as earthquakes, floods, and outbreaks of cholera and bubonic plague.

Clearly this section is not intended as a history of Mallorca, but simply aims to point out the significance of some of the features seen on the island. The castles and the watch towers are among the most striking features, but *ermitas*, or sanctuaries, are also found on mountain tops. One crowns Puig de María, near Pollença (Walk 13), and many others are in use, some offering refreshments and accommodation. (See Appendix 4 for books on the history of Mallorca.)

CULTIVATION

One of the most impressive sights in Mallorca is the blossoming of the **almond trees** in early spring, when large areas of the island become pink and white (if you arrive by plane during daylight in February you can see this from the air). There are said to be over six million almond trees and most of the crop is exported.

Planting of almonds began in 1765, but the **olive tree** has been cultivated for much longer. Some of the trees are believed to be 1000 years old or more, and their gnarled and twisted trunks are seen on many of the walks. Sometimes you will see almonds or olives being harvested, the almonds being shaken

Oranges are cultivated, and a freshly squeezed orange juice is most refreshing

from the trees onto sheets spread on the ground, and the olives being knocked down by long poles.

Orange trees and other citrus fruits are also sights to delight and interest the walker. The main crop is in January, but fruit seems to be on some trees all year round. The scent of the blossom is wonderful, and sometimes in winter you can see blossom, green, unripe fruit and bright-orange or bright-yellow ripe fruit all at the same time. Sóller is famous for its orange groves, but they can be seen in other places, for example in the hortes, or market gardens, near Pollença. **Strawberries** are already ripening under cloches in February and March, and other fruits grown are **mandarins**, **peaches**, **apricots**, **melons** and **figs**. **Vines** grow at Binisalem and near Felanitx, where some very good wine is made.

Vegetables grow all year round, thanks to the sunshine and the irrigation system – **broad beans** and **peas** are often grown on terraces between the fruit trees. Several crops can be grown in succession, and the first peas and beans will be harvested in February. **Potatoes** are another crop grown for export, many on the central plain near Inca and Sa Pobla, including 'earlies' for export to England.

The village markets all have fine displays of fruit and vegetables, most of them grown locally. It is a splendid treat to buy delicious fresh oranges, still with leaves attached, two or three kilos at a time.

The methods of cultivation are a pleasure to watch too. Horses and mules can still be seen pulling primitive ploughs along narrow terraces where it would be impossible to use a tractor. Seed is often hand-sown from a sack hanging round the neck, in a manner that may seem archaic, but is obviously still efficient. **Corn** and **cereal** crops are produced, and grass for grazing is often sown on the olive terraces.

There are few **cattle** on Mallorca, and much milk and dairy produce is imported from Menorca, although there are large flocks of **sheep** and many **goats** in the mountains. These are usually belled and sometimes hobbled. **Pigs** are sometimes seen foraging about in oak woods in a semi-wild state (besides acorns they dig up roots, and can make a real mess of some of the woodland paths in their search for food).

One of the main animal markets is at Sineu, near the centre of the island, and is held on Wednesdays. Here can be seen magnificent rams, tiny lambs and goats, cages of birds and all manner of livestock.

RURAL INDUSTRIES

The remains of two major 'rural industries' will be seen time and again on many walks in this book, and they are in fact intimately connected with these walks, because many of the footpaths were made in association with them. These rural industries are **snow collecting** and **charcoal burning**, and knowing something about them adds greatly to the interest of the walks.

Snow Collecting

The highest manmade paths on Mallorca were all built by the *nevaters*, or snow collectors. Snow was collected on all the highest mountains to make ice for use in the summer, and conserved in snow-pits or buildings known as *casas de neu*. There were seven snowpits on Puig Major,

seven on Puig de Massanella, two on Puig Tomir, on Es Teix, and several on the Serra d'Alfàbia. Most were at an altitude above 900m, sometimes circular and sometimes rectangular, and partly or wholly below ground level. The most unusual, which is roofed over, is on Puig Tomir, below the Coll de Fartàritx (Walk 20).

In winter, when the mountains were covered with snow, groups of men from the nearest villages went up to gather the snow in carriers and baskets made from cane or grass. To make collecting easier, flat platforms were often made and cleared of vegetation, and these can still be seen. The snow was arranged in layers and trampled down hard to pack it into ice, in time to the following rhyme:

Pitgen sa neu, pitgen sa neu,
i tots estan dins ses cases.
Peguen potades, peguen potades,
en Toni, en Xisco, en Juan i N'Andreu.

Tramp the snow, tramp the snow,
and throw it in the pit.
Beat it down, beat it down,
on Tony, Harry, John and Andrew.

The packed snow was put in the pit, and each layer covered with thin layers of grass (probably *càrritx*) to make it easier to extract the blocks when required. When the pit was full it was protected with a layer of ashes, and finally a thick covering of branches. One man stayed on duty all year to keep the covering in perfect condition. On summer nights huge blocks of snow-ice were taken down by mule to the villages and towns. It was not only used for ice-creams and cooling drinks, but also medicinally. An

A poor carboner's hut is often found alongside sitges, or charcoal-burning sites (Walk 63)

emulsion with olive oil was used for dressing wounds and was believed to stop bleeding.

The local authority controlled the price and limited the production of ice, supposedly to prevent speculation, and a specific tax was put on it. Sometimes ice had to be imported from Catalunya by boat, but other years there was over-production and ice was exported to Menorca.

It appears that the last occasion on which a snowpit was used was in 1925 on Puig de Massanella. The casa de neu on the Son Moragues estate was built in the 17th century, but abandoned in the 18th century, as it was not really at a high enough altitude. It is seen on Walk 55, and nearby the hut where the nevaters lived has been made into a *refugi* for walkers.

Charcoal Production

Many other paths used by walkers today were made by the charcoal workers. Almost every wood of evergreen oak was once used for the production of charcoal and there are still plentiful signs of this activity. The former charcoal hearths, or pitsteads (also known as *sitges* – singular *sitja*), appear as flat, circular areas, often ringed by stones and covered with bright-green moss, and pieces of charcoal can still be found on them. (Many of the sites are pointed out as landmarks in route descriptions).

The production of charcoal in Mallorca continued until butane gas became popular, around the 1920s, although in some areas it continued for longer, and there are still people alive today who worked in this industry in their youth. Charcoal's only use in Mallorca was for cooking, being preferred over wood because it gave a cleaner and steadier heat.

The charcoal burners began work in April and lived and worked all summer in the woods with their families. They could not leave the site because charcoal burning is a delicate operation and everything could be ruined in a moment of neglect.

51

For this reason they built huts to live in, the remains of which are often seen in the woods, together with a stone oven used to bake bread. These ovens are a beehive shape and instantly recognisable.

The process of making charcoal began with the felling of large oaks, of a diameter stipulated by the landowner. Each *carboner* had his own area, known as a *ranxo*, and axes and enormous two-handed saws were used to fell the trees. Meanwhile a perfectly flat and circular site had to be prepared, and stones were carefully arranged so that a sufficient circulation of air would carbonise the wood without igniting it.

On the platform cut logs and branches were arranged in a 'cupola', leaving a narrow central chimney, and over all this was laid a covering of gravel and clay. A ladder was needed to reach the top of the chimney, through which the *carboner* dropped live coals to start the process, and to feed the fire from time to time with small pieces of dry wood. Constant vigilance and expertise were needed on the part of the worker.

During the process the weight of the wood was reduced by 75–80%. Each firing lasted 10–12 days and would produce around 2800kg of charcoal. When the operation was complete the covering was removed and hot pieces extracted with a shovel and rake. Sieved earth was used for quenching, as using water caused a loss of quality.

Finally the charcoal was sorted into a number of different grades and taken by muleteers for sale at special shops in the villages. As a by-product, bark from the oak trees was collected and used for tanning.

Lime Burning

Mention must be made of the limekilns that will be seen from time to time – there are three of them in the Cairats valley (Walk 55), but they will be seen in almost every woodland. They are rather different from those seen in the British Isles, in that they are normally cylindrical.

Lime was used for whitening houses, something that used to be done every year, and also for making mortar. As great heat is needed to initiate the reaction $CaCO_3 \rightarrow CaO + CO_2$, these *forns de calç* were always built near a plentiful supply of wood, and great destruction of woodland was often the result. Although there is a vast amount of limestone on Mallorca, the stones used to produce lime were always chosen very carefully, and known as *pedra viva*, or 'living stones'.

From the base of the circular pit used as a kiln, a cupola was built up of large stones with spaces left between them, so that the flames could pass through. Above the cupola the rest of the oven was built up of stones, and the space between the cupola and the outer walls of the kiln filled with pieces of limestone for calcining. The whole structure was then covered with slaked lime and soil, the interior was filled with wood and the fire lit. It was kept burning for a period of time varying from 9 to 15 days, wood being thrown in continually. The quantity required is impressive: 100–150 tons of branches during one firing, and a firing would produce around 10 tons of lime.

It was very hard work, the fire needing to be fed day and night, and it was not financially rewarding – according to the old proverb, 'Qui fa calç, va descalç' ('He who makes lime goes barefoot').

WALKING IN MALLORCA

EQUIPMENT AND CLOTHING

Although the winters in Mallorca are mild and the weather is normally ideal for walking, bad weather is not unknown, as in any area of high mountains. There are days when a **warm sweater**, **anorak**, **hat**, **gloves** and **waterproofs** will be appreciated, especially on the higher tops. There will always be days when these extra clothes will stay in the rucksack, even in January, the coldest month, but it is as well to be prepared.

Boots are advised for most walks, although for those graded C some may prefer **trainers** or **strong shoes**. **Shorts** are not advised, because of the extremely prickly vegetation, unless **long trousers** are taken along too. **Sunglasses** and a **sunhat** might be needed, even in winter for those sensitive to hot sun. It is advisable to carry **water** or other drinks, as dehydration can be very unpleasant and debilitating. (The local oranges are both thirst quenching and cheap.)

Snow falls on the high tops most years, but it is very rare for it to fall at sea level as it did in December 1984 and January 2005. When this happens, the roads to the mountains are cut off for days on end, not only by snow but also by fallen trees. The snow is usually wet and soft, so ice axes and crampons can be left at home.

Of standard walking equipment, take a **whistle**, **compass** and **torch** – darkness falls early in mid-winter, at 17.30 on the shortest days, and some walks are long.

This book deals only with walks and occasional scrambles, none of which requires a rope, although some parties prefer to take a short length for the Serra del Cavall Bernat (Walk 9), the Torrent de Pareis (Walk 26) and one of the ascents of Puig de Massanella (Walk 27). The whole island abounds in steep rock and there is much good rock climbing, with many crags hardly developed (see *Rock Climbs in Mallorca, Ibiza and Tenerife*, by Chris Craggs, Cicerone).

MAPS

One of the best maps for getting around the island is the AA Island Map: Mallorca, at a scale of 1:75,000 (which is actually a Kompass map in an AA cover). It shows walking routes, but it is not accurate enough to be used as a walking map, and is best used as a motoring or cycling map and to aid general exploration of the island.

Originally, the only decent maps of Mallorca were the Mapa Militar, or Military Maps series. In recent years the Instituto Geográfico Nacional (IGN) has published topographic maps of Mallorca at scales of 1:50,000 and 1:25,000. These are part of the Mapa Topográfico Nacional (MTN) series, and referred to throughout this guidebook by the reference MTN50 for the 1:50,000 scale, and MTN25 for the 1:25,000 scale. The names following each reference are the names of the individual sheets.

Mallorcan roads can be very scenic and quite exciting to walk, let alone drive (Walk 54)

8

Up-to-date information on IGN mapping can be checked on the website **www.mfom.es/ign/**.

Three new maps, published by Editorial Alpina, at a scale of 1:25,000, are far and away the best to use in the Serra de Tramuntana, but they do not cover walks in the outlying parts of Mallorca. The three sheets are: Mallorca Tramuntana Nord, Mallorca Tramuntana Central and Mallorca Tramuntana Sud. Together they cover nearly three-quarters of all the walks in this guidebook, including most of the walks numbered 13 to 74. The relevant sheets are mentioned, where appropriate, in the route information box at the beginning of each walk.

These maps show more walking routes, greater detail and better use of place names than any other maps available. They were created using Spanish IGN mapping and local expertise, including that of Mallorcan hiking guide Jaume Tort.

Alpina have also produced a 'Mallorca Hiking Guide' incorporating a pack of seven handy maps at a scale of 1:50,000. These cover the same area as the 1:25,000 maps, but also extend further westwards. As a set, they cover all but the last nine walks in this guidebook, from 72 to 80. The maps are indexed from A to G and are mentioned where appropriate throughout this guidebook.

Maps can be purchased in Mallorca at La Casa del Mapa, Costa Santo Domingo 11, Palma de Mallorca, ☎ 971–225945. Maps can also be obtained in advance from Stanfords, 12–14 Long Acre, London, WC2E 9BR, ☎ 0207–8361231; the Map Shop, 15 High Street, Upton-upon-Severn, WR8 0HJ, ☎ 01684–593146; or Cordee, 3a De Montfort Street, Leicester, LE1 7HD, ☎ 0116–2543579.

The Mallorca Tramuntana map, published by Freytag & Berndt at a scale of 1:50,000, only covers the central part of the Serra de Tramuntana. It marks many walking routes, but the information is not always accurate and the map should not be used on its own.

Street plans of Palma can be obtained free from tourist information centres, and a variety of street plans are often found in a wide range of free tourism publications. There is usually no need to buy a more detailed street plan, though these are available from many bookshops and newsagents.

GPS users should select the datum ED1950 on their units, and use either the IGN or Alpina maps.

GRADING AND ROUTE INFORMATION

All the routes in this book have been walked by the author with the objective of assessing the difficulties in such a way that anyone using the book can form a reasonable idea of what to expect. Such assessment is obviously very subjective, and can be influenced by weather conditions at the time and many other factors. When heavy rain occurs, for example, dry streambeds can become raging torrents, landslips may occur, rocks can fall and the ground can become very slippery. At such times it is better to wait for things to improve, as once the sun is out again all the surface water quickly disappears.

Grades

A   Strenuous walk, often pathless in places and on rough ground, with considerable route finding and/or some scrambling. Normally only for experienced walkers. A+ and A++ are **particularly** difficult.

B   Average mountain walk that may call for some skill in route finding, but is mainly on paths.

C   Easy walking along well-defined paths or tracks and with no route -finding difficulties.

Assuming normal conditions, the walks have been graded into three categories, which can be called '**difficult**', '**average**' and '**easy**', or A, B and C. These categories refer to the terrain and route-finding difficulties. The approximate **times**, **distances** and **heights** involved are given separately in the route information box (at the beginning of each walk) in addition to the grading.

Under the heading **type of walk** there are details of what is involved. It cannot be emphasised too much that a great deal of the walking in Mallorca is over very rough ground, and this often takes a lot longer to negotiate than expected. Even the paths are usually rough and stony and require care.

The walking times allow for photography, some birdwatching and flower identification, but do not include long stops for refreshments. On the whole they are for slower-than-average walkers, more interested in enjoying the scenery than setting speed records.

ACCESS

Many of the walks in this book go across private land, and the maps do not show rights of way. However, by Spanish law there is a right of way on any track leading to the sea, to a mountain top, or to monasteries, hermitages, towers, castles or other famous landmarks, which just about covers every walk.

That is the theory, but in practice it seems to be slightly different. For example, access restrictions have been imposed on the Ternelles valley, and in certain areas walkers have even been threatened in a very unpleasant manner. However, we personally have met with nothing but friendliness from the landowners we have encountered. On occasion they have gone out of their way to point out routes, and obviously appreciated our attempts to speak a few words of their language.

One fact worth knowing is that the ubiquitous sign 'Coto privado de caza' only means 'private hunting' and can generally be ignored by walkers. However, if there appears to be a lot of shooting going on, it might be

Access may be restricted in places, but not all forbidding signs deny access to walkers

more prudent to choose another walk. The black-and-white rectangular sign divided diagonally, often seen on fenceposts and gates, also means private hunting.

Many tracks have a standard sign 'Prohibido el paso', meaning 'No entry', which usually means that cars are prohibited and this must be respected, but it should not stop walkers. The sign 'Camino particular' means 'Private road' and does not necessarily exclude walkers – often access gates or stiles are provided when the gate is a locked one, but more of these are needed.

On the other hand there are some private estates where walkers are distinctly unwelcome – exploration stops short when faced with 3m high fences and heavily padlocked gates topped with barbed wire and iron spikes. (Mallorcan walkers have been known to cut wires and bend apart metal bars when they feel unjustly excluded from parts of their island, and some dedicated local walkers are able to find their way around any obstacle placed in their path!)

There is no access to the summit of the highest mountain of Mallorca, Puig Major. A US military radar station was built on its top, and this is now operated by the Spanish military. At one time there was a popular annual excursion to the summit of Puig Major to see the sun rise at the time of the summer solstice. A long walk was made of it, starting at Biniaraix and following the old road up to Monnàber, going up at night to avoid the scorching heat of the sun.

WALKERS' COUNTRY CODE

It goes without saying that all walkers should have the utmost respect for the countryside through which they walk and for the people who live and work there. Although the vast majority of walkers have this ingrained in them, the fact remains that there are always a few people about who are careless or antisocial, and by irresponsible actions do serious damage to natural resources and private property.

For this reason I am spelling out this code here, in the hope that responsible readers of this book will not only continue to abide by the code themselves, but take an active part in seeing that others do so. Even if this is only in minor ways, such as taking back an extra bit of litter or closing a gate that has been left open, it can all help. Watching out for carelessness in the use of matches in dry areas could even prevent the devastation of a fire.

The importance of the Country Code cannot be too strongly emphasised – there is already some evidence that an increase in numbers of walkers has resulted in landowners being antagonised, and discouraging access across their land.

Large parties should take special care over closing of gates, as it is only too easy to assume that the next one through will see to it. Leaders should try to ensure there is a responsible person at the rear. Large parties in themselves, with their tendency to chatter and spread out over a long line, can be resented as an intrusion into the landscape. Please keep to a minimum number in guided parties.

The Country Code

1 Guard against all risk of fire.

Forests, woodlands and scrub are all highly inflammable. Take every care with matches and cigarette ends, and do not light fires except in recognised fireplaces.

2 Fasten all gates.

Do this even if the gate is found open, unless obviously fastened open by the farmer.

3 Keep dogs under control.

Keep dogs on leads whenever there is livestock about. Some farms have clear pictorial signs indicating that dogs are not allowed in at all.

4 Keep to the paths across farm land.

Crops can be ruined by people's feet.

5 Avoid damaging fences, hedges and walls.

Repairs are costly – keep to recognised routes, using gates and stiles.

6 Leave no litter.

All litter is unsightly, and some, such as glass, tins and plastic, is dangerous to livestock. Take all litter back to the town.

7 Safeguard water supplies.

Avoid polluting water supplies in any way. Never interfere with wells, springs or cattle troughs.

8 Protect wildlife, wild plants and trees.

Wildlife is best observed, not collected. To pick or uproot flowers, carve trees and rocks, or disturb wild animals and birds, not only destroys other people's pleasure, but can irrevocably damage the ecology.

9 Go carefully on country roads.

Country roads have special dangers: blind corners, high walls, deep drops at the edge, slow-moving tractors, sheep and goats. Drivers should reduce their speed and take extra care; walkers should keep to the left, facing oncoming traffic.

10 Respect the life of the countryside.

Set a good example and try to fit in with the life and work of the countryside. In this way good relations between walkers and landowners are preserved, and those who follow are not regarded as enemies.

IBANAT

IBANAT is the Institut Balear de la Natura. They do a lot of good work on the island, including acquiring several tracts of land that are being conserved for public use, constructing some excellent paths, and providing well-equipped picnic sites with shelters, cooking facilities and toilets. One of the largest undertakings was the purchase of the Son Moragues estate near Valldemossa, originally a property of the Archduke Lluís Salvador.

Many routes have been signposted and waymarked for the use of walkers

The waymarked GR221 route leads from Font des Prat to Coll des Prat (Walk 27c)

DEPARTMENT DE NATURA I MEDI AMBIENT

FODESMA was established by the Consell de Mallorca to work with stone and traditional crafts. Stonemasons and labourers repaired the retaining walls, or *margers*, on cultivated slopes, restoring and signposting ancient, stone-paved routes for walkers, and built a series of refuges along the course of a long-distance route, the GR221, or Ruta de Pedra en Sec. In 2004 the organisation's activities were taken over by the Departament de Natura i Medi Ambient del Consell Insular de Mallorca.

MOUNTAIN RESCUE

Until 1995 there was only a voluntary mountain rescue service on Mallorca, but now there are two professional teams – one from the fire service, or Bombers del Consell de Mallorca, and the other from the Guardia Civil. The phone numbers are 112 and 062 respectively.

When needed there is a helicopter available, and presently the service is free of charge, and unfortunately has been kept very busy. Walking alone in the mountains is not recommended – there are many places where, if injured, you might not be found for days or weeks.

GUIDED WALKING

Walking is becoming very popular on Mallorca, and there are several individuals and companies offering guiding services or fully packaged guided walking holidays. The following is very much a shortlist.

Mallorcan Hikers Jaume Tort and his wife Aina Escrivà have a knowledge of walking opportunities around Mallorca that is second to none. Jaume helped Editorial Alpina to produce the most detailed walking maps of the Serra de Tramuntana.
Languages: English, Catalan, Spanish, German and French. Website: **www. mallorca-camins.info** (check Jaume's website for news of any alterations or restrictions to any of the walking routes in this guidebook, and to keep yourself up-to-date about walking in Mallorca). See also **www.gr221.info** and **www. torrentdepareis.info**.

Mallorcan Walking Tours Richard Strutt operates out of Port de Pollença and offers an impressive programme of walks.

Languages: English, Spanish. Website: **www.mallorcanwalkingtours.puerto pollensa.com**.

Outdoor Mallorca Frederic Cederlund offers a varied selection of walks around Mallorca.
Languages: English, Spanish, Swedish. Website: **www.outdoormallorca.com**.

Ramblers Holidays A long-established company allied to the Ramblers' Association. Runs walking trips from several bases, mainly using British guides.
Languages: English, Spanish, some Catalan. Website: **www.ramblershol idays.co.uk**.

Exodus A long-established company employing local guides to explore the Serra de Tramuntana.
Languages: English, Catalan, Spanish. Website: **www.exodus.co.uk**.

Explore A long-established company offering walks through the Serra de Tramuntana.
Languages: English. Website: **www. explore.co.uk**.

The view from the terraces surrounding the monastery on Puig de María (Walk 13)

AREA 1

POLLENÇA AND THE NORTH

1 Platja des Coll Baix

Platja des Coll Baix is a small, sheltered and unspoilt beach on the Alcúdia peninsula where the sea is an incredible turquoise colour. It is not safe for bathing as there is a very strong undertow, but it is an excellent place for a picnic on a sunny day in winter or early spring.

The approach through a sheltered valley with both woodland and open scrub is good for birdwatching.

See sketch map 1.

Starting Point	Barrera de sa Muntanya near Alcúdia
Time	3hr
Distance	9km
Highest Point	128m
Height Climbed	300m
Grade	C
Map	Alpina E or MTN25 Mal Pas – Bon Aire

To reach the starting point, take the Mal Pas road 2km from **Alcúdia**, then turn right at a crossroads where there is a bar, the **Bodega del Sol**. Keep straight on along the narrow country road called the **Camí de la Muntanya** to reach the iron gates, the **Barrera des Coll Baix**, and park just inside. Some prefer to drive all the way to Coll Baix along the gravel forest road.

Follow the main **forest road**, avoiding all side turnings. At first there are pine woods on the left, then open scrub, and fields, almond trees and carobs on the right, sheltered by a low ridge. Further on the track runs through more pine woods, which are fairly open and have an undergrowth,

Type of Walk
An easy walk along a fairly level forest track with a gentle rise to Coll Baix. The narrow path down to the sea is good, but rugged towards the end.

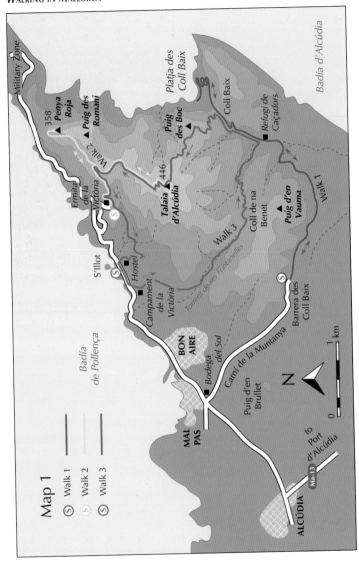

Map 1

Ⓢ Walk 1
Ⓢ Walk 2
Ⓢ Walk 3

mainly of lentiscs and narrow-leaved cistus. There are dwarf fan palms, *càrritx*, euphorbias, asphodels and a few giant orchids.

A long and easy track is followed across sparsely forested slopes to Coll Baix

About 30 minutes after the start there is a private road on the right signposted to the **Finca sa Bassa Blanca**. Avoid this and keep on the main track. The simple shelter of the **Refugi de Caçadors** is later hidden in bushes to the right. A signpost points ahead along the track for the Platja des Coll Baix, while a path to the left is signposted for Coll de ses Fontanelles, used on Walk 3.

The forest track soon rises up to **Coll Baix**, at 128m, where there is a shelter, font and picnic area maintained by IBANAT. Follow the path as signposted down to the beach. This goes quite a long way to the right before descending in zigzags, to avoid the steep and loose cliffs that are in the way of a straight descent from the col to the small sandy beach of the **Platja des Coll Baix**. (A 'Zona perillosa' sign warns against bathing in heavy seas.)

The Talaia d'Alcúdia can be climbed from Coll Baix by a good zigzag path if a longer walk is wanted – see Walk 3.

Simply retrace your steps all the way back along the forest track to return to the **Barrera des Coll Baix**. ▸

Barrera des Coll Baix – Coll Baix	1hr 5min
Coll Baix – Platja des Coll Baix	20min
Platja des Coll Baix – Coll Baix	30min
Coll Baix – Barrera des Coll Baix	1hr 5min

2 Penya Roja and Talaia d'Alcúdia

The Alcúdia peninsula lies between the bays of Pollença and Alcúdia. It is hilly and wooded, and although the Cap des Pinar at the end is a military area and out-of-bounds, the greater part of the peninsula forms a natural park and provides some easy and very attractive walks. Although only a low stump remains of the original watch tower, or *talaia*, on the highest hilltop, it is still a wonderful viewpoint.

The first part of the walk to Penya Roja makes a worthwhile short excursion on its own, along an attractive path undulating below red cliffs and overlooking the sea. An old cannon stands on a flat, circular gun platform on the summit.

See sketch map 1.

Starting Point	Ermita de la Victòria
Time	3hr 10min
Distance	7km
Highest Point	446m
Height Climbed	520m
Grade	B
Map	Alpina E or MTN25 Mal Pas – Bon Aire

Type of Walk
Easy, along wide tracks and well-made footpaths. The last stretch to the top of Penya Roja is by a rocky path that is a steeper scramble.

Take the Mal Pas road from **Alcúdia** and drive along the coast road, turning right approximately 5km from Alcúdia, as signposted for the Restaurant Mirador de la Victòria. There is a large car park, picnic site, and a restaurant with a terrace overlooking the sea.

Walk up past the **Ermita de la Victòria** buildings by a wide track from the corner of the car park. After 20 minutes this makes a sharp bend to the right. Almost immediately,

Seen from Puig des Romani, Penya Roja looks like an unassailable tower of rock

A diversion up to the gap reveals Penya Roja looking like an unassailable tower of rock! The 391m Puig des Romaní can be climbed from this gap.

turn left along a path signposted for **Penya des Migdia**. This path contours along the base of the reddish cliffs, keeping left at a junction below a gap. ◀ The path eventually turns round the end of the rocky ridge by going through a short **tunnel**.

Round the corner the exposed path is protected with a chain and rickety handrail. It leads to an old **stone shelter** with an empty water storage tank behind it. Near this is found the start of the rough, steep path that leads up in about 10 minutes to the top of **Penya Roja** at 358m. A cannon is mounted on the summit, and at one time there was a low stone parapet and a cobbled floor.

Retrace your steps to the wide track, turning left along it as signposted for the talaia. Continue up to a **broad col** at 317m, beyond which the track ends. From here a stony ascent leads up to a well-built zigzag path that once had protective handrails. This winds up to a **large cairn** just below the summit. (A good path will be seen coming up from Coll Baix, used in Walk 3.)

The top of **Talaia d'Alcúdia**, at 446m, bears the stump of a former watch tower. Drop down a short way on the south side to reach two buildings – one is in ruins, while the other is a simple *refugi* with a well on the flat terrace outside.

Retrace your steps down the track to finish back at the **Ermita de la Victòria**.

Ermita de la Victòria – Penya Roja	1hr 5min
Penya Roja – Talaia d'Alcúdia	1hr 15min
Talaia d'Alcúdia – Ermita de la Victòria	50min

3 Talaia d'Alcúdia via ses Fontanelles

This is a circular walk making use of an old footpath in the Fontanelles valley that goes over Coll de na Benet to join a forest road on the south side of Talaia d'Alcúdia. A track continues through the forest and up to Coll Baix, where there is an IBANAT shelter.

A footpath goes down to a small beach from here, as described in Walk 1, and this could be followed if a longer walk is wanted. From Coll Baix there is a good path leading up to the *talaia*. The summit is an excellent viewpoint, described in Walk 2.

See sketch map 1.

Starting Point	Bar S'Illot at Platja de S'Illot
Time	4hr
Distance	11km
Highest Point	445m
Height Climbed	575m
Grade	B
Map	MTN25 Mal Pas – Bon Aire

Take the Mal Pas road from **Alcúdia** and drive along the coast road for approximately 4km. Park opposite the **Bar S'Illot**, not far from the beach at Platja de S'Illot, where there is a small island called S'Illot.

Walk back along the road and turn left up the access road into the **Campament de la Victòria**. Walk straight up through the site and pass a barrier gate at the top end to continue along a clear track. Turn right at a junction of tracks, across fairly level ground towards some new houses on the far side of the **Torrent de ses Fontanelles**. Follow the track upstream and cross where there is a small dam. Continue upstream along a narrow path, crossing at a small rockpool and continuing all the way up to the bushy **Coll de na Benet** at 163m.

Take care on the descent from the col. First head straight across the col, but avoid the narrow path on the left leading straight down into the valley. Turn right to traverse across the valley side using a clearer path marked by cairns, then drop down into the valley of **Coma de s'Egua**. The path continues downstream, crossing the streambed a few times before meeting a broad **forest road** at a junction. Turn left as signposted for Platja des Coll Baix, and in about 15 minutes **Coll Baix** will be reached at 128m.

The path to the beach begins on the far side of the shelter, although it is probably best left for a separate excursion (see Walk 1). The path to the *talaia* rises up through the trees

Type of Walk
Fairly easy on good tracks and rugged paths.

The walk starts on the attractively rugged coast close to the little island of S'Illot

on the northwest side of the col. This well-made zigzag path passes close to the top of **Puig des Boc**, which is an excellent viewpoint, before crossing a gap and going on towards the talaia. Turn left at a signpost and **large cairn** to reach the top of **Talaia d'Alcúdia**, with its summit watch tower stump at 446m, nearby *refugi* and well.

From the summit return to the signpost and cairn and go straight ahead down a steepening zigzag path to a **broad col** at 317m. From here a forest track leads down to the **Ermita de la Victòria** and restaurant, below which is a large car park area.

The last part of the descent begins at the corner of this **car park** at the exact point where the forest track joins it. No path is seen at first, but after a very short but quite steep descent a good path will be found. This leads down steadily to a **streambed** that is crossed, recrossed, and eventually joined and followed to reach a wide cross track. Turn right along this and drop down past the youth hostel, the **Alberg de la Victòria**, to return to the starting point near the **Platja de S'Illot**.

Platja de S'Illot – Coll de na Benet	1hr 10min
Coll de na Benet – Coll Baix	40min
Coll Baix – Talaia d'Alcúdia	1hr 10min
Talaia d'Alcúdia – Platja de S'Illot	1hr

4 El Fumat and Roca Blanca

El Fumat is a spectacular peak that overhangs the Ma-2210 Formentor road near the tunnel at K14. This short excursion is mainly pathless but not very difficult, and on a good day the views are outstanding. It can easily be combined with Walk 5 to Cala en Gossalba and this is strongly recommended. Alternatively there are easy walks down to the sea at Cala Murta and Cala Figuera which are quite short. The route makes use of an old track that was used to reach the lighthouse before the new road and tunnel were constructed in 1968.

Note The old zigzag track continues down from the col between El Fumat and Roca Blanca to Cala Murta, but this is not a recommended route. The gradient is tedious, being made for a heavily laden mule, and the lower zigzags have been incorporated into the gardens of a house.

See sketch map 2.

Starting Point	K14.9 on the Ma-2210 Formentor road
Time	2hr 35min
Distance	4km
Highest Point	335m
Height Climbed	300m
Grade	B
Map	Alpina E or MTN25 Cap Formentor

To reach the starting point drive along the Ma-2210, through the tunnel beneath El Fumat, then park at the *mirador* on the cliff edge at K14.9. Walk back along the road towards the **tunnel**, and at a point marked by a **small cairn** on the left, scramble up the hillside to reach the old track that is just above the road. It has a clearly built-up stone edge, and bears a narrow, trodden path, even though it is very overgrown with *càrritx*.

Follow the zigzag track at a gentle gradient, or take the trodden shortcuts that lead up to the **col** at 242m between Fumat and Roca Blanca. The 335m summit of **El Fumat** is reached quite easily from this col, up rock slabs and stony

Type of Walk
Although only short, the pathless nature of most of this route gives it a B grade.

71

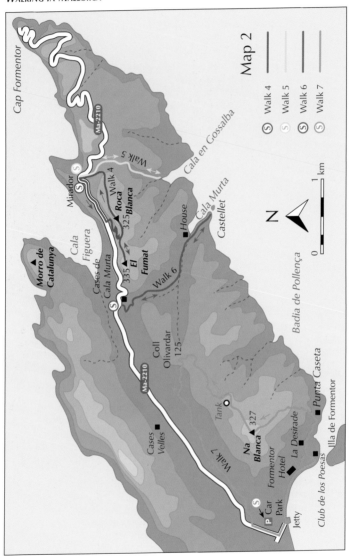

Map 2

Walk 4
Walk 5
Walk 6
Walk 7

Cap Formentor

Ma-2210

Cala en Gossalba

Walk 5

Mirador

Walk 4

Roca Blanca
▲ 325

Cala Figuera

El Fumat
▲ 335

Cala Murta

Cases de Cala Murta

Morro de Catalunya ▲

House

Cala Murta

Castellet

Walk 6

N

0   1 km

Badia de Pollença

Coll Olivardar
125

Ma-2210

Tank ○

Na Blanca ▲ 327

Cases Velles ■

Walk 7

La Desirade

Punta Caseta ■

Illa de Formentor

Formentor Hotel

Club de los Poesas

P Car Park

Jetty

72

ground at an easy angle. After enjoying the view return to the
col and go straight up the ridge ahead to the 325m summit of
Roca Blanca. There is no real path, but neither are there any
particular difficulties.

*El Fumat leans
ominously over the
road, which actually
goes through a tunnel*

From the last top on the ridge continue down in the
same direction, avoiding steep rocks when necessary on the
south side. The ridge ends in a **short cliff**, but an easy way
down can be found leading back to the right. Once on easy
ground walk along to the foot of the cliff, then make for a
large pine tree in the valley below. Follow a red earth path
left, back to the roadside *mirador*, or turn right to reach **Cala
en Gossalba** as in Walk 5.

Mirador – El Fumat	45min
El Fumat – 234m col	15min
234m col – Roca Blanca	25min
Roca Blanca – Mirador	1hr 10min

5 Cala en Gossalba

This tiny bay of bright water on the south side of the Formentor peninsula is an unspoilt gem, inaccessible by car. The path down to Cala en Gossalba was built for the extraction of wood from the forest of pine trees. Some of these pines still stand to provide welcome shade in hot weather. This walk is ideal for a lazy day, or it can be done after the walk over El Fumat and Roca Blanca (Walk 4) to give a longer excursion.

See sketch map 2.

Starting Point	K14.9 on the Ma-2210 Formentor road
Time	1hr 10min
Distance	3km
Highest Point	175m
Height Climbed	Descent and re-ascent 175m
Grade	C
Map	Alpina E or MTN25 Cap Formentor

Type of Walk
Easy, on a good path.

To reach the starting point drive along the Ma-2210, through the tunnel beneath El Fumat, then park at the *mirador* on the cliff edge at K14.9.

Walk straight down the path from the roadside – it is slightly indistinct at first, but soon develops into a clear mule track, following the **streambed** and occasionally crossing it. There are no turnings and no cross-tracks, and the path ends on some rocks on the right-hand side of the little bay of **Cala en Gossalba**. To reach the shore, which is of boulders large and small, go down the remains of **stone steps**.

Return the same way.

Mirador – Cala en Gossalba	30min
Cala en Gossalba – *Mirador*	40min

An easy path makes its way down an attractive, rugged valley to the coast

6 Cala Murta and Castellet

Cala Murta is a small cove on the south side of the Formentor peninsula that can only be reached on foot. Picnic tables, barbecue sites and a toilet have been provided near the stony beach, and a restored footpath leads to a *mirador* looking out to the detached rock of Castellet.

The approach through the woods in the sheltered valley is delightful, and also an opportunity for some birdwatching – in fact it is one of the best areas on the island for observing migrants in both spring and autumn. Look out for crossbills, linnets, black redstarts, warblers, flycatchers and many others.

See sketch map 2.

Starting Point	K13 on the Ma-2210 Formentor road
Time	2hr
Distance	5km
Highest Point	100m
Height Climbed	100m
Grade	C
Map	Alpine E or MTN25 Cap Formentor

Type of Walk
Very easy, on good tracks and paths.

Look up to the left to see some of the endless zigzags on the old mule track, **Camí Vell del Far**, that was built across Fumat to serve the lighthouse at the end of the Formentor peninsula.

There is a car park near the **Cases de Cala Murta** at K13 on the Ma-2210 Formentor road, and actually two beach walks can be accomplished from it. One is a very short descent northwards down a winding path to **Cala Figuera**, though there is also vehicle access to this beach from K12 on the road.

Walk down the main road from the car park at K13 and turn left at the **Cases de Cala Murta**, where there is a signpost for Cala Murta. There are locked gates on the narrow road, but pedestrian access alongside. The road passes a **children's camp** and runs gently downhill through a well-wooded valley. ◂

The quiet lane leads to the gates of a house, where a short track heads right to the nearby shingle beach at **Cala Murta**. Keep to the right side of the bay to follow a clear path to the end of a point, where a *mirador* looks out to the rocky islet of **Castellet de Cala Murta**.

Retrace your steps afterwards to return to the car park.

Car park at K13 – Cala Murta	50min
Cala Murta – Castellet	10min
Castellet – Car park at K13	1hr

A short path leads from Cala Murta to a good viewpoint at Castellet de Cala Murta

7 Na Blanca

This pleasant hill on the Formentor peninsula provides a delightful walk. The broad and rocky top overlooks the colourful waters of the Formentor beach, and on clear days there are views across to the hills on the Alcúdia peninsula and beyond them to Artà. The return route passes the nesting sites of Marmora's warblers and goes through the sheltered wooded valley near the Cases Velles, where birds rest during the spring and autumn migrations. During the winter this is a good place to spot resident birds such as hoopoes, black redstarts, firecrests, crossbills, linnets and great tits.

See sketch map 2.

Starting Point	Car park at a junction at K9 on the PM-221 / Ma-2210
Time	3hr 30min
Distance	8km
Highest Point	327m
Height Climbed	345m
Grade	B
Maps	Alpine E or MTN25 Cala de Sant Vicenç and MTN25 Cap Formentor

Type of Walk
Mainly easy walking on clear tracks, but paths on top are indistinct, rough and rocky.

Start from the large car park on the Ma-2210 at **Formentor**, which can also be reached by bus during the summer. Walk to a nearby **landing stage**, which can be reached by summer ferries from Port de Pollença. Continue walking along the seafront and do *not* use the access road for the Formentor Hotel. You soon have to go onto the sandy beach, then up some steps to use a coastal path in front of the **Formentor Hotel**, but only residents have access to the rest of the hotel grounds.

At the far corner of the fence that encloses the hotel grounds, turn left and follow a road inland from a property called **Club de los Poetas**. Take the second turn to the right, by a house called **La Desirade**, where there is a 'No through road' sign. This road passes a chained gateway and leads to the gates of a house on the **Punta Caseta**. Turn left immediately at the gate to climb steeply up some rough ground, as indicated by a red paint mark.

An **old path** is very soon found, zigzagging up the wooded ridge and away from another gate. Follow the path, well marked with cairns and red paint, up the ridge. Higher up, avoid following a path off to the right and keep left to go up the ridge, where a stony path marked by cairns leads along the edge of steep cliffs to the top of **Na Blanca** at 327m. Enjoy fine views of the Formentor and Alcúdia peninsulas, Serra de Llevant and Serra de Tramuntana.

From the top follow the ridge down in a northeasterly direction. A few cairns mark the way, which in any case is well defined by the proximity of steep crags on the left. Join a track at a **water tank**. (A right turn at this point leads back to the path used on the ascent, for a quicker finish to the walk.)

Follow the track straight ahead, sometimes on the crest of the ridge, and down towards the **Coll Olivardar** at 125m.

Continue downhill by keeping left at all track junctions, entering a wooded valley, then passing close to **cultivated fields**. Keep left at all junctions of stony tracks, bearing in mind that any tracks running right to the road reach locked gates.

After passing through a forest the track reaches a flat area, once a sports pitch called the **Campo de Deportes Formentor**. Walk straight across and turn right down a track, passing a small cave. Fork right at a track junction to reach a **gate** (if it is locked, cross the fence alongside).

Turn left and follow the Ma-2210 back to the car park and bus stop where the walk started. Those who arrived by ferry should return to the nearby landing stage.

Rocky and sparsely forested slopes surround the steep, rugged hill of Na Blanca

Car park – Na Blanca	1hr 50min
Na Blanca – Coll Olivardar	50min
Coll Olivardar – Car park	50min

8(a) Vall de Bóquer from Port de Pollença

This attractive and sheltered valley is much favoured by migrant birds, and in winter is always a good place for seeing some of the residents, such as the beautiful blue rock thrush. It is also interesting botanically, and the flowers of *Cyclamen balearicum* can be found within a few feet of the valley wall under the shelter of other shrubs.

The valley is bounded on the northwest by the splendid Serra del Cavall Bernat ridge, in which there are several spectacular holes or 'windows' – one of these is easily seen from the path. There is a good path right down to the small shingly beach of Cala Bóquer. The end of the Serra del Cavall Bernat dips steeply into the sea and there are views across the bay to the detached rock of El Colomer. (The beach itself is disappointing, with debris washed in by the sea.)

See sketch map 3.

Starting Point	Marina at Port de Pollença
Time	2hr
Distance	6km
Highest Point	85m
Height Climbed	170m
Grade	C
Maps	Alpine E or MTN25 Cala de Sant Vicenç and MTN25 Pollença

Type of Walk
Very easy, along good paths.

Walk along the pedestrianised seafront from the marina at **Port de Pollença** and go straight on along a stone footpath in front of some small apartments. Turn left along the **Avinguda de Bocchoris** and cross the road to follow the **Camí de Bóquer**. The avenue of trees and the path once formed the access road to a farm at Bóquer, and both have been preserved within the expanding sprawl of the port.

Cross the bypass road at a roundabout and continue along the old road up to the finca at **Bóquer**. Go through a gate covered in forbidding notices (walking is allowed) and pass in front of the house. Avoid the chained dog and go through another gate to leave the courtyard. Follow the track

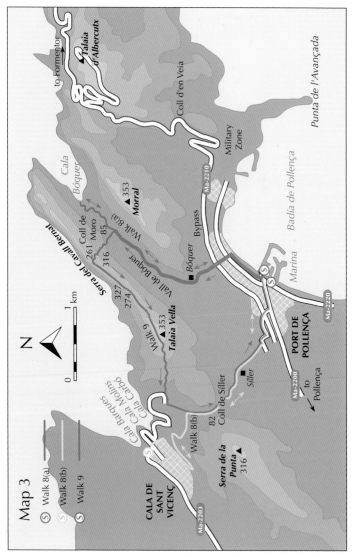

Map 3
- Ⓢ Walk 8(a)
- Ⓢ Walk 8(b)
- Ⓢ Walk 9

N

0   1 km

A clear path leads quickly and easily into the rocky Vall de Bóquer

gently uphill, passing between some immense boulders to enter the **Vall de Bóquer**.

The track then continues through gaps in drystone walls around old fields and crosses over the low **Coll de Moro** at 85m, from where a narrow and winding series of paths continue down to the sea at **Cala Bóquer**. It is possible to walk on past a ramshackle fisherman's shelter to a small platform overlooking the bay. Walk back the same way through the valley to return to **Port de Pollença**.

Port de Pollença – Cala Bóquer	1hr
Cala Bóquer – Port de Pollença	1hr

8(b) Vall de Bóquer from Cala de Sant Vicenç

Walkers staying at Cala de Sant Vicenç can get to Port de Pollença using public buses, or on courtesy buses provided by local hoteliers, or else walk over the Coll de Síller by an easy route taking one hour, described here, to link with Walk 8a.

See sketch map 3.

Starting Point	Cala Molins at Cala de Sant Vicenç
Time	4hr
Distance	14km
Highest Point	85m
Height Climbed	330m
Grade	C
Maps	Alpine E or MTN25 Cala de Sant Vicenç and MTN25 Pollença

Starting from **Cala de Sant Vicenç**, just inland from the tiny beach at **Cala Molins**, go up a flight of steps rising from near a footbridge. Turn right, then left uphill beside the **Hostal Los Pinos**, then right along a track through the woods. Follow this

Type of Walk
Very easy, along good paths and tracks.

83

The Vall de Bóquer as seen from Síller on the way to Port de Pollença

track, which is the **Camí de Can Botana**, then turn left by an electricity substation.

Walk up a concrete track, turn right, then veer left along a track and path leading out of the woods, and follow a cairned footpath across level ground. After going across a little **streambed** the path reaches a track junction at a small building, where you turn right for the **Coll de Síller** at 82m. (**Note** This track is a continuation of the coast road signposted from Cala Molins to Cala Carbo. The coast road could be followed for easier walking or for variety, and it is marked with a 'walking man' signpost at Cala Molins reading 'Pto Pollença'.)

The wide track runs past a waterworks building on the **Coll de Síller** and ends abruptly after another 200m. From the end of the track there is a narrow path running downhill, marked by cairns, leading to a track running to the left of a large house at **Síller**. Go along the access track and road leading away from the house to reach a road junction. Turn left, then right along the suburban **Carrer de les Roses**. This road again turns left and right, then you use a pedestrian crossing to get over the busy bypass road.

Continue straight along the **Carrer de Cala de Sant Vicenç**, and turn left at the **Elf petrol station** to walk to the seafront in **Port de Pollença**. Turn left to pick up the route description for Walk 8(a).

To return to Cala de Sant Vicenç from Port de Pollença, refer to Walk 10(b) to navigate through the suburbs.

Cala de Sant Vicenç – Port de Pollença	1hr
Port de Pollença – Cala Bóquer	1hr
Cala Bóquer – Port de Pollença	1hr
Port de Pollença – Cala de Sant Vicenç	1hr

9 Serra del Cavall Bernat

The Serra del Cavall Bernat ridge lies between the bay of Cala de Sant Vicenç and the Vall de Bóquer. Although its maximum height is a modest 353m, it has very steep cliffs, and those on the Cala de Sant Vicenç side plunge the full height vertically into the sea along a length of 2km. In the evening light the slanting rays of the sun illuminate their intricate structural detail and they glow with changing shades of amber, orange and pink – a most spectacular and beautiful sight.

From the other side it also provides a splendid backdrop to Port de Pollença, seen to particular advantage when driving along the coast road from Alcúdia – the rock towers halfway along the ridge look quite astonishing from many viewpoints. (The traverse of the ridge from end to end is a major undertaking, requiring rock-climbing experience.)

See sketch map 3.

Starting Point	Marina at Port de Pollença
Time	4hr 20min
Distance	9km
Highest Point	353m
Height Climbed	500m
Grade	A+
Maps	Alpine E or MTN25 Pollença and MTN25 Cala de Sant Vicenç

Leave the marina at **Port de Pollença** by walking along the seafront and into the **Vall de Bóquer** as described in Walk 8(a). Walk as far as the last **drystone wall** just short of the highest part of the track on **Coll de Moro** at 85m. Look to the left to see an obvious col on the ridge to the right of a 'window', or hole pierced in the top of the rocky ridge.

A narrow path on the left, beside the wall, leads to some **ruined buildings** in the corner of the old fields. From here look carefully for a steep, narrow, trodden cairned path leading straight up to the **col** at 261m on the **Serra del Cavall Bernat**. There is a sudden view across the col to Cala de Sant Vicenç.

Type of Walk
The route described here is not long, but includes exceedingly rough walking and some quite difficult scrambling.

The Serra del Cavall Bernat is particularly steep and rocky and needs care

From the col turn left and climb up the steep **rock tower** near the edge overlooking the sea – this is a very spectacular and exposed situation, but it is easier than it looks.

The topmost section of the tower is avoided by taking to a **sloping ramp** leading up to the left, to a cairn quite near the top at 316m. From this point onwards the exhilarating route continues southwest along the ridge. To reach the 'window ledge' look for a small cairn that shows the easiest way down on the eastern flank, then regain the ridge the same way to continue the route.

An alternative way to reach the window without climbing the rock tower is by the 'ledge route'. From just below the **col** at 261m turn left and follow an obvious **rocky ledge** at the foot of the tower. This becomes narrow in places, but is not difficult and leads across a subsidiary ridge to a **broad, sloping shelf** below the window. Scramble along this, passing below the window until it is possible to scramble up to the top of the ridge. Walk back along the ridge to find the way down to it on the eastern flank.

Continuing southwest along the ridge, the most difficult part is an awkward move on the descent from the next **rock tower**, whose summit cairn is at 327m. This is technically the most difficult part of the route, and it has to be said that finding the best way is not easy. In places there are **cairns**, scratched rocks and flattened vegetation to indicate the way, but careful route finding is still required. Climb carefully down to the **col** at 274m. Follow a cairned route across the flank of the ridge to avoid further difficulties along the crest of the ridge.

A second window is found just before reaching the last col. On the rise up to the final top, either continue along the edge of the cliffs for spectacular views, or choose easier walking along a cairned path in the **shallow valley** lying between the main ridge and another on the left. A short way up this valley, and on the right, a large hole in gently sloping ground penetrates the sea cliff to form another impressive window.

The final top is a double one, **Talaia Vella**, and is the highest point reached, at 353m. A line of cairns can be followed downhill from between the two tops, crossing **two drystone walls**. Keep following the line of cairns, then the angle eases and the best way down is to go right and pick up another cairned path, which leads gradually into a streambed near the Cala–Síller road, just below a large circular **turning area**.

Either turn right down the road for Cala de Sant Vicenç, which is quickly reached, or turn left at the turning area to return to Port de Pollença. A clear track crosses the **Coll de Síller** at 82m, passing a waterworks building, and ends abruptly after another 200m. From the end of the track there is a narrow path running downhill, marked by cairns, leading to a track running to the left of a large house at **Síller**.

Go along the access track and road leading away from the house to reach a road junction. Turn left, then right along the suburban **Carrer de les Roses**. This road again turns left and right, then you use a pedestrian crossing to go over the busy bypass road.

Continue straight along the **Carrer de Cala de Sant Vicenç**, and turn left at the **Elf petrol station** to walk to the seafront in **Port de Pollença**.

Port de Pollença – Col at 261m	1hr 30min
Col at 261m – Talaia Vella	1hr 30min
Talaia Vella – Coll de Síller	50min
Coll de Síller – Port de Pollença	30min

Avoiding the rock towers

The ascent and descent of the rock towers is not technically difficult, but sensationally exposed and requires a good head for heights - it could be classed as 'easy rock climbing' rather than 'walking'. Nevertheless, it is highly recommended to experienced scramblers, who will find it interesting, strenuous and enjoyable. Those wanting an easier approach are recommended to climb onto the Serra del Cavall Bernat from the Cala de Sant Vicenç side, leaving the Coll de Síller road before the large turning area, and crossing a streambed using a cairned path. It is then comparatively easy to reach the highest top, Talaia Vella, then follow the rocky ridge as far as you wish before returning the same way.

10(a) Serra de la Punta – Ridge Route

This low ridge with several tops lies between Cala de Sant Vicenç and the main road between Pollença and Port de Pollença. Some years ago local cavers found a hitherto unknown cave in this area that proved to be a most important archaeological find. Reconstructions of the wooden burial urns in the form of bulls, found in the cave, can be seen in the museum in Pollença.

As a ridge walk people seem to either love it or hate it. Those who like wandering along easy paths should give this one a miss, but it appeals to those who like the challenge of making their way over rough country. The terrain is almost wilderness, yet it is within sight and sound of the main road, the town of Port de Pollença and the village of Cala de Sant Vicenç.

See sketch map 4.

Starting Point	Cala Molins at Cala de Sant Vicenç
Time	4hr 30min
Distance	9km
Highest Point	316m
Height Climbed	420m
Grade	B+
Maps	Alpine E or MTN25 Cala de Sant Vicenç and MTN25 Pollença

Starting from **Cala de Sant Vicenç**, just inland from the tiny beach at **Cala Molins**, go up a flight of steps rising from near a footbridge. Turn right, then left uphill beside the **Hostal Los Pinos**, then right along a track through the woods. Follow this track, which is the **Camí de Can Botana**, through a gate and cross a stream to join the main Ma-2203 at K3 just outside the village.

Turn left to follow the road to the junction with the much busier Ma-2200 at **La Punta**. There is no need to step onto the busy road, but go up behind some noticeboards and follow the well-defined rocky ridge over several tops. (Most people are surprised by how long and rough this ridge is – the roughest part is the first ascent to a top at 186m.)

The last and highest top of **Serra de la Punta** has a cairn at 316m standing on a distinctive circular buttress. Follow the ridge down towards the **Coll de Síller** – the easiest way is to keep to the ridge at first, then watch out for a way off to the left, following the cairned route that avoids the steep, lower end of the ridge.

Turn left along a clear track, then left again at a junction beside a **small building**, to follow a well-cairned but

Type of Walk
Easy walking along tracks and a road to the beginning of the ridge, then pathless on difficult ground, but no route-finding problems. Boulder hopping and thorny scrub cannot be avoided and the terrain is too rough to be covered in a hurry.

The crest of Serra de la Punta is rough, rocky and pathless most of the time

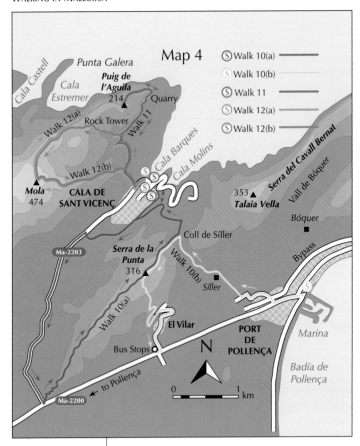

Map 4

- ⓢ Walk 10(a)
- ⓢ Walk 10(b)
- ⓢ Walk 11
- ⓢ Walk 12(a)
- ⓢ Walk 12(b)

narrow path leading back down to **Cala de Sant Vicenç** via the Hostal Los Pinos.

Cala de Sant Vicenç – La Punta	50min
La Punta – Serra de la Punta	2hr 25min
Serra de la Punta – Cala de Sant Vicenç	1hr 15min

10(b) Serra de la Punta from the Coll de Síller

This alternative route from Port de Pollença is less strenuous than the main ridge route. It follows the ridge leading up to the highest top of Serra de la Punta from the Coll de Síller, but avoids the lower part of the ridge, which is very steep and rocky. All the same, this is still no hands-in-the-pockets stroll, and it provides a good introduction to the type of steep and rocky terrain often encountered in Mallorca. The route ends on a main road at El Vilar where there are regular bus services.

See sketch map 4.

Starting Point	Marina at Port de Pollença
Finishing Point	PM-220 / Ma-2200 at El Vilar
Time	3hr
Distance	6km
Highest Point	316m
Height Climbed	315m
Grade	B
Map	Alpine E or MTN25 Pollença

Start from the bus stop and taxi stand at the marina at **Port de Pollença** and follow the Palma road as far as the **Elf petrol station**. Turn right along the **Carrer de Cala de Sant Vicenç** and go over the bypass road using the pedestrian crossing. Continue along the suburban **Carrer de les Roses**, which turns left, then right, then left to reach the edge of town. Take the next right, which is marked for 'Síller'.

Parallel tracks are reached, separated by a wall and tall fence. Follow the one on the left to pass the last building at **Síller**. Walk along a track beside a fence, then turn right to follow a rugged path up to the **Coll de Síller** at only 82m. Pass a waterworks building and walk along a track for about 200m.

A gap in a drystone wall on the left marks the start of the ascent, and some conspicuous **cairns** can be seen heading uphill. There is barely a path, but it is easy to choose a

Type of Walk
An easy approach, followed by a rugged climb.

Looking towards a fine, golden sunset from the summit of Serra de la Punta

way using the cairns as general directional guides. The cairns indicate the point where the rocky ridge is most easily gained and followed to the distinctive cairn on top of **Serra de la Punta** at 316m.

From the summit walk along the ridge for about 5 minutes to a second little top nearby. Turn left here and the houses of El Vilar soon come into view. Go down the broad ridge, then after reaching some cairns on a rocky outcrop bear right to pick up a path, which is in fact the edge of a **wide track**.

Follow the track in a sweeping zigzag down to a road, then turn right to follow the road down past the houses of **El Vilar** in another sweeping zigzag. The main **Ma-2200** is too busy to walk along in safety, but there are bus stops on either side with regular buses between Pollença and nearby **Port de Pollença**.

Port de Pollença – Serra de la Punta   1hr 50min
Serra de la Punta – El Vilar   1hr 10min

11 Puig de l'Aguila

The small hill of Puig de l'Aguila (Eagle Peak) overlooks the sea and makes a worthwhile short excursion from Cala de Sant Vicenç. There are excellent views, especially in the afternoon when the sun is shining on the magnificent cliffs of the Serra del Cavall Bernat ridge across the bay – this view is irresistible to painters and photographers. (Take a torch if you are interested in exploring the rock tunnels of an old ammunition store beneath the peak.)

The old quarry road used for most of the route is occasionally closed by local hunters in the autumn and winter, and this will be realised only minutes after starting the walk. Notices may explain the extent of restrictions, or you could enquire in advance by contacting the tourist information office in Cala de Sant Vicenç, ☎ 971–533264. (Any restriction will also affect the routes on Mola, Walk 12(a) and Walk 12(b).)

See sketch map 4.

Starting Point	Cala Barques at Cala de Sant Vicenç
Time	2hr 15min
Distance	6km
Highest Point	214m
Height Climbed	200m
Grade	C
Map	Alpine E or MTN25 Cala de Sant Vicenç

From the circular car park at Cala Barques in **Cala de Sant Vicenç** walk up the main road, **Avinguda del Cavall Bernat**, inland for about 100m and then turn right up a flight of steps between two houses. At the top of the steps turn right along a track and go right again at a nearby junction. The track leads to a **locked gate** at the entrance to an old quarry road. Access for walkers is through a small gate alongside (if the small gate is locked, there is a way round the fence on the left).

Follow the wide but stony track, which makes several bends to cross streambeds, then passes an **old quarry** where a beautiful white, pink and black rock has been extracted.

Type of Walk

Easy walking along a good but stony track as far as the tunnels, then a narrow path to the top – only a short distance, but rather stony.

93

The old quarry road runs easily round rugged slopes to Puig de l'Aguila

After a sharp bend left a **tunnel** leading into the old ammunition store is reached. (**Note** The ammunition-store tunnel runs straight in for some 40m, then makes a right turn and divides, one part going straight on and the other turning left, then right and right again to meet up with the first part. **Do not attempt to explore without a torch**.)

When the stony track comes to a sudden end, a clear path marked by cairns continues – along the level at first, then zigzagging up to a low top at 166m. (Care is needed near the top as there is a **deep mine shaft**, easily recognised by the gravelly spoil heap at the side.)

The prominent cairn on this little summit is the point of return for many walkers, and is a worthwhile objective, but continuing to the main summit is highly recommended.

Away to the west Cornavaques can be seen, and so can the Castell del Rei, with the cairned route to Mola ahead.

Follow the narrow path on across a small depression and then fairly steeply up to a top where there is a **large cairn**. From here there is a fine view of the Punta Galera, a long and bare rocky point jutting into the sea. ◄ From this viewpoint leave the main path and turn left to cross a low saddle and rise easily to **Puig de l'Aguila**, to be rewarded by outstanding views from the 214m summit.

To return to Cala de Sant Vicenç, either retrace your steps, or vary it slightly by going down the shallow valley on the north side where another line of cairns marks the way back towards the lower top. Just before reaching this you can, if you wish, take a short cut down the gully towards the quarry road.

Cala de Sant Vicenç – Puig de l'Aguila	1hr 15min
Puig de l'Aguila – Cala de Sant Vicenç	1hr

12 MOLA

The area between Ternelles and Cala de Sant Vicenç is mountainous and uninhabited, except for wild goats. The mountains are not high, but would give some very rough walking if access was not completely barred – they are in the form of parallel ridges with very steep cliffs on the northwestern side. Mola, at the eastern end of the Serra de Sant Vicenç ridge, is the only accessible top in the range, and this circular route is a good introduction to the sort of terrain often encountered in Mallorca.

Note There are sometimes restrictions on access – see comment at the start of Walk 11.

See sketch map 4.

12(a) Normal route via East Ridge

Starting Point	Cala Barques at Cala de Sant Vicenç
Time	4hr 30min
Distance	7km
Highest Point	474m
Height Climbed	490m
Grade	B+
Map	Alpine E or MTN25 Cala de Sant Vicenç

From the circular car park at Cala Barques in **Cala de Sant Vicenç** walk up the main road, **Avinguda del Cavall Bernat**,

Type of Walk
Rough and rocky
ground with
occasional traces of
paths. Easy return
along the quarry
road from Puig de
l'Aguila.

inland for about 100m and then turn right up a flight of steps between two houses. At the top of the steps turn right along a track and go right again at a nearby junction. The track leads to a **locked gate** at the entrance to an old quarry road. Access for walkers is through a small gate alongside (if the small gate is locked, there is a way round the fence on the left).

Immediately after the gate turn left on a **rough path**, and after about 100m leave it and make for the ridge to the left of a **rock tower**. Walk up the first section of the ridge on easy, bare rock to reach a **cairn**, then cross a stretch of level ground to the right to reach the offset continuation of the ridge.

At the top of this section there is another **cairn**. Continue up in the same direction, passing the top of a gully that goes down steeply on the right. Go up the broken ground ahead towards a **shoulder**, slightly to the right of the little peak ahead – occasional goat tracks and some outcrops of solid rock are a help. ◄

From this shoulder
it is worth making a
short diversion to a
little top on the left
from where there is
a clear view back
down the ridge to
Cala de Sant Vicenç
and the Serra del
Cavall Bernat.

Ahead is a **rock tower**, steep at the bottom. Cross a little col and go up to the left of the tower on easy rock and scree below the steepest rocks – there is a path and some cairns. Higher up, look for a break in the steep rocks that allows a **rising traverse** right to be made to the summit of **Mola**. This top is the highest of three, at 474m.

Leave the summit by descending to the north and cross the hollow straight ahead to a **small rocky top** on the far ridge. Turn right, northeast, along this ridge and descend on good rock, keeping to the edge of the steep ground on the left. The way gradually downhill is cairned, though trodden paths are intermittent. The route gets closer to the edge of the cliffs again, offering splendid views.

Continue down to the lower top of **Puig de l'Aguila** at 166m. On this top there is a hollow with a **deep mine shaft** and further on is a group of three shafts with paths on either side. Reach the **quarry track** by keeping straight on towards the sea and bearing slightly right.

Follow the bendy old quarry track and pass the **locked gate** seen at the start of the way. Turn left and keep left to reach the steps leading back down onto the **Avinguda del Cavall Bernat**. Turn left to return to the **Cala Barques** car park.

Cala de Sant Vicenç – Mola	2hr	
Mola – Puig de l'Aguila	1hr 30min	
Puig de l'Aguila – Cala de Sant Vicenç	1hr	

Looking back downhill towards the little resort of Cala de Sant Vicenç

12(b) Mola via a rock scramble

This route gains the Serra de Sant Vicenç ridge by way of a pleasant scramble up an unnamed rock tower, reaches the top of Mola from the northeast, then descends the east ridge of Mola back to Cala de Sant Vicenç.

Note You need a clear view throughout this descent, as there are unseen cliffs along the way. If in doubt about your ability to descend safely, then choose the easier descent via Puig de l'Aguila described in Walk 12(a).

See sketch map 4.

Starting Point	Cala Barques at Cala de Sant Vicenç
Time	4hr
Distance	5.5km
Highest Point	474m
Height Climbed	480m
Grade	A+
Map	Alpine E or MTN25 Cala de Sant Vicenç

Type of Walk
A rock scramble
followed by rough
and often pathless
terrain. The direct
descent from Mola
needs particular
care.

From the circular car park at Cala Barques in **Cala de Sant Vicenç** walk up the main road, **Avinguda del Cavall Bernat**, inland for about 100m and then turn right up a flight of steps between two houses. At the top of the steps turn right along a track and go right again at a nearby junction. The track leads to a **locked gate** at the entrance to an old quarry road. Access for walkers is through a small gate alongside (if the small gate is locked, there is a way round the fence on the left).

Follow the wide but stony track, until it makes a **hairpin bend** across a bridge. A little further on there are **two bridges** close together. Follow the streambed uphill from the first bridge and make for the foot of the right-hand rocky peak at the **valley head**.

The route goes up by the ridge that forms the right-hand skyline, and this can easily be gained if the rock is dry by climbing the **head of the gully** direct. (If wet, go up diagonally left, then back right to the notch above the steep section.) The ridge is mainly good, clean rock with ample holds, although there are one or two patches of dense and trying vegetation. The scramble ends at a pleasant little **rock tower**.

From this cliff there
are spectacular
views down to
the sea and up the
Ternelles valley to
Castell del Rei, with
the steep face of
Cornavaques forming
the continuation of
the cliffs.

From the top cross two small rocky knolls and keep going in the same direction to a **wall**. After crossing the wall continue up the vague ridge ahead, choosing bare rock for the easiest walking, and making for the **cliff edge** on the right. ◀

Follow the ridge up until the ground levels out a little with a **rocky top** on the left. Go up this by a small but obvious groove to reach one of the three tops of **Mola**, which have between them a grassy depression. Cross over to the east and reach the highest top at 474m.

To descend, go down at first towards the southeast to avoid some steep ground and find the **obvious break** in

View along the rugged northern slopes of Mola towards Ternelles

a little escarpment, then down to the right to reach some **bare rock ledges**. From here go back left and continue in this direction at the foot of some steep rocks to arrive at a **small col**. Cross this col to the left of a small top ahead and continue down by easy rocks and boulders to another **small col**.

Continue over the next little top and on down towards the end of the ridge. Descend to easy ground on the right before reaching the **final tower** and make for the **locked gate** on the quarry road to return to **Cala de Sant Vicenç**.

Cala de Sant Vicenç – Unnamed top	1hr 10min
Unnamed top – Mola	1hr 20min
Mola – Cala de Sant Vicenç	1hr 30min

13 Puig de María

Looking down on the historic little town of Pollença from Puig de María

The Puig de María is a small but distinctive hill near Pollença. There has been a chapel on the top since 1348, and in 1362 this was in the charge of three women, the first female hermits in the history of the Baleares. At one time there was accommodation for as many as 70 people, and in recent years this was available to anyone. There was a large refectory and kitchens for the use of day visitors, for which a donation was requested.

In 1988 the elderly nuns who had run the place for years decided the time had come to retire, and for a while the chapel's future was uncertain. However, it is now in private hands, and the bar and restaurant services are once again available. (Rooms are also available but it is best to enquire beforehand, ☎ 971–184132.)

Outside there are terraces and a cactus garden from which there are extensive views. Many local people go up there on Sundays, and on Easter Monday it is a place of pilgrimage for all Pollença.

See sketch map 9(b).

Starting Point	Plaça Major in Pollença
Time	2hrs
Distance	5km
Highest Point	325m
Height Climbed	275m
Grade	C
Maps	Alpina Tramuntana Nord, Alpina E or MTN 25 Pollença

From the **Plaça Major**, or the nearby bus stop in **Pollença**, head for the little park where the tourist information centre is, then follow the **Carrer del Roser Vell**. Turn left along the **Carrer del Puig de María**, which leads to the Repsol filling station and Bar Ca'n Bach. Cross the road and turn right, then quickly left, right and left again along a back lane. Cross the busy main **Ma-2200** with care. There is a small parking space for vehicles beside this busy road, where a signpost reading 'Puig de María' points up a lane.

Walk straight up the narrow tarmac lane, which turns sharp right and then left past a few houses and several terraced gardens. At first the road has a patchy surface, is very narrow and climbs in steep zigzags. There is a **turning space**

Type of Walk
Very easy, but steadily uphill on a country lane that becomes a narrow but well-made mule track near the top.

halfway up the hill, but very little parking. From the end of the road a wide path with a cobbled surface and steps leads in 15 minutes to a walled terrace at the side of the summit **chapel** at 325m.

Be sure to go through the gate on the left side of the chapel to reach an open picnic site behind, as well as exploring the buildings, which contain bygone artefacts in a museum-like setting. Access to the chapel is usually through the house. There are bedrooms and dormitory accommodation available, as well as a bar–restaurant.

On the way back downhill, consider branching off to the right along a narrow path signposted for the **Mirador del Molí Vell** for a bird's-eye view of Pollença.

Pollença – Puig de María	1hr 10min
Puig de María – Pollença	50min

14 Rafal d'Ariant and Torrent de Mortitx

The area of the Mortitx gorge is one of the roughest and wildest places in the Serra de Tramuntana. Ecologically important, it is under the protection of IBANAT, and the property occupies dozens of square kilometres and slopes down from the foot of Tomir towards the sea. There are incredible rock formations in the karst landscape, old olive trees with gnarled and twisted trunks, and the sea cliffs are pocked with caves and holes. The gorge itself is interesting botanically, with plants that prefer moister conditions to those that prevail elsewhere.

The ruined house of Rafal d'Ariant is situated on a shelf overlooking the sea, where sheep graze among a few almond and fig trees on the once-cultivated fields. Remote and utterly peaceful, this place is about as far removed from the crowded and noisy resorts of the south of Mallorca as it is possible to be. As such it has an irresistible appeal to all lovers of wild country and solitude.

See sketch map 5.

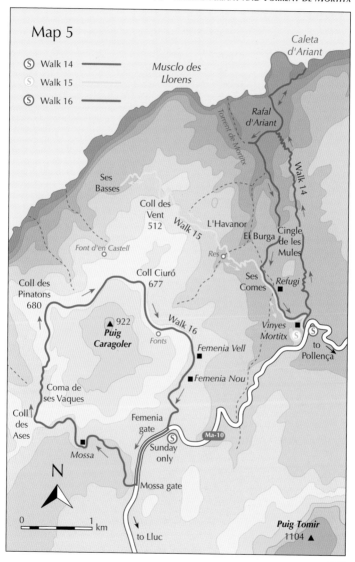

Map 5

- Ⓢ Walk 14
- Ⓢ Walk 15
- Ⓢ Walk 16

Caleta d'Ariant

Musclo des Llorens

Torrent de Mortitx

Rafal d'Ariant

Ses Basses

Coll des Vent 512

Walk 15

L'Havanor

El Burga

Res

Walk 14

Cingle de les Mules

Font d'en Castell

Coll Ciuró 677

Ses Comes

Refugi

Coll des Pinatons 680

▲ 922 Puig Caragoler

Fonts

Walk 16

Femenia Vell

Vinyes Mortitx

Ⓢ Ⓢ

to Pollença

Coma de ses Vaques

Femenia Nou

Coll des Ases

Mossa

Femenia gate

Ⓢ Sunday only

Ma-10

N

0 — 1 km

Mossa gate

to Lluc

Puig Tomir 1104 ▲

Starting Point	Vinyes Mortitx gate at K10.9 on the C-710 / Ma-10
Time	5hr
Distance	10km
Highest Point	400m
Height Climbed	500m descent and re-ascent
Grade	B+ (or A to return by the gorge)
Maps	Alpina Tramuntana Nord, Alpina D or MTN25 Son Marc

Type of Walk
Very rough and rocky, with difficult route finding. Some scrambling is required in the gorge.

There is room for a few small cars to park by the **Vinyes Mortitx** gate at K10.9 on the Ma-10. Go through the gate, pass a **tennis court**, then turn right through a gate on the left of a **stone building**. Continue through orchards to another gate with an access stile nearby. A notice warns about 'big game hunting', but do not be deterred, and a Govern Balear notice warns of difficult route finding and danger of death! This refers to the lower part of the Torrent de Mortitx, however, which is not visited on this walk.

The track rises slightly and turns left at a junction. After about 50m a **cairn** marks a vague path on the right. Follow this path down through olive trees, thorny broom and other shrubs – there are a few **red paint marks** and cairns, but they are not always easy to see.

Go through a **gate** at a junction of two stone walls and continue to follow the path through the wild and rocky area around **Cingle de les Mules**. Cairns and red paint marks will be found in places, but it is still difficult to find the way. The path twists and turns tortuously through the incredible landscape, but makes steady progress downhill towards the coast.

Look out for two places where the path makes a sharp right turn. The path rises slightly, then more distinctly, to cross two spurs on the right-hand side before later reaching a **stone wall**.

The path now turns left and descends a cliff in tight zigzags to reach the plain beside the ruined house at **Rafal d'Ariant** at 150m. From there it is a further 10 minutes or so to the edge of the cliffs, where there is a view of an impressive cave high up on the right. Another narrow path leads over the low **Coll de la Caleta** and descends towards the

coast. This becomes steep and loose, but is worth the effort for the view of the cliffs around **Caleta d'Ariant**.

The **Cova de ses Bruixes** (Witches' Cave) is high up in the cliff on the left and cannot be seen except by crossing very rough ground on the right of the path, leaving this at an extremely large boulder encountered some 20 minutes after leaving the ruined house. Allow an extra hour if you want to do this.

Most walkers will be content to return to Mortitx by the same path used on the descent, although finding the way back is not all that easy, because of the confusing nature of the ground – it is as well to pay attention to the twists and turns on the way down. ▶

A return by the **Torrent de Mortitx** makes a rewarding and slightly more adventurous alternative. This involves some easy scrambling, and is not recommended after rain, which makes the rocks slippery, but it is unlikely that the gorge is often rendered impassable due to flooding.

From the ruined house at **Rafal d'Ariant** follow a path west, passing some old fig and olive trees to reach a streambed, then continue alongside it. After passing a **large pine**

Approaching the remote and abandoned farmhouse at Rafal d'Ariant (photo: Jaume Tort)

Bear in mind that smugglers used to carry contraband inland under cover of darkness along this path!

It is worth detouring to enjoy the dramatic cliff coastline around Caleta d'Ariant (photo: Jaume Tort)

tree a cairn in the bed of the **Torrent de Mortitx** marks the place where the ascent begins. ▸

Turn left at the cairn and start walking up the bed of the stream. After about 15 minutes a **rock slab** on the left of a pool has to be negotiated, which is not technically difficult, but may be a little alarming. It is best crossed either low down near the water or higher up, but not in the middle.

About 5 minutes after this, turn left into a narrower gorge, clearly marked by **paint signs and cairns**. This is an important junction, as the right branch, which looks easier, becomes really difficult higher up. The left branch continues upwards with alternate sections of walking and easy scrambling. Finally at **El Burga** the path tops out onto a flat area at 350m covered in cistus bushes.

After 10 minutes the path joins the Mortitx–L'Havanor track (Walk 15) among olive trees. Turn left and pass a *refugi* hut and noticeboards. Cross a ladder stile by a gate, then pass an orchard and avoid a right turn. Follow the track uphill and turn left by the large **fruit storage sheds**. Follow the dirt road back past the **tennis court** to return to the **Vinyes Mortitx** gate.

A diversion downstream for 5 minutes to see a deep pool of clear water below an immense rock tower is recommended before beginning the ascent.

Note To find the way to the Torrent de Mortitx from the top, look for a path on the right about 5 minutes beyond the *refugi* hut.

Vinyes Mortitx gate – Rafal d'Ariant	2hr
Rafal d'Ariant – Caleta d'Ariant return	1hr
Rafal d'Ariant – Rock slab	30min
Rock slab – *Refugi*	1hr
Refugi – Vinyes Mortitx gate	30min

15 L'Havanor and Coll des Vent

The area around Mortitx, which is of outstanding natural beauty and great scientific interest for its flora and geology, is under the protection of IBANAT. Although this walk goes through wild and spectacular scenery, it is entirely along a narrow road and is highly recommended. The road was improved in 1990 with some concrete stretches, and although there are gates to prevent vehicular use, each has a pedestrian access stile.

This route is in the centre of the area where black vultures live, and it is essential that these rare and magnificent birds are not disturbed. Visitors are requested to keep to the dirt road and only to go in small, quiet groups.

Note Access is discouraged during the long breeding season from January to July and may not be allowed at all during this time; large groups should avoid this area altogether.

See sketch map 5.

Starting Point	Vinyes Mortitx gate at K10.9 on the C-710 / Ma-10
Time	3hr
Distance	10km
Highest Point	512m
Height Climbed	400m
Grade	C
Maps	Alpina Tramuntana Nord, Alpina D or MTN25 Son Marc

Type of Walk
Very easy, along a narrow gravel or concrete road.

There is room for a few small cars to park by the **Vinyes Mortitx** gate at K10.9 on the Ma-10. Go through the gate, pass a **tennis court**, and after passing some **fruit storage sheds** the track swings right and heads towards the coast. Avoid a track to the left and keep on the main track all the way.

An **orchard** lies on the left, then a gate and ladder stile are reached. After passing the gate there are notices and a *refugi* hut on the right. The exit route from the **Torrent de Mortitx** (Walk 14) may be noticed after 5 minutes, on the right among an open area of mature olive trees.

The track has been level up to now, but soon begins to rise and then passes by a **small reservoir** fringed with reeds. (Access, into the Zona Biologica Critica, may be restricted beyond this point, in which case a notice will advise.)

The track climbs further uphill and passes close to a small building and a field at **L'Havanor**. A short descent is followed by another ascent, through a rock cutting, then over the **Coll des Vent** at 512m.

The track winds gradually downhill through an area where young trees have been planted, ending by a field at

Ses Basses, beyond which there is no further access. At this point you simply turn around and retrace your steps back to the road at **Mortitx**. The peak of Puig Tomir dominates views on the return.

The track to Coll des Vent passes the entrance to the Torrent de Mortitx (photo: Jaume Tort)

Vinyes Mortitx gate – Reservoir	40min
Reservoir – Ses Basses	50min
Ses Basses – Vinyes Mortitx gate	1hr 30min

16 Circuit of Puig Caragoler

The rocky massif of Puig Caragoler rises to 922m and lies between the well-known Puig Roig and the Puig Gros de Ternelles, in a wild and virtually uninhabited area north of the C-710 / Ma-10. The route described is not as popular as the circuit of Puig Roig, but is extremely attractive and deserves to be better known.

The views are extensive and varied. At first the outlook on the ascent to the Coll des Ases is of Tomir across the valley. Next, the whole of the northeastern slopes of Puig Roig come into view across a trackless valley. From the Coll des Pinatons to the Coll Ciuró there is a rocky wilderness sloping down to the sea. At the end of the day the eye is drawn to the steep and craggy Puig Gros de Ternelles, and across the plain to the bay of Pollença.

In view of the current access restrictions at Mossa (see Access box, Walk 17) walkers must choose a Sunday for this route, and complete the circuit clockwise as described. There are often objections to walkers passing through Mossa late in the day, as well as on any day except Sunday. Walkers may choose to walk from Femenia anticlockwise part-way round the circuit on any other day, retracing their steps before reaching the Coll des Ases.

There are restrictions on the behaviour of walkers around Femenia, where notices forbid cycling, camping, dumping rubbish, picking mushrooms, walking dogs, lighting fires, making noise or hunting. Please keep quiet and respect the wishes of residents.

See sketch map 5.

Starting Point	Femenia gate at K14.2 on the C-710 / Ma-10
Time	4hr
Distance	10km
Highest Point	680m
Height Climbed	400m
Grade	B+
Maps	Alpina Tramuntana Nord, Alpina D or MTN25 Son Marc

The route begins at the entrance gate to **Femenia** at K14.2 on the Ma-10 Pollença–Lluc road. A parking space is available for one car a few metres towards Lluc, and there is not much space to park anywhere else nearby. It is better to arrange to be dropped off at the nearby Mossa gate, and be picked up at the Femenia gate at the end of the day. Anyone using the summer bus service can ask to be dropped at the Mossa gate and catch a return bus from the Femenia gate.

Start walking along the Ma-10 in the direction of Lluc to reach the **Mossa gate** at K15.3. A concrete access road crosses a wooded area to reach the large sheep farm at **Mossa** – go through the gate at the far side of the house. Cross the clearing straight ahead to find the beginning of the excellent **mule track** that leads up to a high pass. This path slopes up the side of a very steep cliff, and at one time had protective handrails, now disappeared. From the **Coll des Ases**, at 623m, turn right to look down a rugged valley.

The route is a bit vague here, although there are some cairns and traces of a very overgrown path, leading down to the **Coma de ses Vaques**. Keep to the right of a pine tree down this slope if in doubt.

When a flat area is reached in a hollow, cross a streambed and look for small cairns, which reveal traces of a carefully built **mule track** climbing up through a narrow rocky gully. Again, look carefully for small cairns to continue the ascent, weaving between rock outcrops and *càrritx*.

Bear right at a higher level and the cairns lead across the **Coll des Pinatons** at 680m. The cairns lead downhill and to the right, then reveal a roughly contouring route across the northern slopes of **Puig Caragoler**. Keep an eye open and look downhill to spot the **Font d'en Castell**, which is roofed – from above this can be recognised by the green, damp area below it surrounded by a wall. Look ahead to spot a wall with a **tall gate** in it (there are rungs built into the gate to facilitate walkers). Keep to the top side of a field, passing above a **ruined building**, to reach another gate, then continue along a clear track. This traverses a hollow and rises slightly to cross the **Coll Ciuró** at 677m.

Follow the clear track gradually downhill, passing **wayside *fonts*** (one with a push-button tap) and gates with rungs alongside. Watch carefully to spot a short cut through a loop

Type of Walk
No steep gradients, but almost pathless in places, where careful route finding is essential. Not recommended in mist.

Looking along the track to Coll Ciuró, at 677m on the shoulder of Puig Caragoler

of the track just before the farm of **Femenia Vell**, and thus avoid setting the farm dogs barking.

Continue along the access track, crossing a stile beside a gate and passing behind the buildings at **Femenia Nou**. The farm road later swings left, then right, then finally reaches a gate and ladder stile leading out onto the Ma-10.

Femenia gate – Coll des Ases	1hr
Coll des Ases – Coll des Pinatons	1hr
Coll des Pinatons – Coll Ciuró	1hr
Coll Ciuró – Femenia gate	1hr

17 Circuit of Puig Roig

Puig Roig is the lowest and most northerly of the 1000m summits of Mallorca, rising to 1003m, but with its encircling red cliffs it is one of the most attractive mountains on the island. It is especially striking seen in evening light from the C-710 / Ma-10 Sóller–Lluc road, and it is well worth stopping at the small *mirador* near Escorca.

On this classic circular walk around the mountain new views are constantly being revealed, and give endless pleasure no matter how many times the walk is repeated. There are a number of excellent bivvy sites under overhanging rocks, and local walkers used to start the walk in the late afternoon and sleep out there. The route also passes the interesting old cave houses of Es Cosconar, built under overhanging rocks and still in occasional use.

The circuit of the mountain is a delightful excursion, far preferable to a climb to the top. The traverse of the mountain from south to north can be done, but this is an arduous route over very rough ground.

Access
Access through Mossa farm is only allowed on Sundays, and a direct return from Es Cosconar to Mossa is not allowed, so the circuit is only allowed in an anticlockwise direction to Lluc. This means that walkers should be prepared to cover a long road walk between Lluc and the Mossa gate, or arrange for a drop-off and pick-up, or use the summer bus service to join and leave the route.

See sketch map 6.

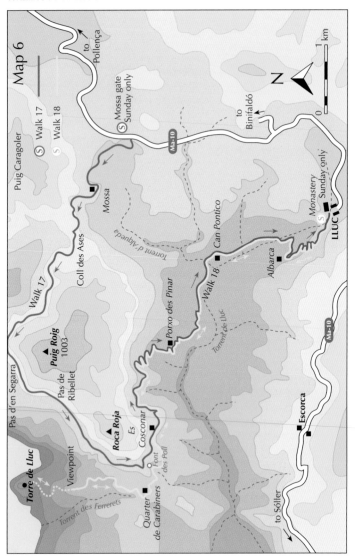

Map 6

— Walk 17
— Walk 18

Starting Point	Mossa gate at K15.3 on the C-710 / Ma-10
Finishing Point	Lluc Monastery
Time	5hr 30min
Distance	18km
Highest Point	700m
Height Climbed	250m
Grade	B+
Maps	Alpina Tramuntana Nord, Alpina D or MTN25 Son Marc and Selva

There is no parking available near the Mossa gate, so either arrange to be dropped off there and collected at Lluc Monastery at the end of the day, or arrive and leave using the summer bus service. (The nearest car parks are around Lluc and at a recreational area south of the Mossa gate at Menut.)

Leave the **Mossa gate** at K15.3 on the Ma-10. A concrete access road crosses a wooded area to reach the large sheep farm at **Mossa**. Go through the gate at the far side of the house. Cross the clearing straight ahead to find the beginning of the excellent **mule track** that leads up to a high pass. This path slopes up the side of a very steep cliff, and at one time had protective handrails, now disappeared.

From the **Coll des Ases** at 623m follow the path around the northern slopes of **Puig Roig** towards the coast. At the most northerly point the path turns a corner above the **Pas d'en Segarra**, around 650m, then runs southwest, contouring below the cliffs around 700m (beware of rockfalls while passing the base of the cliffs). ▸

After crossing a stile by a sheepfold the restored customs house of **Quarter de Carabiners** comes into sight below, with Puig Major towering beyond. Go through a gap in the wall above the barracks and the path then traverses across the slope and joins the track from the customs house after around 500m. (Alternatively, follow the wall down to the ruined barracks and pick up the track there. There is a spring-fed water tank at the Font des Poll, on the way to Es Cosconar.)

After leaving the cave houses at **Es Cosconar** the dirt road makes a couple of short zigzags downhill. Beyond **Font Amitgera** the road embarks on another series of zigzags

Type of Walk
On good but in places very stony paths.

There are excellent views of the old **Torre de Lluc** and the spectacular headland, the Morro de Sa Vaca.

115

A little tower of rock is passed as the path turns a corner at the Pas d'en Sagarra

down a steep slope covered in olives, levelling out to pass a crumbling building at **Porxo des Pinar**.

The dirt road gives way to a narrow tarmac road as it crosses the **Torrente d'Alqueda**. Pass a large finca called **Can Pontico** (where the barking dogs are usually chained). The road runs through fields, crosses the **Torrent de Lluc**, then climbs to **Albarca**. A series of zigzags gives way to a level stretch of road that leads directly to **Lluc Monastery**.

Walkers who insist on closing this loop by returning to the Mossa gate can either follow the main road or use routes based on the first stretches of Walk 22 or Walk 24.

Mossa gate – Mossa	30min
Mossa – Coll des Ases	30min
Coll des Ases – Pas d'en Segarra	1hr
Pas d'en Segarra – Es Cosconar	1hr 30min
Es Cosconar – Lluc Monastery	2hr

18 Es Cosconar and Torre de Lluc

Es Cosconar is a fascinating place with a number of cave houses built under a huge overhanging rock. They face south and have a very impressive view of Puig Major. These houses can also be seen on the walk around Puig Roig (Walk 17), but the walk described here, although slightly longer, is a very much easier one.

Before rising to Es Cosconar the route crosses an absolutely flat plain that looks as though it once held a lake. Now there are cereal crops, olive trees, and sheep with tinkling bells grazing among them. Impressive cliffs dominate this plain at the beginning of the walk, with the red walls of Puig Roig in full view straight ahead. Further on a restored customs house stands in a prominent position overlooking the deep cleft of the Torrent de Pareis. Although this makes a worthwhile objective in itself, the walk can be extended further on towards the old Torre de Lluc, perched on a headland overlooking the sea.

The way to the *torre* has been declared public, but this decision has been contested by the landowner. Access to this walk is restricted to Sundays only (as is Puig Roig). Parking restrictions also add a considerable distance to the route, as walkers must start from Lluc, and only the most active stand a chance of reaching the *torre* itself.

See sketch map 6.

Starting Point	Lluc Monastery
Time	5hr 40min
Distance	22km
Highest Point	540m
Height Climbed	420m
Grade	C to the customs house and B beyond
Maps	Alpina Tramuntana Nord, Alpina D or MTN 25 Son Marc and Selva

At the front entrance of **Lluc Monastery** turn left along a road at the side of a bar–restaurant. The road may be barred to traffic, and leads to a **gateway** and cattle-grid (a notice points out that access is allowed only on foot and only on Sundays).

Type of Walk
Very easy walking along a track. After the customs house there is only a narrow and almost completely lost path to the Torre.

The road descends in a series of zigzag bends, though if you look carefully you will find stone steps allow a couple of short cuts. Turn right at the large house of **Albarca** and the road levels out as it crosses the valley, also crossing the **Torrent de Lluc**.

Follow the level road to a large finca called **Can Pontico** (where the barking dogs are usually chained). The tarmac road becomes a dirt road as it crosses the **Torrent d'Alqueda**, and it is simply a matter of following it all the way through olive groves (there are gates along the way).

After a lengthy level stretch the road passes a crumbling building at **Porxo des Pinar** and begins to rise in zigzags – and occasional short cuts are worthwhile. About 1hr 15min from the start of the walk there is an open gateway, and it is a further 25 minutes from this gateway to the cave houses at **Es Cosconar**.

After the cave houses continue along the track, which descends a little, then swings past a spring in a shallow valley at **Font des Poll**. The track then reaches the restored barracks of **Quarter de Carabiners**. The house itself is not exactly attractive, but the situation is a magnificent one.

It is well worth the extra effort to follow the vestigial remains of a path that goes on to the old watch tower (torre) near the sea. Turn left along a **wall** before reaching the barracks, passing a pair of **olive trees**. Turn right further along, to pass a larger olive tree, then look for traces of the old path, which is built up at the edges and marked by a few small cairns. Keep to the left of a low hill ahead, then bear right to cross a small col and descend slightly to cross a **streambed**.

Continue on fairly level ground and make towards a fence near **two pine trees**. Just to the left it is possible to pick up the old path marked by cairns as far as a little knoll where there are more pine trees. A descent can be made to the right to cross another **streambed**, then the cairned path leads further downhill towards a **rocky crest**.

The **Torre de Lluc** can be seen on a fine headland below, but you need to decide how far downhill you wish to go, bearing in mind that you have to return the same way. Perhaps the best thing is to choose an agreeable viewpoint, then turn around to climb back to the barracks and walk back to Lluc.

Lluc Monastery – Es Cosconar	2hr	*The 'cave houses' at*
Es Cosconar – Quarter de Carabiners	20min	*Es Cosconar are still*
Quarter de Carabiners – Viewpoint	30min	*inhabited on a*
Viewpoint – Lluc Monastery	2hr 50min	*part-time basis*

19 Cuculla de Fartàritx

The impressive peak of Cuculla de Fartàritx, although of no great height at 711m, dominates the town of Pollença and the Vall d'en Marc with its spectacular cliffs facing west, north and east. It is approached by a very interesting old mule track as far as a high farm on the Fartàritx plateau. An intermittent and narrow path skirts the farm and leads to the summit via a natural break in the cliffs.

Note An alternative ascent (Grade A+) involving a steep scramble up an interesting little chimney is also described.

See sketch map 7.

Starting Point	Plaça Major in Pollença
Time	6hr 30min
Distance	16km
Highest Point	711m
Height Climbed	665m
Grade	B+
Maps	Alpina Tramuntana Nord, Alpina D and E or MTN25 Pollença and Son Marc

Type of Walk
Level, easy road walking as far as Can Huguet, then uphill steadily along a well-made mule track to the high plateau. After this the mountain path is less well defined but not too difficult.

Walk from the **Plaça Major** in the centre of **Pollença** to the **Plaça dels Seglars**, at the foot of over 400 **Calvari** steps. Turn right to follow the **Carrer de l'Horta** almost to a bridge on the outskirts of town. Turn left along an old unnamed road, signposted as the GR route to Lluc. After 1km a **broken footbridge** will be seen on the right. Cross the streambed, which is usually dry, and go straight on along a broad dirt road.

Turn left to follow a minor road over a bridge near **Can Pontico**, after which it swings right, then keep straight on alongside the stream. After about 700m turn left, as signposted along the **Camí de la Coma**. Almost immediately turn right and follow the minor road until it rises and ends near a house called **Can Huguet.** Climb in front of and behind a house to reach an **old abandoned house** above it. Go up some steps, passing an old well, and keep straight on, outside a wall, and into an oak wood by a gateway.

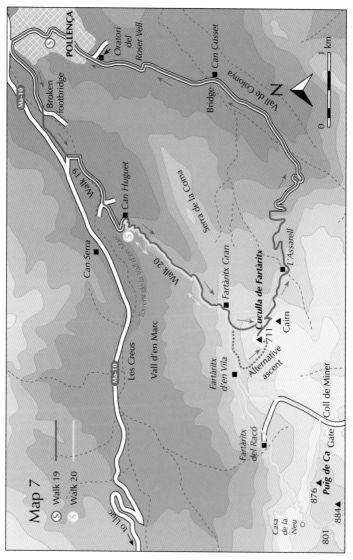

Map 7

Ⓢ Walk 19
Ⓢ Walk 20

POLLENÇA
Oratori del Roser Vell
Broken footbridge
Ma-10
Can Gisset
Bridge
Vall de Colonya
N
0 — 1 km
Walk 19
Can Huguet
Serra de la Coma
Can Sera
Walk 20
Torrent de la Vall d'en Marc
Fartàritx Gran
Cuculla de Fartàritx
L'Assarell
Les Creus
Vall d'en Marc
Ma-10
Fartàritx d'en Vila
711
Cairn
Alternative ascent
to Lluc
Fartàritx del Racó
Coll de Miner
Puig de Ca Gate
876
884
801
Casa de la Neu

A fine view from Cuculla de Fartàritx stretching far into the Serra de Tramuntana

Follow the old track up through the woods, where there may be pigs foraging for acorns. The path goes through a gap in a stone wall, then another gap at a higher level. Turn left here and go through a **metal gate**. After a further 5 minutes there is a left turn along a broader path, then the old mule track is picked up again after 10 minutes, winding upwards through an attractive natural garden of flowering shrubs and fan palms. In about 45 minutes more, this leads to a high farmhouse, **Fartàritx Gran**, near a stream.

Turn right alongside the wall enclosing the fields. The wall turns left to go up several zigzags, while the main path continues across the plateau and is not followed any further on this walk. (Refer to Walk 20 for its continuation towards Puig de Ca.)

Follow the wall uphill from a red paint mark not far beyond **Fartàritx Gran**. A narrow trod can be followed up above the enclosed fields contouring towards some large oak trees. Continue to contour from the wood along open, easy ground, with occasional cairns, until after passing a *sitja* and a **ruined shelter** the path leads uphill towards Cuculla de Fartàritx.

The path turns left below some pinnacles, then slopes up to the base of the cliffs. After turning a little corner, **sloping rocky ledges** lead up to reach the top of the cliffs through a natural break. Turn right at a **prominent cairn** on top of the cliff and go up easy grassy slopes, following smaller cairns for about 400m to reach the top of **Cuculla de Fartàritx** at 711m.

Alternative Ascent, Grade A+

Instead of going round the outside of the **Fartàritx Gran** fields, where the wall turns at right angles, follow the main path that continues in the direction of **Fartàritx d'en Vila**, a restored house completely hidden in a clump of trees. If you want to look at this, stay on the path, which leads to a gate and then a flight of old stone steps. If not, bear left as you approach the trees, then make towards a tall **palm tree**.

From the palm tree choose any way up into the **wide upland valley** of old neglected terraces backed by **high cliffs**. Beware of thorny scrub and make use of animal tracks. There may appear to be no way up these cliffs, but such a way can be found from the obvious corner where there is a notch in the skyline.

At the foot of the corner there is a large **rocky outcrop** covered with ivy – go up past this to reach the foot of the **chimney** (which shows obvious signs of previous use). There are no difficulties, and plenty of comforting hand and foot-holds, although long legs are an advantage in a couple of places. The chimney is surmounted in about 10 minutes, passing a cairn at the top, and a further 10 minutes of easy walking leads to the 711m summit of **Cuculla de Fartàritx**.

Descent

It is possible to enjoy a circular walk by descending to the high farm of L'Assarell at 400m, and walking down the road through the Vall de Colonya, arriving in Pollença by way of the old church at Roser Vell.

To try this descent, return to the **prominent cairn** at the cliff edge some 400m southeast of the summit. Follow the twisting path down **sloping rocky ledges** and keep right to hug the base of the cliffs – there is plenty of awkward scrub, but look ahead to see a length of **drystone wall** on a col. Take any route that seems best and carefully climb over the wall. Make for the farm of **L'Assarell** below, choosing a way among the multitude of animal tracks through thorny scrub (care should be taken not to disturb the many animals here).

Once through the gate there is a surfaced road all the way back to town – at first this zigzags steeply down to the valley floor, then is level most of the rest of the way. Take a left turn over a bridge opposite a large house at **Can Cusset**. The Oratori del Roser Vell is passed, and the **Carrer del Roser Vell** is followed back into **Pollença**.

Pollença – Fartàritx Gran	2hr 30min
Fartàritx Gran – Cuculla de Fartàritx	1hr
Cuculla de Fartàritx – L'Assarell	45min
L'Assarell – Pollença	2hr

20 Puig de Ca

Puig de Ca lies between Tomir and Cuculla de Fartàritx, these three being the peaks that overlook the town of Pollença on the south of the Vall d'en Marc. Although not as spectacular as Cuculla de Fartàritx, Puig de Ca has steep cliffs and provides an interesting walk. A particularly unusual feature is an old snow house with a curved roof – the only one of this type on the island.

See sketch map 20.

Starting Point	Can Huguet reached by road from Pollença
Time	5hr 45min
Distance	12km
Highest Point	884m
Height Climbed	800m
Grade	A
Maps	Alpina Tramuntana Nord, Alpina D and E or MTN25 Pollença and Son Marc

Going from Pollença towards Lluc, turn left at K2.7 on the Ma-10, cross a bridge and turn right, then park somewhere along this lane beside the river. Refer to the route description in Walk 19 to follow the old mule track from **Can Huguet** uphill to **Fartàritx Gran**.

Cross the stream and walk alongside the wall enclosing the fields. Where the wall turns left, go up a little zigzag and then keep on the path, which continues west to the ruined house of **Fartàritx d'en Vila**. There is a gate just before and below the house. Turn left up steps half-hidden among the trees and go between the old buildings.

Behind the property turn right and continue along the track in the same direction as before. There is a **locked gate** to surmount at a boundary fence, after which it is better to avoid going too close to the next house, **Fartàritx del Raco**, where walkers are not welcome. It can be bypassed by crossing the access track and using a path well to the left of the buildings.

Once the farm is passed, head uphill roughly southwest, below the **sheer cliffs** of the mountain, using traces of an

Type of Walk
Partly on good tracks and a well-made mule track, and partly on pathless ground with some route finding required. Rocky on the top but not difficult.

The steep northern cliffs of Puig de Ca as seen from near the Coll de Miner

The old path must once have been an excellent mule track serving the snow house, but unfortunately it has fallen into almost total disrepair.

old path where found. ◀ Above the snow house, or **Casa de la Neu**, the ground becomes steeper, but the remains of the path are more evident. Go through what's left of a fence to reach the **Coll de Fartàritx**, at 801m, where a wide track leads south.

Follow the track to a **boundary wall** and then turn left into a shallow gully, making for a low crag at the top. There is an easy way up a sloping ledge and the west top of **Puig de Ca** is reached at 863m in a further few minutes. Double back to continue over the main top at 884m, then head for another top at 876m and walk along the rocky ridge down to the **Coll de Miner**.

Cross a wall on the col close to the crag, as there is a high **locked gate** on the col itself at 635m. Follow the tarmac track down towards **Fartàritx del Raco**, but leave it where it bends left towards the farm. Cut across country to return to the ruined house at **Fartàritx d'en Vila**, finding your own way rather than looking for the defunct path shown on the map.

From the ruins, follow the path back to **Fartàritx Gran** and walk down the mule track to **Can Huguet** to reach the road and finish.

Can Huguet – Fartàritx Gran	1hr 15min
Fartàritx Gran – Coll de Fartàritx	1hr 30min
Coll de Fartàritx – Puig de Ca	45min
Puig de Ca – Coll de Miner	30min
Coll de Miner – Can Huguet	1hr 45min

21 Puig Tomir

Because of its commanding position at the head of the Pollença valley, and its accessibility, Puig Tomir is a well-known and popular mountain.

It can be reached in 1 hour 30 minutes from the road end at Binifaldó by a well-defined path, and is one of the places where black vultures are sometimes sighted, and for this reason it is a mountain where other walkers are likely to be met, especially at weekends. Most people go up and down from Binifaldó – a short but enjoyable excursion.

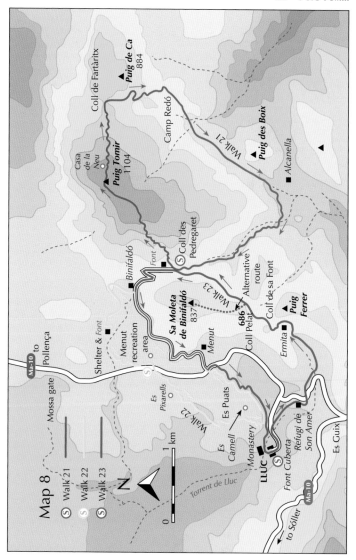

Map 8

Ⓢ Walk 21
Ⓢ Walk 22
Ⓢ Walk 23

N

km

The views from the top are extensive, and it is an interesting summit with a deep, circular snowpit nearby. All the summit area itself is bare and rocky and there are steep crags on the northern side. This walk is an interesting circular route returning via Alcanella.

See sketch map 8.

Starting Point	Coll des Pedregaret at Binifaldó
Time	5hr
Distance	9km
Highest Point	1104m
Height Climbed	630m
Grade	A
Maps	Alpina Tramuntana Nord, Alpina D or MTN25 Son Marc and Selva

Type of Walk
Mainly on rough and stony paths, and including a short but easy scramble. There are some route-finding problems around Alcanella where trees and scrub obscure the way.

Menut and Binifaldó are signposted through a gateway at K17.4 on the Ma-10 Pollença–Lluc road. The gate may be closed to traffic at weekends, in which case use the nearby Es Pixarells car park, adding 7km and 2 hours to the day's walk. Drive up the road and keep left at **Menut**. The road passes an education centre called **Binifaldó**, but climbs further and ends at the Agua Binifaldó bottling plant on the **Coll des Pedregaret**, where there is a parking place at 660m.

The walk starts between the gate to the bottling plant and a gate onto a forest track. Follow the **boundary fence** of the bottling plant uphill until a sharp right turn is marked. The path begins to wind up through the trees. After leaving the woods there is a rising traverse across a **scree slope** directly above the bottling plant. After crossing a second and wider scree the path rises steeply, keeping close against the rocks on the right.

The path is mostly a good one, with **rock steps** built up in the steeper places, and leads to a little **rock slab** about 4m high. Although this is easily surmounted by means of a groove sloping up diagonally from right to left, and well supplied with hand and footholds, it comes as a surprise to those unused to using their hands on a walk. The **metal cable and**

rungs fixed to the rock can be a real help if the rocks are icy – thankfully a rare condition.

Above the slab the path continues up through a shallow valley that leads directly to the crest of the mountain. The path keeps just to the right of the crest, and it is simply a matter of following the cairns up gently rising ground to the summit of **Puig Tomir**. The altitude is 1104m and views are extensive.

From the top go down east to reach the ruined snowpit of **Casa de la Neu** in 10 minutes, then continue following a rocky, cairned path down towards the **Coll de Fartàritx.** ▶ Aim slightly to the right of the col at first to avoid some steep ground, then aim for the centre where a vehicle track will be found at 800m. Turn right along this and follow it down past a small hollow, the **Clot Fondo**, where young trees have been planted.

When another track is met, turn right again to reach a flat plain known as **Camp Redó**. From the turning circle at the end of the track a narrow path leads to a high wooden stile beside a gateway in a boundary wall. Follow the cairned path on through a narrow and rugged valley that skirts the southeast slopes of Puig Tomir.

The rocky slopes of Puig Tomir are seen on the way back to Coll des Pedgregaret

In places the remains of the old track used by the snow workers can be picked out.

Cross a ladder stile and walk through an enclosure, leaving it at another ladder stile. A sizable flat area below 500m in the valley contains the ruined house of **Alcanella**. This was once a cultivated clearing, but became quite overgrown, although a **vehicle track** has recently been bulldozed through and some plots are again under cultivation (there is no access to the house).

Follow the track at first, but watch out for a narrow, **cairned path** on the right. Follow this, which is the old mule track, and cross the vehicle track a little further along. The path passes a man-made **rockpool** of water, then crosses the vehicle track again. (**Note** If you choose only to follow the vehicle track, be sure to turn right along the old path before the track crosses a streambed, or you will end up well off-route.)

The path is fairly vague as it crosses the **streambed**, but as height is gained it becomes clearer. It rises high on the left side of the valley where it is rocky and well marked by cairns. Higher up it goes into the forest, then descends a little and crosses a streambed to join a **wide track**.

Keep right and this track rises steadily to return to the **Coll des Pedregaret** by the forest gate at **Binifaldó**.

Binifaldó – Puig Tomir	1hr 30min
Puig Tomir – Coll de Fartàritx	45min
Coll de Fartàritx – Camp Redó	30min
Camp Redó – Alcanella	1hr
Alcanella – Binifaldó	1hr 15min

22 Es Camell (Camel Rock)

The well-known 'Camel Rock' has been sculpted by natural forces to look almost exactly like a camel. If any member of your party is agile enough they can climb to the neck and pose for a photograph, emulating the postcards on sale in the shop at Lluc Monastery. The rock is partly hidden among trees on the rocky ridge between Lluc and the Es Pixarells recreation area, and used to be quite difficult to find. The whole area is covered with oak trees and karstic rocks eroded into incredible shapes, with undershrubs of cistus, euphorbia and lentisc.

Lluc Monastery is an impressive building with a museum, gallery, shops, bar–restaurants, ATMs, picnic areas and accommodation. The Menut picnic area where the walk starts has ample parking and toilets, but can be crowded on Sundays and holidays.

See sketch map 8.

Starting Point	Menut recreation area at K16.6 on the C-710 / Ma-10
Time	2hr 40min
Distance	8km
Highest Point	600m
Height Climbed	160m
Grade	C
Maps	Alpina Tramuntana Nord, Alpina D or MTN25 Son Marc and Selva

Start at the **Menut recreation area** at K16.6 and cross the Ma-10. Turn left along a footpath running roughly parallel to the road. This is marked with **wooden posts** and it twists and turns through amazing rock formations as though through a maze. In about 10 minutes it joins a wide track that leads to the **Es Pixarells recreation area**.

Follow the main track downhill a little, away from the main road, then along and uphill to a fine *mirador*. Further along, turn right at a path junction and cross a slight rise at **Es Puats**. The track begins to descend, but on reaching a *sitja* and a stone bench, a narrow path on the left leads to **Es Camell**, or Camel Rock. The path continues past the outcrop to a rocky viewpoint. The climb up to the 'neck' is a rock climb of about 7m and is not easy.

Return to the path junction, turn left to descend to the valley floor and cross a **footbridge** to reach a track beside a football pitch. If you wish to visit nearby **Lluc Monastery**, return to this point afterwards. (**Note** If you start this walk at Lluc, then watch carefully to spot the football pitch on the left of the access road leading away from the monastery. Cross the pitch to reach the track beside the footbridge.)

Type of Walk
Easy and pleasant on good paths.

A view of Lluc Monastery, showing its remote and secluded mountain location

The track is the beginning of the **Camí Vell**, or 'old road', from Lluc to Pollença and is followed uphill to reach the main **Ma-10** at a gate. Turn left along the road and after 100m turn right through a gateway signposted for Menut and Binifaldó. The tarmac road leads up to **Menut**, where you turn left to avoid the forest nursery.

Continue up the road almost to the **Binifaldó** education centre, which is operated by IBANAT. Look out for the old road signposted for Pollença on the left, and follow the track for about 400m. Take a branch track on the left, and in a little under 20 minutes it passes a stone **shelter and *font***.

Follow the track onwards, despite many bends, and it crosses a wooded rise and reaches the main **Ma-10**. Do not step onto the road, but turn left and go up through the wood, where stone steps lead back to the **Menut recreation area** where the walk began.

Menut – Es Camell	1hr
Es Camell – Binifaldó	1hr 10min
Binifaldó – Menut	30min

23 Binifaldó and Menut

Binifaldó and Menut are two publicly owned *fincas* in the mountains not far from Lluc Monastery, managed and conserved by the Govern Balear in association with IBANAT. The houses at Binifaldó have been restored and are used as an education centre, while the house at Menut has a defensive tower and the land nearby is used as a forest nursery. The main Ma-10 passes through the Menut area, and excellent recreation opportunities have been provided. Some camping is also permitted here, on application to the *conselleria* in Palma.

This walk explores the typical mountain landscape in which the two *fincas* sit. There are large expanses of oak woodlands and pines growing higher up the slopes here and there, replacing the oaks. The bedrock is permeable limestone with karstic erosion, producing some very curious rock formations, such as the well-known Es Camell (Camel Rock), seen in Walk 22.

The high rainfall has produced a series of springs, of which one, the Font des Pedregaret, is exploited commercially at Binifaldó. Ses Fonts Ufanes is different from the other springs in that rainwater and melting snow from Puig Tomir and Sa Moleta drain into a phreatic tube. This emerges in the woods at the side of the track in Es Bosc Gran and is said to flow all the year round.

The top of Sa Moleta de Binifaldó can be reached from the Coll Pelat.
See sketch map 23.

Starting Point	Lluc Monastery car park
Time	3hr
Distance	10km
Highest point	690m
Height Climbed	280m
Grade	C
Maps	Alpina Tramuntana Nord, Alpina D or MTN25 Son Marc and Selva

Leave the main gateway of the monastery at **Lluc** and turn left along the road. The road is straight at first, but before it bends right, turn right at a gateway and cross a ladder stile. A track leads gently onwards then a path climbs a wooded slope to a gate. Cross a track and continue straight up a cobbled zigzag path to reach the **Refugi de Son Amer**.

Type of Walk
Easy, on good tracks all the way, with some ups and downs, but nothing very steep.

Looking southwest towards the rugged mountains from Coll Pelat

Abundant signposts and marker posts lead to an access track. Follow the GR221 signs to turn left for Pollença, pass a car park and avoid the main **Ma-10 road**. Walk parallel to the road at first, then veer away from it, turning right to cross a stone-lined channel. A clear path leads up a slope of scrub to join a track going through a gap in a wall. Follow the bendy track until a path is marked off to the left. This winds uphill to the restored chapel of S'Ermita de Son Amer.

Walk up to a track and turn left further uphill, passing more *sitges* and a limekiln. Further up the track, head right as marked and cross a ladder stile over a wall and fence on the **Coll Pelat**, around 690m (2265ft). ◀

From the Coll Pelat a diversion can be made up the rugged ridge running north to Sa Moleta de Binifaldó, returning the same way. The 837m summit is crowned with an aerial. An ascent would give this walk an overall B grade and take an extra hour.

A path leads quickly to a track, which is followed straight ahead past a few *sitges* in rocky woodland. Turn right at a signposted track junction. The track runs gently up and down before climbing to pass a gap in a wall, where there is a view of the bulky Puig Tomir ahead. Walk down the track but when it bends sharply right, keep straight ahead along a narrow, rugged path. This features plenty of ups and downs but remains obvious as it crosses a forested slope to reach the broad **Coll des Pedregaret** at around 650m (2130ft).

Beyond a gate in a wall lies a car park and the access road to the Agua Binifaldó water-bottling plant. Follow the road downhill and note that there is access on the right up to a *font* below the plant, where water is freely dispensed. The road bends and there are unofficial short-cuts on the way to **Binifaldó**, where a large building serves as an education centre.

Continue down the road to pass the forest nursery at **Menut**, then later turn left along the main **Ma-10**. After 100m turn right down a wide track from a wooden gate – this is the **Camí Vell**, and another part of the old road from Lluc to Pollença. A path goes across a **football pitch** to arrive back at **Lluc Monastery**. Turn left and then right along the road to return to the starting point.

Lluc Monastery – Coll des Pedregaret	1hr 50min
Coll des Pedregaret – Lluc Monastery	1hr 10min

24 Lluc to Pollença via Camí Vell

The new road between Pollença and Sóller has resulted in the old road, or Camí Vell de Pollença, becoming a quiet and attractive byway through delightful countryside, making a pleasant and easy walk. It has been adopted as part of the waymarked GR221 through the Serra de Tramuntana. The only snag is that some walking has to be done along the main Ma-10, from the junction at K5.4 to K2.8.

A party that has the use of two cars might prefer to leave one car at K5.4 and the other at Lluc. Alternatively, aim to tie this linear route in with the schedule of the summer bus service running between Pollença and Lluc.

See sketch maps 9(a) and 9(b).

Starting Point	Lluc Monastery car park
Finishing Point	Plaça Major in Pollença
Time	4hr 45min
Distance	17km
Highest Point	620m
Height Climbed	150m
Grade	C+
Maps	Alpina Tramuntana Nord, Alpina D or MTN25 Son Marc, Selva and Pollença

From **Lluc Monastery** go out of a side entrance marked for the Botanic Garden. Just before this traffic-free road meets the main access road, turn left at a gateway and go across a **football pitch** to join a track near a footbridge. The old road, or **Camí Vell**, begins here, level at first, then rising in a series of bends to reach the **Ma-10** at a wooden gate.

Type of Walk
Easy, along tracks and mostly downhill. In mid-winter it can be mainly in the shade.

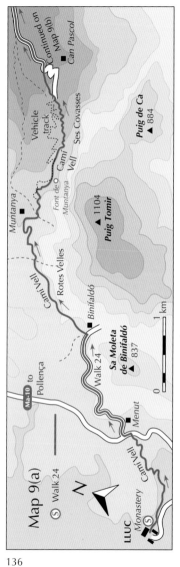

Map 9(a)

- Ⓢ Walk 24

N

LLUC
Monastery — Ⓢ

Cami Vell

to
Pollença — Ma-10

Menut ■

Walk 24

Sa Moleta
de Binifaldó
▲ 837

Binifaldó ■

Rotes Velles

Cami Vell

Muntanya ■

Font de ○
Muntanya

Cami
Vell

Rotes Velles

Puig Tomir
▲ 1104

Vehicle
track

Ses Covasses

Puig de Ca
▲ 884

Continued on Map 9(b)

Can Pascol ■

0 ——— 1 km

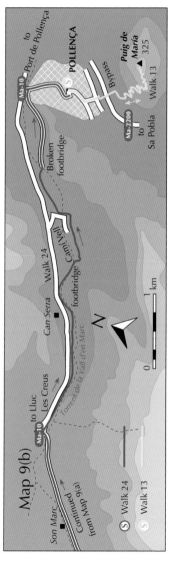

Map 9(b)

to
Port de Pollença

Ma-10

Pollença

Ⓢ

Bypass

Puig de
Maria
▲ 325

Walk 13

Ma-2200
to
Sa Pobla

Broken
footbridge

Cami Vell

Walk 24

footbridge

Can Serra ■

Cami Vell

Torrent de la Vall d'en Marc

to Lluc
Les Creus

Ma-10

Son Marc ■

Continued from Map 9(a)

N

0 ——— 1 km

- Ⓢ Walk 24
- Ⓢ Walk 13

Turn left along the road, and after 100m turn right through a gateway signposted for Menut and Binifaldó. The tarmac road leads up to **Menut**, where you turn left to avoid the forest nursery. Continue up the road to 620m, then down the road almost to the **Binifaldó** education centre, which is operated by IBANAT.

Turn right along a track, where fields rise behind a wall on the right, towards Puig Tomir. The track rises gently and is joined by the **Camí Vell**, or old road, from Lluc. Walk straight ahead and gently down into a forest with limited views. Pass some gates and follow the track beneath the rocky face of Puig Tomir, heading down through sparser woodland with an undergrowth of heather and cistus.

Step down a cobbled path on the left to short-cut a bend from the track. Cross the track and go down a winding path that features old cobbles and restored surfaces. Pass the **Font de Muntanya** and land on the track again beside a bridge. Continue straight ahead downhill until two tracks diverge. Between them, signposted as the GR221, is a stone-paved path. Go down it to cut out a bend in the track then beware of any unmarked short-cuts you might see, and stay on the track unless clearly directed off it. A marker post indicates a right turn to short-cut a bend in the track, then follow the track across a steep and well-wooded slope, noting its neatly buttressed edge and gentle gradient.

When a hairpin bend is reached, head straight along a narrow path, and soon step down to the left as marked at a *sitja*. Walk down a wooded slope alongside a wall and go through a gate. The path runs down a steep, rugged, bouldery, wooded slope. Pass a couple of *sitges* and a limekiln and continue roughly parallel to a wall. Fork right as marked, and don't go through a gap in a wall, but follow the woodland path downhill beside a tall fence. Cross a tarmac access road and continue down the woodland path, which becomes rough and stony, and is fenced on both sides.

Turn left down a narrow tarmac road, leaving the woods and turning right to pass small fields. Turn right again at the gates of Can Melsion and follow the road past larger fields around **Son Marc**, eventually crossing a bridge over a river to reach a junction with the main **Ma-10 road**.

Turn right but almost immediately turn right again to follow a riverside path, rather than the main road. Always

The Camí Vell in cultivated countryside between Can Pascol and Can Melsion

follow the **Torrent de la Vall d'en Marc** unless clearly signposted to the contrary. The main road is very close to hand at **Can Serra**, then a couple of footbridges lead walkers across to the other bank, where a tarmac access road is reached, the Camí de Can Romí, and this is followed straight ahead beside the river.

Turn left to cross a bridge and leave the river, then turn right along the **Camí Vell**, now a dirt road flanked by walls. Turn right at another junction to return to the river and cross the bridge. Turn left along another road and follow it straight ahead. It passes the **Refugi del Pont Romà**, the end of the GR221, as it reaches the outskirts of **Pollença**, around 60m (195ft).

Lluc Monastery – Binifaldó	1hr
Binifaldó – Muntanya	35min
Muntanya – Can Pascol	1hr 20min
Can Pascol – Can Pontico	1hr 25min
Can Pontico – Pollença	25min

25 Caimari and Ses Figueroles

The old farmhouse of Ses Figueroles can only be reached by mule track. The fig trees after which it is named grow on terraces surrounding the house, which is still in occasional use. It lies in a narrow valley south of Alcanella and is approached by the same mule track from Binibona. On this circular walk an ascent is made to the Coll de Sa Batalla, then the recently restored Camí Vell de Lluc is followed back down to Caimari.

See sketch map 10.

Starting Point	Plaça Major in Caimari
Time	5hr 15min
Distance	16km
Highest Point	640m
Height Climbed	600m
Grade	B
Maps	Alpina Tramuntana Nord, Alpina C, D and F or MTN25 Selva

Start in **Caimari**, where the road to Binibona is signposted from the main Ma-2130 and leads to the **Plaça Major** in the middle of town. Pass in front of the church, then turn left up **Carrer de Sant Jaume**. Turn right along **Carrer de Binibona**, which becomes the Camí de Binibona on the edge of town. Fork left at a road junction where several signs indicate accommodation options (there are two small hotels in the little village of **Binibona**).

Turn left along a country road signposted for two agro-turismo establishments – **Can Beneït** is passed on the way out of Binibona, while **Ets Albellons** is further along the road. Two minutes after passing the gate to the latter, when following a track, turn right as marked by cairns to cross the **Torrent de Sant Miquel**, using a narrow path. On the other side go through a gate made of an old bed and cross the **Torrent des Picarols** to reach a wide forest track.

Turn left and continue walking up the valley. Follow the track past a **limekiln**, then fork left at a junction and pass

Type of Walk
Varied terrain with country roads, forest tracks, mule tracks and a restored pilgrim track. The higher paths are overgrown in places and need careful route finding.

139

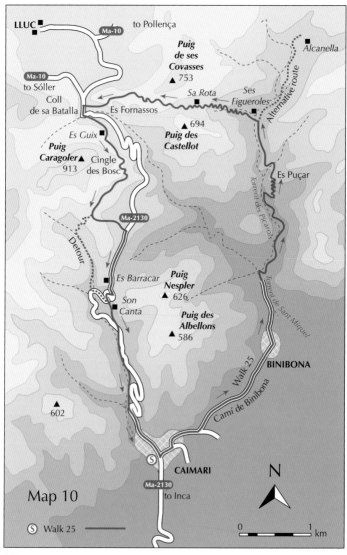

another limekiln. Ten minutes later, look out for a **cairn** denoting a short cut on the right. After rejoining the rugged main track turn right, then 2 minutes later find the continuation of the old path marked by **cairns** on the left. (Don't worry if you miss the short cut – the track bends right later, but you must be sure to spot the left turn marked by cairns.)

An old **mule track** zigzags up out of the woods to cross a rocky shoulder at 320m on **Es Puçar**, then veers into a streambed and up out again to a rocky cleft. The scenery is a wilderness of huge boulders and steep rocky bluffs, yet the main road up from Inca to Lluc is but a short distance west.

The path descends gently into the valley, passing through a gap in a **boundary wall**. A few minutes after this, keep left to go through a gate in a fence close to where the Alcanella path rises up to the right. Cross the bed of the **Torrent des Picarols**.

When the house of **Ses Figueroles** is reached, keep left and watch carefully to spot a vague path marked by small cairns. Follow this up through pine woods (the path is not always easy to trace, so watch carefully for the trodden line). After about 20 minutes' ascent the path crosses a **streambed** onto open ground, then follows the course of the original zig-zag track, which is overgrown with *càrritx*, but in fairly good condition. Some abandoned terraces are reached, where a **well** has been restored to feed Ses Figueroles. Further uphill is the large ruined house of **Sa Rota**.

After this the old path is not always clear, but the way is marked by small paint signs and cairns – watch for these with great care and attention. Go through a gap in a wall to reach the 595m col between **Puig des Castellot** and Puig de Ses Covasses, and here enjoy views across to Massanella.

The path now winds about between rocks and *càrritx*, gradually ascending towards a rocky shoulder at 640m on **Puig de Ses Covasses**. Again, watch very carefully for the trodden path and small cairns. Go through the gap in a wall then descend to reach a wide forest track at **Es Fornassos** – this leads to the **Coll de Sa Batalla** and comes out by a café at the side of a petrol station (there is a bus service to Caimari at this point).

Turn left along the **Ma-2130** and cross a bridge, then turn right along the wide track that leads to **Es Guix** in about 10 minutes, passing on the way the track to Comafreda and

View of the rugged valley on the mule track from Es Puçar to Ses Figueroles

Massanella (Walk 27). The restored track we follow down to Caimari is easy and obvious, signposted and waymarked as the **Camí Vell de Lluc**, or PRM4. It rises to a prominent rock cutting in the cliffs at **Cingle des Bosc**, at around 600m, then descends gradually through woods to a *refugi* on the way to the main road. The road must be followed downhill for about 1km.

(**Detour** If you do not mind a little more uphill, then take the clear track branching right from the Camí Vell and go over to the Coveta Negra valley, to then join the main road lower down at K10. In this case, turn left up the main road to rejoin the Camí Vell where it is signposted downhill from the access road serving Son Canta.)

Staying on the main route, the path is picked up again on the right after passing the large house at **Es Barracar** at K11. It is well signposted and obvious throughout, cutting across the main road to pass **Son Canta**, and again at a lower level, continuing down the valley to reach it again on the outskirts of **Caimari**.

Simply follow the road straight back into town to finish.

Caimari – Binibona	30min
Binibona – Ses Figueroles	1hr 30min
Ses Figueroles – Coll de Sa Batalla	1hr 30min
Coll de Sa Batalla – Caimari	1hr 45min

Alternative Route

An alternative to this circular walk is to continue up through the valley to Alcanella and come back again the same way. The area around Alcanella, which is passed on Walk 21 around Puig Tomir, is accessible by mule track and makes an ideal picnic site. Instead of branching left to **Ses Figueroles**, take the right fork uphill. Rather overgrown, the path is arduous at first, until the edge of some old, neglected fields is reached near **Alcanella**. (There is no access to the old houses here.)

View from the col at 595m between Puig des Castellot and Puig de Ses Covasses

THE CENTRAL MOUNTAINS

26 TORRENT DE PAREIS

Pareis means 'couple', and this gorge has been cut by the action of a couple of streams, the Torrent de Lluc and Torrent des Gorg Blau, which meet at a place known as S'Entreforc, where the Torrent de Pareis continues down to the sea at Sa Calobra.

This route is one of the most popular on the island, going through a narrow gorge between cliffs over 300m high. The scenery is wild and spectacular, and the stream disgorges into the sea at a lovely bay, with clear turquoise and deep-blue water, between rocky headlands.

However, it is more of a scramble than a walk, and only recommended for those who are agile enough and suitably experienced. In places the scrambling is more of a rock climb, and many people take a short rope to safeguard the ascent or descent of the difficult places. Fixed ropes are sometimes found, but more often than not they have broken or are worn out, although the bolts may remain in place. Some of the smooth boulders have been hammered rough to give a better grip, and although experienced climbers will have no trouble making a descent through the whole gorge from Escorca to Sa Calobra, it is suggested that others take two bites at the cherry, and make approaches from both top and bottom.

Logistics can be a problem for the through-route, especially in winter. Some leave a car at Escorca and count on getting a lift back (and bear in mind the Radio Taxi Escorca, ☎ 608–631707 or 639–287055). In summer the bus can be used from Sóller or Pollença to Escorca or Sa Calobra, and it is also possible in summer to get a boat from Sa Calobra to Port de Sóller (at the time of writing the last boat is at 16.45, but check in advance). The whole descent takes from 3½ to 5 hours, depending on conditions and the fitness and ability of the party.

It is essential to choose a day during a period of dry weather. After rain the rocks will be wet and slippery, and there are deep pools which have to be waded or even swum across. People have been injured and drowned here, and the mountain rescue service has been kept busy with incidents in the gorge. Summer is the recommended season for this excursion, but

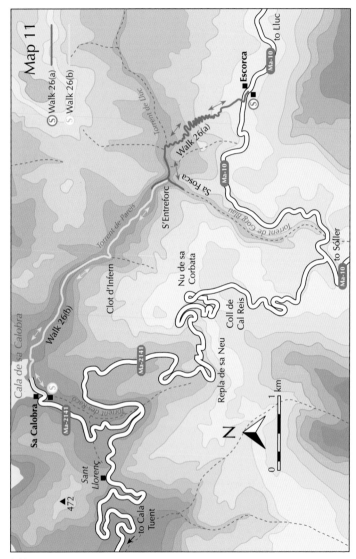

Map 11

Ⓢ Walk 26(a)
Ⓢ Walk 26(b)

The deep cleft of the Torrent de Pareis as seen on the descent from Escorca

suitable conditions sometimes occur during the winter after an extended period without rain.

Check the website www.torrentdepareis.info for current conditions on this route. Information points at Escorca (morning) and Sa Calobra (afternoon) operate from May to October, tel 971–517100.

26(a) Escora to S'Entreforc and return

This section is the easiest part of the gorge, but still takes you into very impressive places. It also allows time for a diversion to the entrance of the narrow, rock-walled ravine at La Fosca, and leads beyond S'Entreforc to the top of a large bouldery section that is one of the more difficult places.
    See sketch map 11.

Starting Point	Bar Restaurante Escorca at K25.2 on the Ma-10
Time	3hr 30min
Distance	6km
Total Height	Descent and ascent of 490m
Grade	B
Maps	Alpina Tramuntana Nord, Alpina D or MTN25 Son Marc and Selva

Type of Walk
Narrow, stony paths lead down a steep slope into a bouldery gorge, coming back uphill the same way.

Start at a small car park opposite the **Bar Restaurante Escorca**, on the Ma-10, and read the multilingual warning sign about the Torrent de Pareis. Step down from the road and follow a path through a nearby gate (this bypasses the original way by the small 13th-century church of **Sant Pere**).

Follow the path alongside fields through a rocky woodland. Go through an **iron gate**, and continue along the path in the same direction for 5 minutes, looking out for a sharp left turn marked with an **arrow and cairn**. (**Note** If you reach a spectacular rock 'window', you have gone too far and must go back, though it might be considered worthwhile to miss this turn deliberately to enjoy the view – it takes only a minute.)

From the sharp left turn the path zigzags down a steep, rocky slope, after which it becomes easier to follow down a series of increasingly wider bends. Lower down in the gorge, look out for a right turn some 20m after passing a **fig tree**. A narrow path leads through clumps of *càrritx* into the bouldery bed of the **Torrent de Lluc**. (Note this point, which otherwise might be missed on the way back – there is only an unobtrusive arrow painted on a boulder.) Once in the

Awesome vertical rock walls rising 300m enclose the Torrent de Pareis

streambed turn left and look out for another narrow path on the left, which avoids part of the bouldery streambed and leads to **S'Entreforc**.

For the diversion to **Sa Fosca**, keep near the rock wall on the left where there is a trace of a path leading into a narrow ravine. After about 20 minutes the rock walls virtually meet overhead and increasing darkness makes a return to S'Entreforc advisable.

Back at **S'Entreforc** turn left down the gorge, but follow a narrow path on the right-hand side, indicated by green paint arrows – this leads down through the **Torrent de Pareis**, towards Sa Calobra. Twenty minutes later the top of some enormous blocks will be reached and it is recommended that a return to **Escorca** is made from this point.

Descent	1hr 30min
Ascent	2hr

26(b) Sa Calobra to S'Entreforc and return

Sa Calobra is a tiny cove with a shingle beach between rocky cliffs, with a small harbour where boats from Port de Sóller ply in the summer. It is a deservedly popular place, but an early start will avoid the crowds who arrive by coach and boat.

The drive down the Ma-2141 is spectacular, with one hairpin bend after another, and even a 'knot' where the road passes under itself at Nu de sa Corbata. However, it is a wide, well-maintained road and the coaches are usually concentrated in the middle of the day.

All the difficulties of the Torrent de Pareis are in this section of the gorge and it should only be attempted after a dry period. Sometimes bad flooding can occur after heavy rain and flash floods are not unknown. Normally, the vast amphitheatre at the exit only has a trickle of water going out to sea, and is even used for open-air concerts in the summer.

See sketch map 11.

Starting Point	Sa Calobra
Time	5–6hr
Distance	7km
Total Height	200m
Grade	A+
Maps	Alpina Tramuntana Nord, Alpina D or MTN25 Son Marc and Port de Sa Calobra
Note	All lefts and rights in the following description are for those looking **up** through the gorge.

Type of Walk
An easy beginning gives way to several rock scrambles and boulder-chokes in a narrow, rocky gorge. Remember that ascents also need to be reversed.

Leave **Sa Calobra** and pass the Restaurant Bar Mar Azul and Restaurant Brisamar. Follow a paved path onwards and go through a **tunnel** (this has electric lighting, but if it was to fail, you would need a torch.) Emerge into a wide amphitheatre near a small **bandstand** and read the warning notice about the **Torrent de Pareis**. If the conditions are right for the walk there will be little or no water flowing across the shingle beach at the mouth of the gorge.

Start walking into the gorge along level **shoals of pebbles and gravel**. In about 10 minutes some easy boulders are surmounted on the left, where there may be a **pool**. Few of the many visitors venture beyond this point.

After stretches of relatively easy walking interspersed with clambering over **boulders**, there is a narrow section requiring care. Look carefully to spot the best way, where polished rock has been hammered rough to offer a grip up **short rock pitches** where seasonal waterfalls spill. There are a series of these, which are either seen easily, or are hidden beneath chockstone boulders. In dry conditions it will be possible to circumvent any rockpools, but take note of the 'tide marks' well above your head to realise how deep the water can be in some parts of the gorge.

An easier section of boulders and pebbly shoals comes next, but watch out for a path on the right, nipping briefly into a **side gully**, to avoid difficulties. After this there is a varied stretch, with a couple more **rock pitches** and a wriggling manoeuvre up a gully beneath a chockstone boulder.

If the mouth of the Torrent de Pareis is full of water, then proceed no further! (photo: Jaume Tort)

The gorge narrows again and is filled with a chaotic mass of huge blocks. Watch carefully for red arrows that point out the easier pitches, as well as indicating a **couple of paths** high on the left, avoiding difficulties in the bed of the gorge. Eventually, relatively easy walking leads to a confluence of rocky ravines at **S'Entreforc** (the forbidding ravine of **Sa Fosca** is to the right).

If you are intending to continue up to **Escorca**, use the path avoiding the bouldery bed of the **Torrent de Lluc**. There are no further difficulties, but you need to look out for the exit from the streambed, on the right, marked by a painted arrow on a boulder, indicating the path uphill.

Walkers who turn around to retrace their steps to **Sa Calobra** will find that green arrows painted on rocks and boulders point the way to the easiest pitches, though some of these are more difficult to descend than ascend. Bear this in mind on the way up – do not climb anything that you cannot confidently reverse!

Ascent 2hr 30min		3hr
Descent 2hr		2hr 30min

27(a) Puig de Massanella – Normal route

The Puig de Massanella is the highest accessible peak in Mallorca, as Puig Major is prohibited. As such it is very popular, and other walkers are often met, especially on Sundays when many local walkers take to the hills. Because of its height and situation the views are outstanding, so if possible choose a fine clear day for the ascent.

Twin peaks at the top are visible from many places and make the mountain instantly recognisable. A freshwater spring, the Font de s'Avenc, not far below the summit, is approached by stone steps leading down into two caves. Water dripping down the rocks collects in a series of stone troughs in the lower cave, and this is a very attractive place on a hot day.

Note A charge of 4 euros per person may be made by a 'guard' at the gates of Comafreda to cover 'destruction of the countryside'. If you pass the gate early or late in the day, then the 'guard' may not be present.

See sketch map 12.

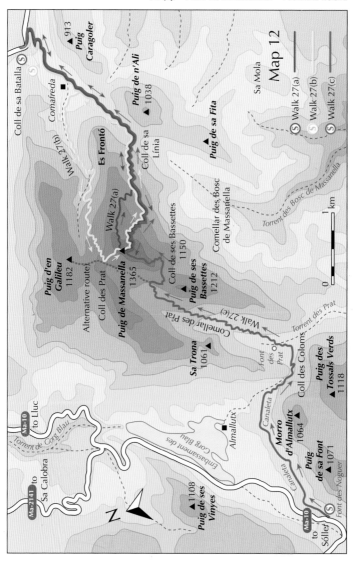

Map 12

Ⓢ Walk 27(a)
Ⓢ Walk 27(b)
Ⓢ Walk 27(c)

Sa Mola

Coll de sa Batalla Ⓢ

▲ 913 Puig Caragoler

Comafreda ■

Puig de n'Ali ▲ 1038

Es Frontó

Walk 27(b)

Coll de sa Línia

Puig de sa Fita ▲

Walk 27(a)

Comellar des Bosc de Massanella

Torrent des Bosc de Massanella

Puig d'en Galileu ▲ 1182

Alternative route

Coll des Prat

Puig de Massanella 1365 ▲

Coll de ses Bassettes 1150

Puig de ses Bassettes ▲ 1212

Sa Trona ▲ 1061

Comellar des Prat (Walk 27(c))

Font des Prat

Torrent des Prat

Coll des Coloms

Puig des Tossals Verds ▲ 1118

0 —— 1 km

Ma-10 to Lluc

Torrent de Gorg Blau

Ma-2141 to Sa Calobra

Embassament des Gorg Blau

Almallutx ■

Canaleta

Morro d'Almallutx ▲ 1064

Puig de sa Font ▲ 1071

Canaleta

Font des Noguer

Ⓢ Ma-10 to Sóller

▲ 1108 Puig de ses Vinyes

N

153

Starting point	Coll de sa Batalla on the Ma-2130 near Lluc
Time	5hr 15min
Distance	11km
Highest Point	1365m
Height Climbed	795m
Grade	B+
Maps	Alpina Tramuntana Nord, Alpina C and D or MTN25 Selva

Type of Walk
Quite strenuous, but mainly on reasonably good paths. In the upper part the paths are very rocky in places and not always easy to follow.

Park near the petrol station at **Coll de sa Batalla** on the Ma-2130, avoiding the lay-by which is used by coaches stopping at the restaurant. Walk towards Inca and cross a bridge over the **Torrent des Guix**, then go through the gates on the right. Follow the stony track uphill, doubling back up to the right about 250m from the start. The track straight ahead leads to the farm of Es Guix and is used on Walk 25.

After zigzagging uphill, then levelling out, the track passes a **locked gate** with pedestrian access on the right (a charge of 4 euros per person may be demanded at this point). Beyond the gate is a cultivated valley with the farmhouse of **Comafreda** set back on the right.

Avoid the farm by bearing left and take the path on the left-hand side of the wall bounding the fields. The path follows the wall at first and then rises through the woods and is marked by painted arrows. Join a wider track at **two painted boulders** – right is marked 'Prat' and left is marked 'Puch'.

Turn left and follow the track up to the **Coll de Sa Línia** at 824m. Turn right at the two **marker stones** indicating 'Puig'. A good path leads uphill fairly steeply in zigzags, arriving at another engraved stone at a bifurcation in the path at **s'Avenc del Camí**. The left-hand path is signposted 'Font y Puig' and the right-hand path 'Puig y Font'. Either route may be taken to the top by fairly well-marked paths. (The one to the right is slightly easier to follow, but the one to the left leads to a water source first!)

Taking the left-hand route, a keen eye must be kept for paint marks and **cairns**, as it is easy to wander off the route on one of the many natural ledges that look like paths. There is a **large cairn** marking a place where the path begins to rise

towards an isolated alzine or **evergreen oak**. Above this a roughly level section leads to the spring at **Font de s'Avenc**.

From the spring the path continues level for about 20m before leading up a **rocky staircase**. Stones have been jammed or cemented into cracks in the slabs, and these, along with small cairns, help show the way to the sloping shelf, **Pla de sa Neu**, that lies below the summit. On this shelf another **marker stone** reads 'Puig'. ▶

Take care on the descent, going down onto the shelf below the summit and following another cairned path. If there is mist on top, start by heading east, then swing more to the southeast and keep an eye open to spot the **cairns**. The path is well marked once located, and rejoins the route of ascent at the bifurcation beside the engraved stone at **s'Avenc del Camí**. From there it is simply a matter of retracing your steps back to the **Coll de sa Línia**, Comafreda and **Coll de sa Batalla**.

A view from the steep and rocky southern slopes of Puig de Massanella

Take care near the 1365m summit of the **Puig de Massanella**, as there is an impressively deep pothole once used as a snowpit.

Coll de sa Batalla – Coll de sa Línia	1hr
Coll de sa Línia – Font de s'Avenc	1hr
Font de s'Avenc – Puig de Massanella	45min
Puig de Massanella – Coll de sa Batalla	2hr 30min

27(b) Via Coll des Prat

The Coll des Prat is a high pass at 1220m, lying north of Puig de Massanella. There is a very good track all the way up, passing the old snow houses, or *cases de sa neu*, just below the pass. Pilgrims also used the path on their way from Sóller to Lluc Monastery.
See sketch map 12.

Starting Point	Coll de sa Batalla on the Ma-2130 near Lluc
Time	5hr
Distance	12km
Highest Point	1365m
Height Climbed	795m
Grade	A++
Maps	Alpina Tramuntana Nord, Alpina C and D or MTN25 Selva
Note	This is graded A++ as several readers have found it to be very difficult and some take a rope to safeguard the exposed part.

Type of Walk
Quite strenuous. The scramble from the Coll des Prat to the summit is steep and exposed, requiring experience and a head for heights.

Follow the 'normal route' in Walk 27(a) for about 40 minutes to the track where there are **two painted boulders** – left is marked '*Puch*' and right is marked '*Prat*'. Turn right and follow the track through a **gateway** in a wall. Keep left along a good forest track leading up through the trees. When the trees thin out the old trail continues all the way up to the top of the **Coll des Prat**, also known as the Coll de ses Cases de sa Neu. Take care around the ruined buildings and crumbling snowpits, before reaching a wall on the pass at 1220m.

Turn left and go up to the **foot of the crags** on the left-hand side of the wall, looking for a **gully** that can be ascended fairly easily at first. Where this becomes steep, traverse right until a way can be found up a steep but easy **chimney**, reaching the summit ridge about 70m to the right of the 1365m summit of **Massanella**. (People have also been observed ascending a gully on the right-hand side of the wall, but this appears to be rather loose.) ▶

A descent can be made either by the direct route to Coll de sa Línia or by way of Font de s'Avenc – the latter is recommended. From the summit of **Puig de Massanella** follow the path slightly east of south to the lip of the sloping shelf below the summit. An **engraved stone** reads 'Font' and points the way to a **rocky staircase** that leads down to the spring at **Font de s'Avenc**. The path from the spring is quite well marked, but surprisingly easy to lose, so keep looking for cairns and paint marks.

This path leads to a junction with the more direct route from the summit, at a marker stone at **s'Avenc del Camí**. The path down to the **Coll de Sa Línia** is now obvious. At this col turn left down a clear track marked for Lluch, and in about 15 minutes turn right at the **two painted boulders**.

Follow the path down through the woods to Comafreda and so retrace your steps to **Coll de sa Batalla**.

Coll de sa Batalla – Coll des Prat	2hr 15min
Coll des Prat – Puig de Massanella	50min
Puig de Massanella – Font de s'Avenc	30min
Font de s'Avenc – Coll de sa Línia	50min
Coll de sa Línia – Coll de sa Batalla	50min

*If this route does not appeal, it is easy enough, but longer, to go over the **Coll des Prat** and then join Walk 27(c) coming up from Font des Noguer.*

A flight of steps leads down into a cave where the Font de s'Avenc is located

27(c) Puig de Massanella
via Font des Noguer

This interesting route makes use of an old track that is part of the ancient pilgrims' way from Sóller to Lluc. The first part over Coll des Coloms is also used on several other walks, even as far as the well-known covered spring, Font des Prat, with its crystal-clear water.

The continuation of the route up the long Comellar des Prat, although a popular route for Mallorquíns, was for a long time virtually unknown to most British walkers. It is now fully waymarked as part of the GR221.

See sketch map 12.

Starting Point	Font des Noguer at K33.7 on the Ma-10
Finishing Point	Coll de sa Batalla on the Ma-2130 near Lluc
Time	6hr 20min
Distance	12km
Highest Point	1367m
Height Climbed	800m
Grade	A++
Maps	Alpina Tramuntana Nord, Alpina C and D or MTN25 Selva

Type of Walk
A good path leads all the way up to the Coll des Prat. A rock step can be difficult to reverse, hence the descent to Coll de sa Batalla.

Start from the car park at **Font des Noguer** at K33.7 on the Ma-10. Follow the water-filled *canaleta* upstream, using the well-trodden level path alongside. After crossing the flow, the path is more rugged and leads up a wooded slope to the **Coll des Coloms**, at 808m. Continue across the col and follow the path downhill, then turn left as signposted for the **Font des Prat**.

Just before reaching the font a path to the right is signposted for the Cases de sa Neu and Lluc. This path immediately crosses a **bridge** and continues away from the streambed for 100m or so, rising slightly on the east side of the valley, the **Comellar des Prat**. The path then bends left through the trees to traverse the valley side well above the

streambed. The path is well defined throughout and eventually leaves the woods to climb higher, open slopes.

Watch carefully around 1100m for a **narrow path** branching off to the right. This is marked with cairns, and passes below some large **rocky outcrops** towards the col between Massanella and the Puig de Ses Bassetes. A **rock step** to the col is mounted by stepping up on adequate but sloping footholds for two or three moves, until a large and comforting 'jug handle' can be gripped with the right hand. A few easier moves and it is done.

Once on the **Coll de ses Bassettes at 1150m** the only difficulty is in deciding the way through the rocky wilderness ahead. There are few cairns, which in any case are difficult to see amongst the rocks.

Rock climbers may like to turn left and go straight up the steep ridge leading to the top. Walkers should make a very slightly rising traverse across easy ground to the foot of a **rocky spur** about 300m away. Look out for the easiest ways up sloping ledges and gullies until it is possible to go back left to join the ridge above the steep section. Follow the ridge up to the top of **Puig de Massanella**. There is quite

The Puig de Massanella rises to the right of the Coll des Prat in this view

a prominent cairn on the first top at 1347m, then a twin top can be visited before crossing over easy ground to the main summit at 1365m.

If transport can be arranged from Coll de sa Batalla at the end of the day it makes an enjoyable excursion to descend Massanella via the 'normal route'. Do this by following the descent described in Walk 27(b), otherwise it is necessary to reverse the route on the rock step to return to **Font des Noguer.**

Note The climb up the rock step to the col at 1150m may be too much for some walkers to attempt in the first place. In this case a good alternative is to make for the Coll des Prat, from which it is not much further to turn left and reach the 1882m top of Puig d'en Galileu. From there either return to the Font des Noguer, or descend to Comafreda and Coll de sa Batalla by the reversing the ascent described in Walk 27(b), depending on transport.

Font des Noguer – Font des Prat	1hr 10min
Font des Prat – Col at 1150m	1hr 20min
Col at 1150m – Puig de Massanella	1hr 30min
Puig de Massanella – Coll de sa Batalla	2hr 20min

28 Canaleta de Massanella from Font des Noguer

This old *canaleta* carries water from the Font des Prat, high up in the mountains, to the village of Mancor de la Vall, on the edge of the plain to the north of Inca. The project was accomplished by a local man, Montserrat Fontanet Llabrés, in 1748, after it had been declared an impossible feat by various prestigious foreign engineers. It still functions as well as it did when it was built two and a half centuries ago.

Before modernisation in 1983, when the water was piped, it used to flow in an open channel and was even more attractive. There are water taps at intervals along the pipeline, but in dry weather hardly a trickle comes out, so don't count on being able to quench your thirst.

See sketch map 13.

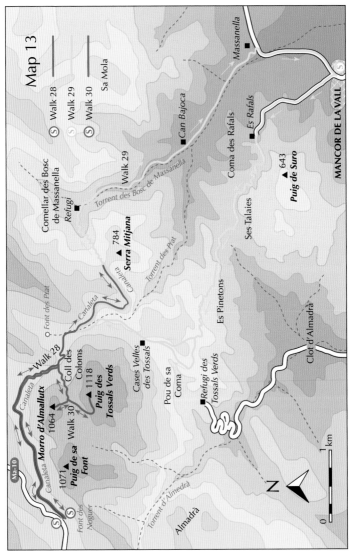

Map 13

Ⓢ Walk 28
Ⓢ Walk 29
Ⓢ Walk 30

Sa Mola

Massanella

Can Bajoca

Es Rafals

MANCOR DE LA VALL

▲ 643
Puig de Suro

Comellar des Bosc
de Massanella
Refugi

Walk 29

Coma des Rafals

Torrent des Bosc de Massanella

▲ 784
Serra Mitjana

Ses Talaies

Canaleta

○ Font des Prat

Torrent des Prat

Es Pinetons

Clot d'Almadrà

Canaleta

Walk 28

Coll des
Coloms

Cases Velles
des Tossals

▲ 1118
**Puig des
Tossals Verds**

Pou de sa
Coma

■ *Refugi des
Tossals Verds*

1064 ▲

Walk 30

1071 ▲
*Puig de sa
Font*

Morro d'Almallutx

Ma-10

Canaleta

Ⓢ Font des
Noguer

Torrent d'Almedrà

Almadrà

N

0   1 km

Starting Point	Font des Noguer at K33.7 on the Ma-10
Time	4hr 20min
Distance	12km
Highest Point	808m
Height Climbed	250m
Grade	B
Maps	Alpina Tramuntana Nord or Central, Alpina C or MTN25 Sóller and Selva

Type of Walk
Not strenuous, but somewhat exposed on the aqueduct.

Start from the car park at **Font des Noguer** at K33.7 on the Ma-10. Follow the water-filled *canaleta* upstream, using the well-trodden level path alongside. After crossing the flow, the path is more rugged and leads up a wooded slope to the **Coll des Coloms** at 808m. Continue across the col and follow the path downhill, then turn left as signposted for the **Font des Prat**. The spring is situated in an open glade inside a small stone building.

Cross the nearby **streambed** and walk downstream for about 300m to an open area where large clumps of summer snowflake, Leucojum aestivum, flourish in late winter and early spring, in pools of water fed by the stream. The *canaleta* begins here, with the **pipeline** buried by earth and stones in between the stone walls that used to flank the open channel.

In about 5 minutes an **arched aqueduct** carries it across a ravine, then it continues along the wooded slopes of **Puig des Castellot des Rafal**. Soon it goes round a rocky corner by means of a small **tunnel**, then drops down gradually to a wooded col at 692m, beside **Serra Mitjana**. After this it falls, gently at first then more rapidly, to the long and narrow Massanella valley (this can be followed on the longer Walk 29, starting at Mancor de la Vall).

Follow the pipeline as far as the place where it begins to plunge steeply down the hillside – this is your turning point, so retrace your steps back along the *canaleta* and return to **Font des Noguer**.

Font des Noguer – Coll des Coloms	50min
Coll des Coloms – Font des Prat	15min

Font des Prat – Turning point	1hr 10min
Turning point – Coll des Coloms	1hr 15min
Coll des Coloms – Font des Noguer	50min

A walker crosses stone arches while following the canaleta across the cliff-face (photo: Alan Parker)

29 Canaleta de Massanella from Mancor de la Vall

This walk starts from the village of Mancor de la Vall, which is northeast of Inca and served by buses from that town. It is a very interesting circular walk making use of country roads, old mule paths, the *canaleta* path, and forest paths and tracks. The scenery is varied and it is a good walk for seeing wild flowers. The descent down the Massanella valley goes through a very narrow and wild gorge between vertical rock walls, gradually giving way to olive terraces and almond groves.

See sketch map 13.

Starting Point	Plaça de Baix in Mancor de la Vall
Time	5hr 50min
Distance	16km
Highest Point	710m
Height Climbed	720m
Grade	A
Map	Alpina Tramuntana Central, Alpina C or MTN25 Selva

Type of Walk
Easy walking on roads, good tracks, paths, and easy but spectacular walking along the *canaleta*. Descend by a path to the Massanella valley.

There are parking spaces around the streets and squares of **Mancor de la Vall** (the central areas are attractively stone-paved, with a few shops and bar–restaurants). If arriving by bus, walk through the town by following the Carrer Principal up to **Plaça de Baix**, then walk up the Carrer Major to **Plaça de Dalt**. Turn right along the **Carrer Bartolomeu Reus**. This road bends right, then left at a restaurant and climbs uphill.

Continue ahead as signposted **Camí des Rafal** from a road junction. After crossing a streambed, avoid the Camí d'Escorques, which branches left, and go straight ahead instead. Five minutes further on the road swings right and left and a footpath cuts out the first bend on this road.

There is a 'private' notice, which applies to cars, at an **unlocked gate** across the road. Continuing uphill, a covered well is passed. The road ends at over 400m at a large finca,

Es Rafals, but a good track continues through a gate to the left of the house. Keep following this track until it turns right through a **gap in a wall**.

Go straight ahead along another track just before this point, descending from olive terraces into an **oak wood**. In a few minutes the track approaches an obvious **boundary wall**, very high and with a fence on top. The track turns right downhill and is no longer any use.

The way to continue is to walk alongside the wall, but watch for **cairns** leading off to the right, which reveal an **old mule path** leading up to a **gateway**. (Don't worry if the old path isn't seen, as the wall leads to the gateway anyway, where a pine tree grows in the gap!)

On the other side of the wall the well-made mule path continues, sometimes contouring and sometimes rising gently. Occasional **cairns** and red paint marks are useful, as vegetation has obscured the way in places. After almost 2km this path turns a corner and rises in a few bends to a gap in another **boundary wall** at 650m. The path splits beyond the gap and either way can be used to progress onwards.

A length of water pipe is exposed in the old stone channel of the canaleta

The left-hand branch simply contours around a valley and reaches a signposted path junction at 650m on a shoulder of a hill. The **Refugi des Tossals Verds** is down to the left, but turn right to continue, as signposted along the GR route for Font des Noguer. The right-hand branch climbs over a **col** at 710m and goes through a gap in a wall, then descends gently to a signposted junction. Again, turn right to follow the GR route uphill. (Both paths are signposted back for Mancor, should you ever walk this route in the opposite direction.)

The path leads up to a col at 707m, where ruins of the **Cases Velles des Tossals** lie to the left. There is an old well, the Font de sa Basola, off to the right. Keep walking straight ahead, however, to descend from the col into woods. The path is signposted at intervals for Font des Noguer, and it swings left to run parallel to the **Torrent des Prat**. Before the streambed is reached the old *canaleta* can be seen on the other side of the valley, carried across a cliff on an arched aqueduct. Go through a gate and cross the **streambed** as marked, then scramble up the bank to find the *canaleta* path.

Follow the **Canaleta de Massanella** to the right, along the top of the **aqueduct**, then it continues along the wooded slopes of **Puig des Castellot des Rafal**. Soon it goes round a rocky corner by means of a small **tunnel**, then drops down gradually to a wooded col at 692m, beside **Serra Mitjana**. After this it falls, gently at first then more rapidly, to the long and narrow Massanella valley. Look out for a **narrow path** leading into the oak woods on the left – this is a key point and is marked by a **cairn**.

The path beginning here can be followed easily down through the trees, being well constructed and marked by blue painted arrows and a number of cairns. It is narrow at first, crosses a **stile over a fence**, then becomes wider after passing two sitges, and leads down to a track junction beside a forest house, or *casa forestal*. ◄

The casa forestal has been refurbished as a refugi.

Turn right and follow the main track down beside the **Torrent des Bosc de Massanella,** going though a deep, rock-walled gorge, then passing a house called **Can Bajoca**. Lower down the broad valley the dirt road bends left, then goes through a gate near the large property used by the **Massanella Adventure Centre**. Use the small side gate provided for walkers. (Signs point out, in retrospect, that this is a private road and dogs are not permitted.)

Turn sharp right, then the dirt road bends left to reach the car park of the **Son Catlar** bar–restaurant. Turn right here and walk along the road to **Mancor de la Vall**. The road, the **Carrer de Massanella**, enters town by way of the **Plaça d'Espanya**, where a memorial font celebrates the town's connection to the Font d'es Prat via the *canaleta* on 9 April 1983. Walk straight ahead to finish back in the **Plaça de Baix**.

Mancor de la Vall – Es Rafals	40min
Es Rafals – Boundary wall	35min
Boundary wall – Cases Velles	1hr 30min
Cases Velles – *Canaleta*	25min
Canaleta – *Casa forestal*	1hr 20min
Casa forestal – Massanella	1hr
Massanella – Mancor de la Vall	20min

30 Puig des Tossals Verds

Puig des Tossals Verds is the highest of a group of peaks that lie south of the Gorg Blau and east of the Cúber reservoirs. It is an easy top to reach and an ascent can be combined with the neighbouring Morro d'Almallutx. There are splendid views of Puig de Massanella and Puig Major, with its impressive cliffs. On the col between Puig des Tossals Verds and Morro d'Almallutx are the remains of an old *casa de sa neu*, where snow collectors lived.

See sketch map 13.

Starting Point	Font des Noguer at K33.7 on the Ma-10
Time	4hr 20min
Distance	9km
Highest Point	1118m
Height Climbed	475m
Grade	B
Maps	Alpina Tramuntana Nord or Central, Alpina C or MTN25 Sóller and Selva

Type of Walk
Some route finding required on a steep, wooded slope. Cairned path to Puig des Tossals Verds. Pathless and rocky, but not too difficult, on Morro d'Almallutx.

View of the Cúber reservoir from Puig de sa Font near Morro d'Almallutx (photo: Alan Parker)

Start from the car park at **Font des Noguer** at K33.7 on the Ma-10. Follow the water-filled *canaleta* upstream, using the well-trodden level path alongside. After crossing the flow the path is more rugged and leads up a wooded slope to the **Coll des Coloms**, at 808m. A signpost to Puig des Tossals Verds points right. The path used to be a good one, as it once served the needs of the snowpit on the col above, but is now rather vague in places, although there are some **cairns** and paint marks.

A *sitja* is passed and the path is easier to spot at a higher level where it crosses and recrosses a less wooded valley. Make for the left-hand side of a large **rock pinnacle**, after which the col between the two peaks is easily reached beyond a gap in a wall at 954m. The path splits – left for Puig des Tossals Verds, and right for Morro d'Almallutx – but first take the time to have a look at the old **snowpit** on the col.

The left-hand path is narrow but cairned, and climbs roughly southwest up a vegetated slope to reach a rocky shoulder. Here it swings left as it climbs, then heads straight

for the top of **Puig des Tossals Verds**, where a trig point stands at 1118m. Enjoy extensive views, then retrace steps to the **snowpit**.

The other path from the col heads north and soon expires on a rocky slope, almost bare of vegetation. Follow a sparse line of cairns up easy-angled rocks to reach the summit cairn on top of **Morro d'Almallutx** at 1064m. Views over the reservoirs and across to Puig Major are excellent.

Walk back down to the **snowpit** and continue down to the **Coll des Coloms** to retrace your steps to **Font des Noguer**.

Font des Noguer – Coll des Coloms	50min
Coll des Coloms – Puig des Tossals Verds	1hr
Puig des Tossals Verds – Morro d'Almallutx	1hr
Morro d'Almallutx – Font des Noguer	1hr 30min

31 Circuit of Tossals Verds

The four peaks of Tossals Verds lie south of the Gorg Blau and east of the Cúber reservoirs. This walk follows a pipeline through very interesting country, and a torch is essential for use in the tunnels along the way.

The Refugi des Tossals Verds, which is passed on the walk, was the first of a network of mountain huts built to provide accommodation for walkers through the Serra de Tramuntana. Since it opened in April 1995 it has proved very popular, with accommodation in dormitory rooms, a restaurant service and a bar. (There is a central reservation number for all the *refugis* – 971–173700. The direct telephone number for the Refugi de Tossals Verds is 971–182027.)

Note A payment of 3 euros per person is required to enter the property of Finca Solleric. If you wish to avoid this, and also avoid the tunnels, then use the waymarked course of the GR221 on the other side of the valley.

See sketch map 14.

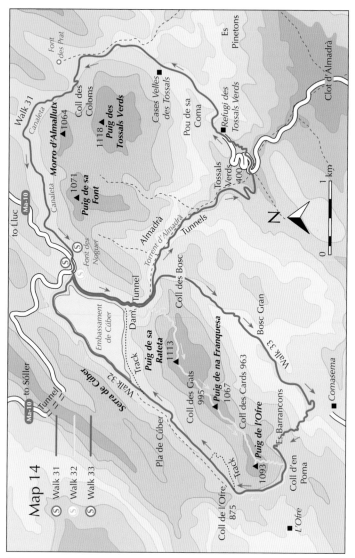

Map 14

- Ⓢ Walk 31
- Ⓢ Walk 32
- Ⓢ Walk 33

N

0   1 km

to Lluc

to Sóller

Ma-10

Ma-10 Tunnel

Es Pinetons

Clot d'Almadrà

Font o des Prat

Coll des Coloms

Cases Velles des Tossals

Pou de sa Coma

Refugi des Tossals Verds

Walk 31

Canaleta

Morro d'Almallutx ▲1064

1118 ▲ Puig des Tossals Verds

Tossals Verds 400

▲1071 Puig de sa Font

Canaleta

Almadrà

Tunnels

Torrent d'Almadrà

Font des Noguer

Ⓢ Ⓢ

Tunnel

Dam Tunnel

Coll des Bosc

Bosc Gran

Walk 33

Embassament de Cúber

Puig de sa Rateta 1113 ▲

Puig de na Franquesa ▲1067

Coll des Gats 995

Coll des Cards 963

Es Barrancons

Comasema

Serra de Cúber

Track

Walk 32

Pla de Cúber

Track

Coll de l'Ofre 875

Puig de l'Ofre ▲1093

Coll d'en Poma

L'Ofre

170

Starting Point	Cúber gate at K34 on the Ma-10
Time	4hr 45min
Distance	12km
Highest Point	808m
Height Climbed	470m
Grade	B
Maps	Alpina Tramuntana Central, Alpina C or MTN25 Sóller and Selva

Park beside the Ma-10, clear of the locked entrance to the reservoir, the **Embassament de Cúber**. Go through the pedestrian access gate and walk along the road towards the **reservoir dam**. Just before reaching the dam take the stony track descending into the gorge below.

In 5 minutes either go straight on along the main track, or branch right by a large boulder to go through the a **tunnel**. The track is very rough and stony, but the walking becomes easier after following the pipeline across the **Torrent d'Almadrà**. Later there is another rough section where the path has been washed away.

Ahead lie 5 more tunnels, none of which takes more than 5 minutes to pass through, though a torch helps considerably. The **first tunnel** is no problem. The **second tunnel** ends with low headroom. The **third tunnel** has an interesting 'window' cut halfway through it. The **fourth tunnel** is little more than a rock arch. The **fifth tunnel** might be a bit muddy towards the end.

If preferred, the old *canaleta* can be followed across the cliff face instead of going through the last two tunnels. It carries a small-bore water pipe, but previously the water was carried along an open channel. ▸

After the last tunnel, turn right to follow a wide track, which provides easy walking and leads down to a valley above **Almadrà**. Follow the track downhill and take a left fork, which is marked 'Tossals'. The track leads quickly down to a **locked gate** with a stile on the left. There is a tarmac road from Almadrà on the other side. Turn left here and follow this road up through olive terraces, enjoying dramatic views of the valley.

Type of Walk
Rough walking on the downhill section from Cúber – a torch is needed for the tunnels. An easy middle section leads up to the Refugi des Tossals Verds, then a restored path and an easy *canaleta* path.

Note Walkers emerging from the tunnels into the property of Finca Solleric are required to pay a fee of 3 euros per person. There are abundant notices warning of this.

Looking back through the valley from a point above the Refugi des Tossals Verds

Watch out for a sign revealing a short-cut path up the terraces to the splendid **Refugi des Tossals Verds** – the tarmac road ends here. Go through the gates into the *refugi* compound and leave through another gate at the left-hand side of the house. A well-made path twists and turns uphill and is signposted for the Cases Velles. In fact there are two roughly parallel routes signposted – keep to the right-hand one, a popular mule track offering the best views as it climbs. The ruins of the **Cases Velles des Tossals** lie to the left of a col at 707m, and there is an old well, the Font de sa Basola, off to the right.

Keep walking straight ahead to descend from the col into woods. The path is signposted at intervals for Font des Noguer, and swings left to run parallel to the **Torrent des Prat**. Go through a gate and cross the **streambed** as marked, then shortly afterwards cross back again using a **footbridge**.

Follow the track up to the **Coll des Coloms** at 808m and walk down the other side, still following GR signposts reading

Font des Noguer, and passing several sitges. When a concrete *canaleta* is reached, turn left and go with the flow to follow it all the way to the main Ma-10 at **Font des Noguer**, about 5 minutes before the car park by the reservoir gate at **Cúber**.

Cúber gate – Almadrà gate	1hr 40min
Almadrà gate – Refugi des Tossals Verds	35min
Refugi des Tossals Verds – Cases Velles	45min
Cases Velles – Coll des Coloms	50min
Coll des Coloms – Cúber gate	55min

32 Puig de Sa Rateta and Puig de l'Ofre

Puig de l'Ofre is a distinctive triangular peak when seen from Sóller, from where it is usually climbed. The walk described here, however, starts and finishes at the Embassament de Cúber, a large reservoir where ospreys may sometimes be seen fishing. Many other birds may be seen, including red kites and black vultures.

This route is a high ridge walk from Puig de Sa Rateta to Puig de l'Ofre, returning through the Cúber valley.

See sketch map 14.

Starting Point	Cúber gate at K34 on the Ma-10
Time	4hr 20min
Distance	10km
Highest Point	1093m
Height Climbed	560m
Grade	B+
Maps	Alpina Tramuntana Central, Alpina C or MTN25 Sóller

Park beside the Ma-10, clear of the locked entrance to the reservoir, the **Embassament de Cúber**. Go through the pedestrian access gate and walk along the road towards the **reservoir dam**.

Type of Walk
Not too strenuous but rough, rocky ground and tricky route finding on the initial ascent of Sa Rateta. Easy return route along a track.

Walkers approach the Coll de l'Ofre, with the mountain crest stretching beyond

(**Note** Study the next part of the route even while approaching the dam – look straight ahead to spot a narrow, scree-filled gully with a sharp right-angled bend in it, falling into the gorge below the dam. The aim is to reach this gully at the 'elbow' halfway up. **Be sure to identify this feature before proceeding** – if you cannot clearly identify the way, then consider instead the path to Sa Rateta in Walk 33.)

The easiest way to continue is to follow the dirt road beyond the dam for some 50m or so, then turn uphill to the left on reaching a **small quarry**. Climb over a rocky spur and contour round a shallow valley of *càrritx*, rising towards a cluster of evergreen oaks, following a vague path. A **broken wall** and fence are crossed just before the 'elbow', and from this point a series of cairns will be found leading up the **gully**.

This ascent is quite easy, but steepens further up. Exit from the gully is by a conspicuous **pine tree** seen on the skyline. On the other side of this skyline ridge is a hidden valley. Cairns continue to mark the route, which progresses upwards at a fairly easy angle, making use of natural **ledges of rock** and scree. It emerges finally from the head of the valley. Swing round to the right and make for the top of **Puig de sa Rateta**, across rocky but easy ground, reaching the summit cairn at 1113m.

From the top the ridge continues level at first to the southwest, and then drops down quite steeply to the **Coll des Gats** at 995m, following traces of a path alongside a wall. There is an unusual and conspicuous patch of short grass on this col, free of thorny scrub – quite rare in Mallorca. Going up the next ridge from here, the steep crag ahead is avoided by making for an obvious **shelf** on the left. Easier rocks lead round behind the steep crag to regain the ridge. Continue over the double top of **Puig de na Franquesa** at 1061m and 1067m, and cross a wall on the descent to **Coll des Cards** at 963m. ▸

There is a way down into the Cúber valley from here if a shorter walk or escape route is needed.

The next part of the ridge is gained by easy slabs to the left of an **electricity pylon**, and a cairned path leads along the crest to the top of **Puig de l'Ofre**, at 1093m, which is a splendid viewpoint.

To descend, go back along the ridge for about 150m to a small shoulder and find the path down to the south, to reach a track on the **Coll d'en Poma**. Turn right along the track, through a gateway in a wall, and follow it through forest round to a junction with a wider track. Turn right to follow the wider track onto the 875m **Coll de l'Ofre**, where there is a large cairn and metal cross.

The wide track could be followed back through the Cúber valley, or **Pla de Cúber**, to cross the **reservoir dam** and return to the starting point. However, the waymarked GR route is to be preferred. Follow the path down from the col, away from the track. The path leads back to the track, which you follow as far as a **gate**. Branch left here to follow another path round the opposite side of the **reservoir** instead. ▸

Note the little *refugi* at the head of the reservoir, which offers shelter, a picnic area and toilet.

Whether you choose to follow the path or the track, you will end up back at the gate leading onto the **Ma-10**.

Cúber gate – Puig de sa Rateta	1hr 30min
Puig de sa Rateta – Puig de l'Ofre	1hr 15min
Puig de l'Ofre – Coll de l'Ofre	35min
Coll de l'Ofre – Cúber gate	1hr

33 Cúber and Comasema circular walk

The Cúber reservoir is the starting point for several walks, and the wide track leading past it to the Coll de l'Ofre is well known. The Comasema valley on the other side of the ridge from Puig de sa Rateta to Puig de l'Ofre is less well known, and this circular walk links the two by following little-used paths, giving an interesting round with splendid views.

See sketch map 14.

Starting Point	Cúber gate at K34 on the Ma-10
Time	5hr 40min
Distance	12km
Highest point	891m
Height Climbed	530m
Grade	B
Maps	Alpina Tramuntana Central, Alpina C or MTN25 Sóller

Type of Walk
Mainly easy on fairly level, wide tracks, but some ups and downs on rough and stony paths.

Park beside the Ma-10, clear of the locked entrance to the reservoir, the **Embassament de Cúber**. Go through the pedestrian access gate and walk along the road towards the **reservoir dam**. Just before reaching the dam take the stony track descending into the gorge below. In 5 minutes either go straight on along the main track, or branch right by a large boulder to go through a **tunnel**.

The track is very rough and stony, but the walking becomes easier after following the pipeline across the **Torrent d'Almadrà**. Cross the streambed and turn left, following the concrete wall of the pipeline on the right. In less than 5 minutes look out for a **cairn** (sometimes demolished but always rebuilt) showing the way up onto a **cobbled**

track, which goes up parallel to the pipeline at first. This old track, once part of the pilgrims' way to Lluc, twists and turns and eventually turns right up a rock slope to the **Coll des Bosc**, at the head of the Comasema valley.

The col can be a confusing place because trees hamper visibility. First a false col is reached then the path rises again. When the true col is reached at 799m there are several **prominent cairns**, and the more obvious path turns right to go up Puig de sa Rateta (an alternative ascent to that used in Walk 32). At this point turn left through trees and shrubs to find a broad clearing.

The easy but rather stony old track beginning at the clearing leads down through the woods into the Comasema valley, passing after 15 minutes an old spring on the right, the **Font de sa Cisterna**. The path continues down through the woods, passing signs of charcoal-burning activities and an animal shelter, before reaching a gateway at the edge of the woods.

Some 20 minutes after the gateway and about 200m before reaching the large buildings at **Comasema**, turn right between stone walls into a streambed at 550m. This turning is signposted for Es Barrancons and l'Ofre, as well as back up the valley to Sa Rateta and Cúber. ▶

This is the beginning of an old track, again part of the pilgrims' way, which leads up a steep hillside to **Es Barrancons** by a winding route on the right of the gully. Though well graded, the way is mostly obscured by vegetation, and in a dreadful condition following damage by fire some years ago. It emerges onto a flat shelf below a wood, a good viewpoint. Go through a **metal gate** into the woodland and turn left to follow the main path, marked with blue paint and cairns. Turn right shortly after crossing a **streambed** and look out for cairns, but in general keep straight on uphill to reach a forest track.

Turn left along the track, through a gateway in a wall on the **Coll d'en Poma** at 891m, and follow it round to a junction with a wider track. Turn right to follow the wider track onto the 875m **Coll de l'Ofre**, where there is a large cairn and metal cross.

The wide track could be followed back through the Cúber valley, or **Pla de Cúber**, to cross the **reservoir dam** and return to the starting point. However, the waymarked GR route is to be preferred. Follow the path down from the col, away from

There is also a way signposted to Orient, but no return is allowed by this route!

A placid view of Cúber reservoir, where there are paths on either shore

the track. The path leads back to the track, which you follow as far as a **gate**. Branch left here to follow another path round the opposite side of the **reservoir** instead. ▸

Whether you choose to follow the path or the track, you will end up back at the gate leading onto the **Ma-10**.

Cúber gate – Coll des Bosc	1hr 10min
Coll des Bosc – Es Barrancons	1hr 15min
Es Barrancons – Coll de l'Ofre	1hr 45min
Coll de l'Ofre – Cúber gate	1hr 30min

Note the little *refugi* at the head of the reservoir, which offers shelter, a picnic area and toilet.

34 Castell d'Alaró

Puig d'Alaró is one of the two prominent 'sugar loaf' mountains seen north of the Palma–Inca motorway or railway (the other one is Puig de s'Alcadena, to which there is no access).

Castell d'Alaró, originally a Moorish stronghold, once covered almost the entire top of the mountain and the approaches to it were well defended by steep cliffs. The only way up is by a steep, cobbled path with steps and ramps leading to a fortified gatehouse. The remains are still very impressive and the views extensive.

A narrow road runs up to a col, passing the Restaurant Es Verger on the way. Traditional food is served here and it is very popular at weekends, which are best avoided. On the topmost point of the hill is a small bar–restaurant, while accommodation is available in a restored *hostatgeria*. (The *hostatgeria* is part of the evolving network of simple *refugis*, providing accommodation for walkers, ☎ 971–182112.)

See sketch map 15.

Starting Point	Plaça de la Vila in the centre of Alaró
Time	4hr 30min
Distance	11km
Highest Point	821m
Height Climbed	600m
Grade	C
Maps	Alpina Tramuntana Central, Alpina C or MTN25 Alaró

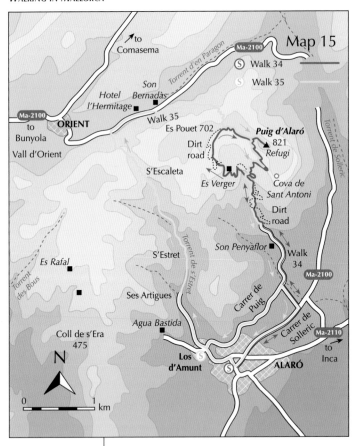

Type of Walk

Easy walking up a narrow road and a good path.

Parking is not allowed beside the road on the approach to Castell d'Alaró. The only car parks are at Es Verger and Es Pouet, within half an hour of the summit! Limited roadside parking is available at K18 on the Ma-2100, as well as around the town of **Alaró**, which also has a good bus service.

The route is structured from the **Plaça de la Vila** in the centre of town. Head northeast out along the Ma-2100, so that **Carrer Ca'n Ros** and **Carrer de Solleric** lead out of town and through the countryside. Turn left as signposted 'Castell d'Alaró', following a minor road gently uphill. Turn right at a junction where a walking signpost also indicates Castell d'Alaró.

Pass through a gateway on the road at the **Son Penyaflor Agroturismo**, then prepare to take advantage of short cuts as the road becomes quite bendy. The first short cut begins just after crossing a **streambed**, at a chained gateway on the left, but this is private property. If you use it, climb past **two enormous boulders** and follow the trodden path up to a road bend. Walk up around a couple of bends to find another short cut on the left, also on private property, following a trodden path fairly close to the road.

There are two short cuts that make use of an old **mule track**, the first signposted 'Castell d'Alaró' and the next marked by wooden posts, winding up through **olive terraces**. There is yet another short cut, not signposted, but found running straight ahead from a bend on the now rather battered road. This last one bypasses a signposted path used on the descent.

Continue up the road, and after passing the **Restaurant Es Verger** the main track continues climbing in a series of bends. Narrow paths short cut the first of these, then a broader path short cuts the broader bends. The main track leads to a forested col at 702m, at **Es Pouet**, where a large open space is used as a car park. The way up to the castle is signposted – a well-built path that joins another path used on the descent.

The **gatehouse** of the castle is reached in 5 minutes by turning left at the path junction. Allow a few minutes for looking round here before continuing to the top of **Puig d'Alaró** at 821m.

Have a look at the buildings, which comprise the santuari, or pilgrim church of Mare de Deu del Refugi, the restored hostatgeria, which provides simple accommodation, and the small bar, which offers food and drink.

Extension to Cova de Sant Antoni

An extension to this walk would be a visit to the **Cova de Sant Antoni**, a large cave with a sloping floor reached in about 30 minutes from the top. It lies at the end of a ridge running southeast then south, culminating in an **old tower** with steep drops almost all around. (The cave and its rather

The gatehouse of the Castell d'Alaró is worth a few moments of exploration

difficult approach are on private property and the landowner does not allow access.)

To leave **Puig d'Alaró** walk back down through the **gate-house** and continue down to the **path junction** passed on the way up. Turn left as signposted 'Alaró' and follow the zigzag path to join the battered road below. Keep an eye open to spot all the **short cuts** used on the ascent, then follow the main Ma-2100 straight back to **Alaró**.

> Alaró – Puig d'Alaró 2hr 30min
> Puig d'Alaró – Alaró 2hr

35 Alaró–Orient circular walk

The walk to the Castell d'Alaró from Alaró is well known and deservedly popular. Less well known is the approach from Orient, a very attractive old village situated in a peaceful valley. This whole walk is full of interest, exploring the length of the s'Estret valley.

Alaró is an old town with narrow streets, many of them one way, and a full range of services. The church tower dominating the central Plaça de la Vila is a landmark at the beginning and end of the walk.

See sketch map 15.

Starting Point	Plaça de la Vila in the centre of Alaró, or Los d'Amunt
Time	4hr 30min
Distance	13km
Highest Point	821m
Height Climbed	895m
Grade	C+
Maps	Alpina Tramuntana Central, Alpina C or MTN25 Alaró

Type of Walk
All the walking
is easy, on roads,
tracks and paths.

The first objective is to walk from the **Plaça de la Vila**, in the centre of **Alaró**, to the outlying quarter of Los d'Amunt. Walk gently uphill to leave the square along **Carrer Calet**. Turn left along **Carrer d'Enmig**. Turn right along **Carrer de Can Coxeti**, then take the second left turn at **Los d'Amunt** to reach the tiny square of **Plaça de Cabrit i Bassa**, where there is a shop and bar.

Walk straight through the little square to follow the road out of **Los d'Amunt**. The road is covered in tarmac until it crosses a streambed at **Font de ses Artigues**, and as it continues up through the **s'Estret valley** the surface varies from concrete to gravel. An attractive plantation of palms is seen at **Can Poleta**, and **rock walls** constrict the road at one point.

Climb steadily through the valley, parallel to the **Torrent de s'Estret**, until the road swings left round the head of the valley. Watch carefully to spot a steep and **stony path** climbing to the right. It runs in a streambed, and stone steps take it uphill to **S'Escaleta**. Continue up a rugged **mule track** in a narrow valley, reaching a broad, wooded gap around 600m.

Turning left, a track runs towards a **gap in a wall** and there is a sudden 'surprise view' of the **Vall d'Orient**. (The track could be followed off-route, down to a road, to reach the village of **Orient**, if desired.) Before reaching the **gap in the wall**, turn right down a path on the wooded slope, dropping straight down to the Ma-2100.

Turn right and follow the road past the **Hotel l'Hermitage**. Just after passing the K11.8 marker near **Son Bernadàs**, turn right through a gate onto olive terraces. Turn left and follow a track that gradually drifts away from the road. Go through a gate with a stile alongside, then the path slopes gently uphill towards a **wooded gully**. The path rises in zigzags on the wooded hillside to reach a col at 702m, used as a picnic area and, regrettably, a car park, at **Es Pouet**.

From here the way is signposted 'Castell d'Alaró' up a well-built path that joins another path used on the descent. The **gatehouse** of the castle is reached in 5 minutes by turning left at the path junction. Allow a few minutes for looking round here before continuing to the top of **Puig d'Alaró** at 825m. ◄

Refer to Walk 34 for details of the summit area and its facilities.

For the descent, walk from the top of the **Puig d'Alaró** back down through the **gatehouse** and return to the **path junction** passed on the ascent. One option is to walk back to

A 'surprise view' of the village of Orient from a track on the forested slopes

Es Pouet and follow the bendy road down to the **Restaurant Es Verger**. However, it is preferable to turn left as signposted 'Alaró' at the **path junction** and zigzag down to the bendy road well below the restaurant.

Turn left and follow the waymarked route down the road, which will reveal two short cuts down an old **mule track**. Watch carefully to spot two other options for short cuts, though on private property. The first stays fairly close to the road, and the second pulls further from the broad bends to pass a couple of **enormous boulders** before rejoining the road to cross a **streambed**. The road continues down through a gateway and passes the **Son Penyaflor Agroturismo**.

When a road junction is reached, there are two options to finish the walk. One is to turn left to reach the main PM210, and turn right to follow it, as the **Carrer de Solleric** and **Carrer Ca'n Ros**, back to the Plaça de la Vila in **Alaró**. The other option is to continue straight along a quieter road, the **Carrer de Puig**, then turn right along the **Carrer del Pujol**, to return to **Los d'Amunt**, if you parked a car there.

Alaró – Vall d'Orient	1hr
Vall d'Orient – Puig d'Alaró	1hr 30min
Puig d'Alaró – Alaró	2hr

185

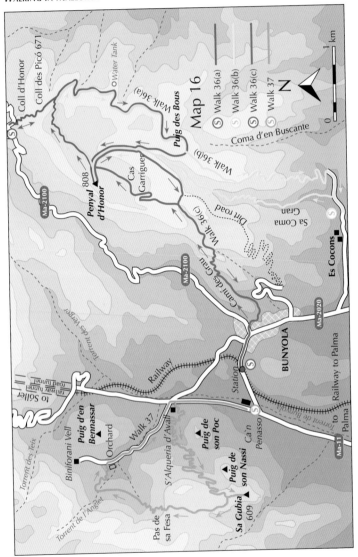

36 PENYAL D'HONOR

Penyal d'Honor is the high limestone escarpment overlooking the narrow valley that links Bunyola with Orient. The main top at 813m is tree girt and difficult to reach, but the slightly lower 808m top offers panoramic views over the south of Mallorca, including the bay of Palma and the high peaks of Galatzó, Puntals de Son Fortesa and Es Teix. Across the valley to the north are close views of the steep slopes of the Serra d'Alfàbia.

Cas Garriguer is a well-equipped, high-level recreation area with picnic tables, barbecues and a toilet, managed by IBANAT and kept in excellent condition. This area can be reached by a long, driveable track from Bunyola and is sometimes crowded at weekends and holidays.

See sketch map 16.

36(a) Penyal d'Honor from Coll d'Honor

Starting Point	Coll d'Honor at K6.1 on the Ma-2100
Time	3hr 25min
Distance	9km
Highest Point	808m
Height Climbed	450m
Grade	C+
Maps	Alpina Tramuntana Central, Alpina C or MTN25 Alaró

Driving from Bunyola or Orient on the Ma-2100, the **Coll d'Honor** is reached at K6.1 and the altitude is over 550m. There are occasional buses over the col, and parking is very limited. (Note that the route does not go through the gates on top of the road.)

Descend on the Orient side to **K6.2** and follow the track blocked by a boulder. Climb easily up the increasingly stony track, and avoid two paths heading off to the left. The main path leads up to **Coll des Picó** at 671m. Cross the broad col,

Type of Walk
Mainly easy, on good tracks and stony paths.

View from the rocky summit of Penyal d'Honor to the twin forested summit

then after a short descent a hairpin bend is reached. Turn right here, in effect walking straight ahead.

The path rises steeply for a short distance below a **rock wall**. When a path is seen at the top of this climb, marked by a small cairn on the right, keep straight on (the path on the right is the return route). Going straight on, the path descends to join an **old track**. Turn right and follow this as it contours round the head of the Torrent des Paguer, reaching a circular **water tank**.

Avoid a branch track on the right just before the tank, but immediately afterwards, turn right to follow the main track westwards. This is soon joined by another track coming up from the valley. Keep on the **main track**, which roughly contours round the wooded slopes of **Puig de ses Cristes** and drops as it swings round the wooded slopes of **Puig des Bous**.

Another clear track comes in from the right, which is used on Walk 36(b), but the main track swings right and runs north to go through a gate and reach the **Cas Garriguer** recreational area.

At this point all the facilities lie down to the left, but the route turns right and climbs directly up a **wide track**, heading north from Cas Garriguer. This gradually becomes a **narrow path**, but is easy to follow and joins a clearer track where there is a signpost reading 'Penyal d'Honor'. A rugged path leads easily to the top in about 10 minutes. **Penyal d'Honor** rises to 808m and is crowned with a small hut in a fenced compound. Enjoy the views, then return the same way to reach the track.

Turn left and follow the track uphill. It then descends and makes a sharp bend to the right. Just before the bend, a **cairn** on the left shows the beginning of a **narrow path**. This twists and turns through the trees and is clear and easy to follow if you keep an eye open to spot **cairns** along the way. At one point the path goes near enough to the escarpment edge for a fine view across the **Vall d'Orient**.

The path leads down to the junction passed on the outward route. Turn left and walk steeply downhill below the **rock wall**, then turn left again at the path junction on a hairpin bend to walk up to the **Coll des Picó**. Simply retrace your steps downhill to return to the Ma-2100 on the **Coll d'Honor**.

Coll d'Honor – Cas Garriguer	2hr
Cas Garriguer – Penyal d'Honor	25min
Penyal d'Honor – Coll d'Honor	1hr

36(b) Penyal d'Honor from Es Cocons

This is a longer walk with 680m of ascent. To reach the start from Bunyola, drive along the Ma-2020 towards Santa María, passing a cemetery. Turn left at K7.9, along a road signposted 'Es Cocons'. Drive straight through the hamlet, and do not be alarmed by the narrow and patchy nature of the road, which soon leads to a wide parking area on the right.

See sketch map 16.

Starting Point	Es Cocons southeast of Bunyola
Time	4hr 30min
Distance	13km
Highest Point	808m
Height Climbed	680m
Grade	C+
Maps	Alpina Tramuntana Central, Alpina C or MTN25 Alaró

Type of Walk
Mainly easy, on good tracks and stony paths.

Walk away from **Es Cocons** along the lane for about 3 minutes, then go straight ahead along a track where the lane turns sharp right at a **house**. There is a small almond grove on the left, as well as fruit and olive trees.

Follow the track through a gate and up through the valley of **Sa Coma Gran**, passing a **cave house** beneath steep crags in a narrow, gorge-like section. Higher up, the valley widens and is again cultivated for a while. Above, the track goes through a gate into **dense oak woods** and continues to climb. Go through a gate near the top of the valley to reach **Cas Garriguer** at 620m.

Cross the wide access road and climb directly up a **wide track**, heading north from Cas Garriguer. This gradually becomes a **narrow path**, but is easy to follow and joins a clearer track where there is a signpost reading 'Penyal d'Honor'. A rugged path leads easily to the top in about 10 minutes. **Penyal d'Honor** rises to 808m and is crowned with a small hut in a fenced compound. Enjoy the views then return the same way to reach the track.

At one point the path goes near enough to the escarpment edge for a fine view across the Vall d'Orient.

Turn left and follow the track uphill. It then descends and makes a sharp bend to the right. Just before the bend, a **cairn** on the left shows the beginning of a **narrow path**. This twists and turns through the trees and is clear and easy to follow, provided you keep an eye open to spot **cairns** along the way. ◄

The path leads down to a junction with a **clearer path**. Turn right and in less than 10 minutes the path descends to join an **old track**. Turn right and follow this as it contours around the head of the Torrent des Paguer, reaching a circular **water tank**. Avoid a branch track on the right just before the tank, but immediately afterwards, turn right to follow the main track westwards. This is soon joined by another track coming up from the valley. Keep on the **main track**, which roughly contours round the wooded slopes of **Puig de ses Cristes** and drops as it swings round the wooded slopes of **Puig des Bous**. Watch out for a clear track on the left.

Turn left along the clear track, and after about 5 minutes go straight ahead at a track junction beside a **well** (the track on the left leads to Puig de Na Marit). The clear track rises gently at first and then descends the forested ridge between **Sa Coma Gran** and the **Coma d'en Buscante**. The track becomes more rugged as it winds down a slope where many of the pines have been toppled.

At the bottom of the path, by the big iron gates of **Can Bergantet**, turn right down the battered access road to return to the starting point just before **Es Cocons**.

A 'cave house' is passed in a rock-walled part of the valley of Sa Coma Gran

Es Cocons – Cas Garriguer	1hr 30min	
Cas Garriguer – Penyal d'Honor	30min	
Penyal d'Honor – Es Cocons	2hr 30min	

36(c) Penyal d'Honor from Bunyola

This walk uses a pleasantly restored path, the Camí des Grau, starting in the old town of Bunyola by climbing flights of steps. Bunyola can be reached by train from either Sóller or Palma, and there are plenty of bus services, too. The little town has shops and bar–restaurants, but no accommodation.

This route is mostly signposted and could be tied into the zigzag access road used by vehicles. This climbs from K8.5 on the Ma-2020 to the recreation area at Cas Garriguer at 620m in a high, forested valley.

See sketch map 16.

Starting Point	Bunyola railway station
Time	3hr 50min
Distance	10km
Highest Point	808m
Height Climbed	640m
Grade	C+
Maps	Alpina Tramuntana Central, Alpina C or MTN25 Alaró

Type of Walk
Easy, on good tracks and paths.

From the **railway station** walk up into the square, **Sa Plaça**, in the centre of **Bunyola** and turn left along the Ma-2100 signposted for Orient. Turn right up the steps of **Carrer de Sant Bartomeu** to reach the narrow tarmac road of **Carrer d'Orient** and turn right to walk more or less on the level. Turn left up more steps at the **Carreró de la Comuna,** signposted 'Sa Comuna' and 'Camí des Grau'.

At the top of these steps a clear track is signposted ahead. Follow the track for about 200m until the **Camí des Grau** is signposted on the left, along a clear path. After a short distance avoid a right fork and continue up the restored path, which is easy to follow and passes a **limekiln**. After rising steadily the path is waymarked to the right and zigzags up a steep slope. Look out for a signpost indicating a short diversion left to a *mirador*.

Ten minutes later the path reaches a junction with a track beside a crumbling **limekiln**. Turn left as signposted

The little building at Cas Garriguer, where there are recreational facilities

'Cas Garriguer' and walk up the valley floor to reach another path junction. Go straight on up the narrow valley of **Comellar d'en Cupí**. The path rises and joins a broad and clear track. Turn left and follow this up past a **double bend** and onwards for a further undulating kilometre.

A signpost on the left reads 'Penyal d'Honor'. A rugged path rises left and leads easily to the top in about 10 minutes. **Penyal d'Honor** rises to 808m and is crowned with a small hut in a fenced compound. Enjoy the views then return the same way to reach the track.

Go straight across the wide track to descend the upper part of the valley of **Sa Coma Gran**. The narrow path becomes a broad woodland track, reaching a wide road at a hairpin bend at **Cas Garriguer**. Either avail of the recreational facilities, or simply turn right and follow the broad dirt road for about a kilometre.

Go straight ahead at a junction with other tracks, as signposted 'Bunyola' and 'Camí des Grau'. Pass a **water tank** in the forest, and after 4 minutes the route used on the ascent is reached. Turn left and follow the path downhill,

The other track signposted for Bunyola and Comellar d'en Cupí could be used, but this simply leads out onto the broad, zigzag dirt road used by vehicles between Bunyola and Cas Garriguer.

signposted 'Bunyola'. Turn right at the next signposted junction to follow the **Camí des Grau** as before. ◄

For a slight variation in town towards the end, descend the steps of the **Carrer de la Lluna** to reach the main square of **Sa Plaça** by the church in **Bunyola**. From here it is 10 minutes down the road to the **railway station**.

Railway station – Bunyola	10min
Bunyola – Penyal d'Honor	1hr 45min
Penyal d'Honor – Cas Garriguer	25min
Cas Garriguer – Railway station	1hr 30min

37 Sa Gubia and Pas de sa Fesa

Leandro Ximenis was a well-known Mallorquín mountaineer, and a *mirador* was erected in his memory on top of Sa Gubia in 1958. The situation is a magnificent one, with panoramic views in all directions. Sa Gubia is a 609m hill west of Bunyola, whose cliffs provide some of the best rock climbing in the area.

Gubia means 'gouge', and from the south the cliffs that tower over the orchards look as though a giant has gouged out a deep groove in the solid rock. The Pas de sa Fesa is a narrow cleft in the rocks, giving an easy but fascinating passage down a cliff into the valley of Biniforani, a quiet place filled with olives, lemons and almonds. This walk is well known and popular, so weekends are best avoided.

See sketch map 16.

Starting Point	Ca'n Penasso at K14.7 on the Ma-11 near Bunyola
Time	4hr 30min
Distance	10km
Highest Point	609m
Height Climbed	450m
Grade	B
Maps	Alpina Tramuntana Central, Alpina B and C or MTN25 Alaró

A view to Biniforani and the Coll de Sóller from the top of the Pas de sa Fesa

Type of Walk

Easy up to the *mirador* using a wide track almost to the top. The descent is steep, but not difficult, and finishes on a narrow country lane.

Leave the restaurant and large car park at **Ca'n Penasso**, at K14.7, and walk north along the busy **Ma-11** to the entrance to **S'Alqueria d'Avall**, at K15.7, a large manorial house on the left. (There is very limited parking beside the main road here, if you arrive early enough to secure a space.)

Keep left of the house to go through gates, then follow a wide, easy, zigzag track uphill. This track passes a couple of shelters on olive terraces, and there are fine views of **Puig de son Poc** and **Puig de son Nassi** on the way up to a col at 539m. On this col is a **stone memorial** to Leandro Ximenis, and a stony path leads easily uphill, crossing a ladder stile to reach the summit trig point at 609m on **Sa Gubia**, as well as the *mirador* and a nearby shelter.

From the top return to the wide track by the **memorial** and turn left. The track continues through a gate towards a property called Muntanya, but leave it at the point where it makes a left turn near a shelter, the **Porxo des Pouet**. Take a clear track on the right, behind the shelter, which rises slightly and becomes an indistinct path to a **col at 533m**. Turn left where a small cairn marks the way down into the narrow cleft of **Pas de sa Fesa**. There is a stile halfway down.

A steep and narrow path, not too clear at first, zigzags down a wooded slope, reaching a clearer track on olive terraces. Turn left along this, then right, then zigzag down from terrace to terrace as marked by **small cairns**. When a **locked gate** is reached, cross it using stones piled up as a makeshift 'stile'.

Continue straight along a track and a narrow, battered road. Turn right down a zigzag access road lined with **cypress trees**. Turn right at a road junction beside an **orchard** of lemon trees and follow the road down past the stout gates marked Biniforani. Turn right to follow the narrow road back to the main Ma-11 near **S'Alqueria d'Avall**. There only remains a final right turn and the walk back along the main road to **Ca'n Penasso**.

The busy road walk can be avoided in both directions by taking a longer, meandering route through Bunyola – this suits walkers who reach Bunyola by bus or train. Walk up into the village and turn left to leave by way of Villa Francisca, following a quiet road to the main road close to S'Alqueria d'Avall.

Ca'n Penasso – S'Alqueria d'Avall	30min
S'Alqueria d'Avall – Sa Gubia	1hr 30min
Sa Gubia – Biniforani gate	1hr 30min
Biniforani gate – Ca'n Penasso	1hr

38 Serra d'Alfàbia

The long, high ridge of Serra d'Alfàbia dominates the Vall de Sóller and presents a constant challenge to walkers based in the area. The ridge is over 4km long with several tops over 1000m, the highest being 1067m.

Although the southwestern top is spoiled by communication antennae, the rest of the ridge is wild and rocky, and being difficult ground to walk on, is rarely visited. The views are extensive, and the glimpses down into the quiet Vall d'Orient especially charming.

See sketch map 17.

Starting Point	Plaça de sa Constitució in Sóller
Time	7hr 40min
Distance	15km
Highest Point	1067m
Height Climbed	1130m
Grade	A+
Maps	Alpina Tramuntana Central, Alpina C or MTN25 Sóller and Alaró

Leave the **Plaça de sa Constitució** in Sóller and go behind the church to find the narrow **Carrer de Reial**. Follow this and take the second turning on the left, which is the **Carrer de la Unió**. Turn right up the **Carrer de Pau Noguera** and follow this road to the **cemetery** on the southern edge of Sóller. Cross a bridge on the right of the road and walk straight ahead up a **narrow path** between terraces, to cut out a bend on the road. Cross the road and go straight up another path from a **gate** made from an old bed!

Type of Walk
Steep but easy at first, then rough and slow along the ridge over tilted and dissected limestone pavement.

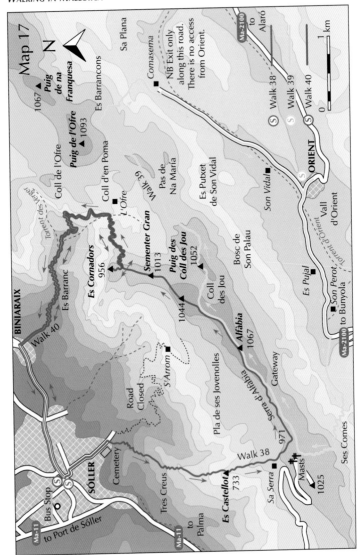

The path uphill is a well-made **mule track**, but narrow and overgrown in places and would benefit from being used by more walkers. The path zigzags up through terraces, and passes a ruined caseta and a **small house**. Shortly after this is a gentler traverse, passing a beautifully carved and painted **heraldic shield** on a boulder. Pass above another small house. When a **boundary wall** is reached the path rises in tight bends on a slope of pines, then goes through a **gateway** in the wall.

About 10 minutes later it goes through another gateway at 550m, after which the path becomes overgrown and difficult to follow. After 40 minutes the path levels off near some **big pine trees**. The communication masts come into sight and there is some relief from the vegetation. The path reaches a ridge at **Es Castellot**, connected by a rocky spur to the main Alfàbia massif. Follow this ridge up towards the masts. The path veers left to go through a **gap in a wall**, then makes the final climb to reach a shelf behind the farmhouse of **Sa Serra** at 850m.

Go to the left of the house and follow the fence to a gate. Cross the farm track and climb straight uphill. When small cliffs block the way, head left along sheep paths to find a way to the lowest point on the ridge. There is a gap in a fence on a **col at 971m**. Turn left to start climbing and grappling with the rock – progress along the crest of the narrow ridge is difficult, slow and a bit exposed in places. (There is a track just down on the Orient side of the ridge, bounded by a high fence, and if you wish to use it, then do so from the col at 971m, otherwise it is almost impossible to approach.)

The last part of the track is followed later from an open **gateway**, and it quickly narrows to a path, with cairns showing the way towards **Alfàbia**. There is a trig point on top at 1067m. The rock ridge broadens later and is easier to follow than it was at the beginning, but the going is quite hard. After crossing a **boundary wall**, and a col at 1018m, the route runs northeast over a top at 1044m.

It may be quite a relief to reach the final top of the ridge, **Sementer Gran** at 1013m. After this it is 20 minutes or less down to a col to join a clear path allowing a quick ascent of **Es Cornadors** as an optional extra. ▶

For the descent, be sure to head east from the col between Sementer Gran and Es Cornadors (there is no access westwards via the remote farmstead of S'Arrom). The path

There is a small *refugi* just below the 956m summit.

Walkers take a break on the rough and rocky crest of the Serra d'Alfàbia

is clear and obvious, zigzagging downhill until it crosses a streambed near the **Cases de l'Ofre**.

At this point turn left to follow the popular path down the spectacular **Es Barranc** to reach the village of **Biniaraix** on the way back to **Sóller**. Full details of this descent are found in the route description for Walk 42.

Sóller – Sa Serra	2hr 30min
Sa Serra – Alfàbia	1hr 15min
Alfàbia – Cornadors col	1hr 15min
Cornadors col – Cases de l'Ofre	35min
Cases de l'Ofre – Biniaraix	1hr 35min
Biniaraix – Sóller	30min

39 Puig des Coll des Jou

Jou means 'yoke', and as the peak is yoked to the main Serra d'Alfàbia by the Coll des Jou it seems an apt name. The col is not easily reached from Orient and has to be approached in a very roundabout direction along the Serra d'Alfàbia. Thereafter a delightful and easy scramble leads to the summit at 1052m, which is a superb viewpoint. The return is by the Comasema valley.

Note The walk can only be done in the clockwise direction described because of a locked gate between Comasema and Orient, which allows walkers to get out of the property, but not into it from Orient. Direct descents from the Coll des Jou to Orient lead to locked gates that are difficult to outflank.

See sketch map 17.

Starting Point	Orient
Time	7hr
Distance	15km
Highest Point	1067m
Height Climbed	600m
Grade	A
Maps	Alpina Tramuntana Central, Alpina C or MTN25 Sóller and Alaró

Leave the attractive hilltop village of **Orient** and follow the Ma-2100 westwards towards the Coll d'Honor. The road runs level and passes a popular track where a walking route to Santa María starts. However, stay on the road, passing an oak tree from which the sign for **Son Perot** hangs.

At a road bend at **K7.9** a boulder on the right is marked 'Camino Publico', and indicates an **old cobbled road** leaving the main road. Follow the old road and it quickly becomes a narrow path up into a wooded valley. This path meets a wider path, where you turn right and pass a **small ruined building**. Continue along the path and cross a **boundary wall** using a stile. Walk straight ahead to follow the track towards the top of a col at 551m, but when it swings markedly left before the col, turn right along a **narrower track**.

Type of Walk
Starting on easy roads and paths, then the traverse of the Serra d'Alfàbia is on pathless, rocky ground and needs an eye for picking the best route.

Follow the track as it winds uphill, again almost to the top of a col at 597m on the forested slopes. Turn right again up an even narrower track, and follow this as it winds further uphill, reaching yet another little col around 720m at **Ses Comes**. Turn right again, this time up a **narrow path** marked with red paint arrows and occasional cairns. After some initial zigzagging the path traverses well to the left before climbing further uphill.

Watch carefully for cairns and paint marks as the ground becomes rocky and the path virtually disappears. Looking ahead, prominent **antennae** will be seen on the **Serra d'Alfàbia**, and you can walk towards them. Turn right before reaching them to find a **clear track**, and follow this to the right, parallel to the rocky crest, along an easy course around 960m.

The track leads through an open **gateway**, then quickly narrows to a path, and cairns show the way towards **Alfàbia**. There is a trig point on top at 1067m. The rock ridge broadens later and is easier to follow than it was at the beginning, but the going is quite hard. After crossing a **boundary wall**, and a col at 1018m, the route swings well to the right to cross rugged ground on the way down to the **Coll des Jou**, a surprisingly level area at 984m.

At first sight the mountain appears intimidating, with formidable crags overlooking the col. In reality there are no difficulties, and some small cairns beginning near an **old wall** show the way up to a sloping grassy ledge on the west side of the ridge. This leads in 10 minutes to a **breach** in the rocks giving access to the Orient side. Ten minutes' easy scrambling now leads to the top of **Puig des Coll des Jou** at 1052m.

The next objective is the shoulder to the right of l'Ofre. Start to descend in a roughly east-northeast direction, following occasional cairns. A good eye for picking the best route comes in useful again. Veer east and find a gap in a **boundary wall**, then gradually descend to a valley floor and into a streambed.

Where this swings right, leave it and start ascending at a gentle gradient to reach traces of a path at the left-hand side of a cliff – this is the **Pas de Na María**, built in the 15th century and used to transport sacred relics from Sóller to Castell d'Alaró. Now little used, there are few cairns, but it is not difficult to find a way that rises and contours along the Sóller side of the broad ridge.

Walkers cross the Coll des Jou to reach the rugged Puig des Coll des Jou

After crossing the tops of a couple of side valleys, go over to the Orient side, before dropping down and then rising slightly to go through a gap in a stone wall at **Coll d'en Poma** at 891m. There is a telescope with a coin slot nearby, then a wide forest track is reached.

Turn right to walk along the track, and in about 5 minutes, after a bend left, look for the start of the descent path via **Es Barrancons**. Follow little cairns and blue paint marks, and cross a streambed to find a **metal gate** in a wall at the edge of an escarpment. An **old mule track** zigzags down from here into the valley of Comasema. A fire contributed to the deterioration of this path, which is badly overgrown with *càrritx*. Pick out and follow the old built-up path wherever possible, as taking short cuts is causing further erosion.

When the main track in the valley is reached, turn right and follow the signposted diversion, avoiding the lovely old house of **Comasema**. This route is marked for Orient, and an additional notice (in Spanish only) requests that walkers keep moving, make no noise, take no photographs, leave no rubbish and respect the surroundings. Follow the access road away from the house.

A **locked gate**, where there are many signs forbidding entry, is surmounted by using a metal ladder beside the right-hand gatepost. A **fireman's pole** is provided to aid descent on the other side. Continue along the road to return to **Orient**.

Orient – Alfàbia	2hr 30min
Alfàbia – Coll des Jou	1hr
Coll des Jou – Puig des Coll des Jou	20min
Puig des Coll des Jou – Coll d'en Poma	1hr 40min
Coll d'en Poma – Orient	1hr 30min

40 Es Cornadors

Es Cornadors overlooks the Barranc de Biniaraix, which contain the well-known Pilgrim Steps, a wonderful old cobbled track originally going all the way from Sóller to the monastery at Lluc. There is a *mirador* near the top of Es Cornadors, as well as a *refugi* hut, from which the conical Puig de l'Ofre is seen to great advantage. The view of the vertical face of Es Cornadors from the path is possibly even more striking than the view from the *mirador*.

The walk up the *barranc* contends for the most popular walk on Mallorca, so weekends are best avoided! The gorge is outstandingly attractive, with hundreds of tiny terraces accommodating olives and oranges, flanked by steep walls on both sides.

(**Note** A popular alternative route to and from the top of Es Cornadors used to lead from Sóller via the farm of S'Arrom, but this route is closed, and any ascent or descent will reach locked gates and forbidding notices.)

See sketch map 17.

Starting Point	Plaça de sa Constitució in Sóller
Time	5hr 40min
Distance	14km
Highest Point	956m
Height Climbed	950m
Grade	C+
Maps	Alpina Tramuntana Central, Alpina C or MTN25 Sóller

Leave the main square in **Sóller**, which is the **Plaça de sa Constitució**, by following the **Carrer de sa Lluna**. Pass the Bar Molino and continue along Carrer de l'Alquería del Comte, then the **Carrer d'Ozones**. Cross a bridge and follow the Camí de Biniaraix into the village of **Biniaraix**. Go up into the village and turn right at the **Plaça de la Concepció**, to follow the **Carrer de Sant Josep** to the public washplace. Turn right along the narrow track signposted 'a l'Ofre i a Lluc a Peu'. There is also a GR221 signpost for the Barranc de Biniaraix.

The track gives way to a path crossing a **streambed**, which is usually dry. The old, stepped, cobbled path has for centuries been used as a pilgrim route to the monastery at Lluc. After crossing and recrossing the streambed, the path goes through a narrow section of the **Barranc de Biniaraix**.

After climbing past a small house, a junction of paths is reached at the corner of another house called **Can Silles**. The left-hand path leads up to Es Verger and is used in Walk 41, so keep straight ahead along the main path. The cobblestone path charts a circuitous course up the cliffs at the head of the *barranc*, then runs almost level along one side of a high valley, not far from the **Cases de l'Ofre**.

Turn right where a concrete structure sits in the streambed, and a signpost indicates 'Es Cornadors'. Follow the most clearly trodden path, which is intended to keep walkers clear of the farm buildings at **Cases de l'Ofre**, though these will be seen sitting in a cultivated hollow surrounded by high mountains. The path zigzags generally westwards and passes striking pinnacles of rock (*cornadors* means 'horns' and the ridge bristles with them!). ▸

When a col is reached at 915m, turn right uphill and quickly reach the refugi, which is remarkably close to the top of **Es Cornadors**. Only a few more paces leads to the summit cairn at 956m and splendid views of the surrounding mountains. There is also the nearby **Mirador d'en Quesada** to visit, for outstanding views into the *barranc*.

The only practical descent to Sóller is to walk back the way you climbed the mountain. Anyone trying to descend via **S'Arrom** will quickly reach a formidable locked gate.

Type of Walk
Almost entirely on clear and well-made paths. No difficulties, but quite a long and strenuous ascent.

Beware of a very **deep hole** just to the right of the path at one point.

Sóller – Biniaraix	30min
Biniaraix – Cases de l'Ofre	1hr 45min
Cases de l'Ofre – Es Cornadors	45min

A view of the sheer face of Es Cornadors above the Barranc de Biniaraix

Es Cornadors – Cases de l'Ofre	35min
Cases de l'Ofre – Biniaraix	1hr 35min
Biniaraix – Sóller	30min

41 Portell de sa Costa

The *portell* is a gateway on the high ridge of the Serra de son Torrelles, where there is a sudden and magnificent view across the Vall de Sóller to the coast with its circular harbour at Port de Sóller.

The Es Verger spring is an attractive place to visit, especially after recent rain, when little waterfalls cascade over mossy rocks, but bear in mind that this is a difficult route. (See the end of the route description for a couple of easier options.)

See sketch map 18.

Starting Point	Plaça de sa Constitució in Sóller
Time	6hr 20min
Distance	11km
Highest Point	940m
Height Climbed	930m
Grade	A+
Maps	Alpina Tramuntana Central, Alpina C or MTN25 Sóller

Leave the main square in **Sóller**, the Plaça de sa Constitució, by following the **Carrer de sa Lluna**. Pass the Bar Molino and continue along Carrer de l'Alquería del Comte, then the **Carrer d'Ozones**. Cross a bridge and follow the Camí de Biniaraix into the village of **Biniaraix**. Go up into the village and turn right at the **Plaça de la Concepció**, to follow the **Carrer de Sant Josep** to the public washplace. Turn right along the narrow track signposted 'a l'Ofre i a Lluc a Peu'. There is also a GR221 signpost for the Barranc de Biniaraix.

The track gives way to a path crossing a **streambed**, which is usually dry. The old, stepped, cobbled path has for centuries been used as a pilgrim route to the monastery at Lluc. After crossing and recrossing the streambed, the path goes through a narrow section of the **Barranc de Biniaraix**. After climbing past a small house a junction of paths is reached at the corner of another house called **Can Silles**.

Type of Walk
The ascent by Es Verger is very strenuous, with loose scree and thorny scrub. A steep and stony descent ends with an easy road walk.

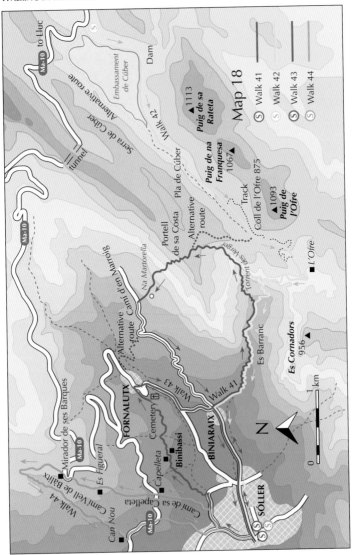

▸ To go up by the Es Verger spring route, turn left at **Can Silles** and in 10 minutes **Can Sivella** will be reached. This is a house in a most attractive situation, having a marvellous view of Sóller framed by the rocky walls of the *barranc*. The path goes straight ahead along a terrace and crosses a **footbridge** over a streambed. Keep following the path that goes up through old terraces, watching out for a right turn indicated by an arrow and the faint words 'Es Verger'.

Zigzag uphill and watch carefully for a right turn along a level path, indicated by another painted arrow and even fainter words. Pass another **small house** to reach the streambed. The **Es Verger** spring is reached within 30 minutes of leaving the main *barranc* path at Can Silles.

The difficult part begins after the spring, with only rough paths up **loose stones** and scree and several patches of **thorny scrub**. The best way is mainly on the right-hand side, although sometimes clambering up **large boulders** in the centre makes a good alternative. Eventually easier ground is reached after passing some **pine trees**, although long before this you may wish you had opted for the easier way up the *barranc*.

When a **drystone wall** is seen across the top of the slope ahead, make for a gap near the middle. A few metres on the other side of the gap there is a splendid view down the attractive and hidden valley of **Coma de son Torrelles**, while on the left the **Portell de sa Costa** will be seen.

Walk towards the *portell*, which is a gap in a drystone wall. Just through the opening is another gateway below which is a rather fine **rock pinnacle**. Here is a good place to rest and admire the view before starting the descent, because although there is an excellent and well-graded path all the way down, it is rather stony and care is needed.

At first there are some **tight bends**, then wider sweeps. There are a couple of places where a fallen tree or minor rock fall has blocked the way. If the path is lost, then backtrack and find it again, though it is well trodden. Halfway down the slope the path goes left and slightly uphill over a **small knoll**, then continues winding downhill.

The path reaches walls, fences and terraces. Simply stay on the old **cobbled path** and do not go through gates on either side or along any access tracks to nearby buildings. The old path leads down past a spring at **Na Martorella** to

Both the left and right-hand paths from here look impossible, although the path on the right, signposted as the GR route to l'Ofre and Cúber, is actually very easy all the way up and can be used as an alternative approach.

A walker passes through the Portell de sa Costa, with the sea in the distance (photo: Jaume Tort)

drop directly onto the **Camí d'en Marroig**. Turn left to follow this winding road downhill (some of the bends can be short cut using well-trodden paths). (**Note** There is also an alternative descent, signposted 'Fornalutx a peu', seen after passing a house called Can Pelat.)

The road leads back to the public washplace at **Biniaraix**. Simply retrace your earlier steps of the day back along the road to **Sóller**, or take advantage of the occasional bus into town.

Sóller – Biniaraix	30min
Biniaraix – Can Silles	50min
Can Silles – Es Verger	30min
Es Verger – Portell de sa Costa	1hr 50min
Portell de sa Costa – Camí d'en Marroig	1hr 30min
Camí d'en Marroig – Sóller	30min

Easier Approaches to the Portell

There are easier approaches to the *portell* via the **Coll de l'Ofre**, either from **Cúber** (Walk 42), or by continuing up through the **Barranc de Biniaraix** (Walk 44).

If the *barranc* is used, turn left before reaching the **Cases de l'Ofre** and follow the track or path to **Coll de l'Ofre.** From the cairn and metal cross at 882m on the col, follow a narrow path meandering roughly northwards towards **Puig des Verger** at 974m. This is fairly well trodden and marked by small cairns. The path veers to the northwest, after passing close to the summit, then runs parallel to a **drystone wall** most of the way to the **Portell de sa Costa**. Alternative timings would be as follows.

Cúber gate – Coll de l'Ofre	1hr 10min, or
Biniaraix – Coll de l'Ofre	2hr 50min, then
Coll de l'Ofre – Portell de sa Costa	40min

42 Cúber and Barranc de Biniaraix

Mallorca has no natural lakes, but the two reservoirs built to augment Palma's water supplies provide satisfactory alternatives. The largest of them, the Embassament de Cúber, occupies a natural basin below the steep buttresses of Mallorca's highest mountain, Puig Major. The mountain looks doubly impressive reflected in the still water. This can be a good place for birdwatching, with red kites seen, for example, sometimes an osprey, and black vultures quite frequently.

This easy, classic walk through the mountains runs mainly downhill, and is accomplished with the aid of the summer bus service that runs along the Ma-10 linking Sóller with Pollença. There is a natural picnic place on a gently sloping grassy shelf overlooking the Sóller, quite close to Coll de l'Ofre.

The descent via the Pilgrim Steps goes down through an impressive gorge, the Barranc de Biniaraix, below the sheer rock walls of Cornadors, with typical Mallorquín terraces growing ancient olive trees, fruit and vegetables.

See sketch map 18.

Starting Point	Cúber gate at K34 on the Ma-10
Finishing Point	Plaça de sa Constitució in Sóller
Time	3hr 45min
Distance	11km
Highest Point	875m
Height Climbed	130m
Grade	C+
Maps	Alpina Tramuntana Central, Alpina C or MTN25 Sóller

Type of Walk
Very easy, along a wide track at first, over the Coll de l'Ofre, then down the excellent mule track known as the Pilgrim Steps to the village of Biniaraix.

Alight from the bus at K34 on the Ma-10, beside the locked entrance gates to the reservoir, the **Embassament de Cúber**. Go through the pedestrian access gate and walk along the road to cross the **reservoir dam**.

Alternatively, use the path along the other side of the reservoir, signposted as the GR221, which is only a little longer, much quieter and completely traffic free. Both routes join again beyond the head of the reservoir near a little *refugi* hut that provides shelter, a picnic area and a toilet.

Continuing through the valley, or **Pla de Cúber**, there are locked gates along the dirt road, which is used by the people who work at the farm at l'Ofre and drive up from Sóller each day, but pedestrian access is provided for walkers.

Where the track bends left near some trees, walkers are directed along an obvious short-cut path up through some woodland, and this is waymarked with wooden GR posts. There is a large cairn surmounted by a metal cross on the **Coll de l'Ofre** at 875m.

On the other side of the col keep right to avoid using the track and follow the short-cut paths revealed by more GR marker posts. At the last bends before the **Cases de l'Ofre**, the way for walkers has been diverted to the right to avoid the farm, and this is well signposted, with steps leading down into **Es Barranc**, signposted 'Biniaraix'.

Walking down the *barranc* is like walking down a stone staircase, but with spectacular views at every turn. (About halfway down you will notice a path climbing to the right from a house called **Can Silles**. This is the way up to the **Es Verger** spring, visited on the way to Portell de Sa Costa during Walk 41.)

Keep walking downhill, crossing and recrossing the *barranc* to reach the village of **Biniaraix** at the public washplace. Turn left through the village, following the **Carrer de Sant Josep**, then turn left down from the **Plaça de la Concepció** to follow the road out of the village (there is a bus stop on the Plaça).

A little waterfall seen from the path running down the Barranc de Biniaraix

213

Cross a bridge over a river and continue along the **Carrer d'Ozones**, Carrer de l'Alquería del Comte and Carrer de sa Lluna to reach the **Plaça de sa Constitució** in the centre of **Sóller**.

Cúber gate – Coll de l'Ofre	1hr 10min
Coll de l'Ofre – Cases de l'Ofre	25min
Cases de l'Ofre – Biniaraix	1hr 40min
Biniaraix – Sóller	30min

43 Fornalutx and Biniaraix

The village of Fornalutx is one of the most attractive in Mallorca. It is very old, with picturesque buildings in narrow, stepped streets and well worth allowing several hours to look round.

The excursion begins among typical Sóller houses, then follows a narrow path up to Binibassi with its splendid 14th-century mansion, where the oranges are reputed to be the best in Spain. The path leads through olive terraces to Fornalutx, where there is a small square with a fountain. The route visits Biniaraix on the way back to Sóller.

See sketch map 18.

Starting Point	Plaça de sa Constitució in Sóller
Time	2hr
Distance	7km
Highest Point	150m
Height Climbed	150m
Grade	C
Maps	Alpina Tramuntana Central, Alpina C or MTN25 Sóller

Type of Walk
Easy, along country lanes and good paths.

Leave the main square in **Sóller**, which is the **Plaça de sa Constitució**, by following the **Carrer de sa Lluna**. Turn left along **Carrer de la Victòria 11 Maig**, which is signposted

Almost an aerial view of the charming and historic little village of Fornalutx

'Palma'. Turn right at the corner of a **football ground**, as signposted 'Fornalutx'. At the next road junction, turn left as indicated by a walking signpost for Fornalutx, among many other destinations (do **not** go the way the traffic goes to Fornalutx). Walk up the road and turn right, then later fork right along the **Camí de s'Ermita**. GR221 signposts confirm the route.

At the end of the road, at a junction beside a large carob tree, turn left up a track as signposted 'Fornalutx', then quickly turn right at nearby gates to follow a narrow cobbled path instead. This leads up to **Binibassí**, where you weave between houses to reach a road end.

Turn left up a stepped path, signposted 'Fornalutx', beside a channel of water flowing from a vigorous spring. Go through a gate bearing a notice requesting 'No Dogs'. Watch out for a right turn down a **narrower path**, which should be clearly marked, descending through olive terraces. This leads to a **concrete track**, which in turn leads to a **cemetery**, and so onwards to **Fornalutx**. Walk straight ahead by road, past the school, until the narrow **Carrer de sa Plaça** leads into the cosy **Plaça d'Espanya**, where refreshments can be obtained.

The **Carrer de Sant Bartomeu** is signposted 'Sóller' down from the square in Fornalutx. Pass a car park and bus stop, then watch for steps and a concrete road on the left. This is the **Carrer Mallorca**, which cuts out a couple of bends from the main road and is signposted 'Sóller a peu'.

Continue down the main road and turn left along a narrow lane signposted for **Biniaraix**. The village is quickly reached near a public washplace, where you turn right down **Carrer de Sant Josep** to reach the little **Plaça de la Concepció**, where there is a bus stop.

Turn left to follow the road out of the village. Cross a bridge over a river and continue along the **Carrer d'Ozones**, Carrer de l'Alquería del Comte and Carrer de sa Lluna to return to the **Plaça de sa Constitució** in the centre of **Sóller**.

Sóller – Binibassí	50min
Binibassí – Fornalutx	20min
Fornalutx – Biniaraix	20min
Biniaraix – Sóller	30min

44 Mirador de ses Barques from Sóller

This *mirador* on the busy Ma-10 is well known as a viewpoint for passing motorists and also as a starting point for a long walk to Sa Costera, Cala Tuent and Sa Calobra. With a bar serving freshly squeezed orange juice and a panoramic view over the Port de Sóller, the *mirador* makes a worthwhile destination for a walk from Sóller.

A combination of old paths and tracks, restored and signposted, can be used to climb to the *mirador* and descend again afterwards.

See sketch map 18.

Starting Point	Plaça de sa Constitució in Sóller
Time	3hr 30min
Distance	9km
Highest Point	439m
Height Climbed	430m
Grade	C
Maps	Alpina Tramuntana Central, Alpina C or MTN25 Sóller

Type of Walk
Easy, on good footpaths and tracks.

Leave the main square in **Sóller**, which is the **Plaça de sa Constitució**, by following the **Carrer de sa Lluna**. Turn left along **Carrer de la Victòria 11 Maig**, which is signposted 'Palma'. Turn right at the corner of a **football ground**, as signposted 'Biniaraix'. At the next road junction, turn left and notice the walking signposts, then turn right. When the first house is reached, called **Villa Ideal**, turn left up a track signposted as the **Camí de sa Capelleta**.

Keep right of one building, then walk up a concrete ramp from another. Cross a track and walk up a **few steps** to follow a path onto a higher part of the track. Turn right along the track, then left up another rugged path. The path and stone steps cut across the winding course of the track, leading up through olive terraces. Pass the **Capelleta**, an unattractive, rustic structure built in 1917. Next to it is the **Santuari de Santa María de s'Olivar**, a larger and plainer building.

Cross the main **Ma-10** at K48.8 and continue up more steps. Again, climb straight uphill and avoid a winding track. The old path is securely fenced off from olive terraces and links with another signposted path climbing from Sóller. When a **house** is reached on a concrete track, walk straight ahead for a few metres, then step to the left to continue along the old path.

Reach a higher concrete track where there is a **signpost**. Walk straight ahead, but step to the left to go through a gate, to follow a pleasant path winding up through terraces of olives and carobs. Go through another gate and follow a track away from a house, passing another house called **Es Figueral**.

Watch out for a marker post on the right revealing an old path climbing through woods onto higher olive terraces. When the path turns right and is signposted 'Fornalutx', go straight through a gate instead as signposted 'Bàlitx'. The path runs just below a bend on the main Ma-10, and quickly reaches the **Mirador de ses Barques**. Apart from the splendid view of Port de Sóller, there is a bar–restaurant and bus stop, and at weekends the place is very busy with motorcyclists.

To leave, follow the path leading north up **stone steps**, signposted 'Bàlitx'. It rises over a small hill to reach the end of a **concrete track**. Walk straight ahead along a track that narrows to a path, going down through a gate to join a dirt road among olives. Cross over the dirt road to follow a narrow path signposted as the **Camí Vell de Bàlitx** for Sóller.

Walk down a narrow, cobbled mule track through olive terraces, passing a **small building** (close all gates along the way, even if one of them is a bed!). When a narrow concrete road is reached, the **Camí de Sa Figuera** is signposted right for Port de Sóller, while the **Camí Vell** is signposted straight ahead down to Sóller.

The old path is obvious and winds downhill to reach a **large house**. Cross its access road and turn left to walk through a gate. A waymark post suggests you walk straight ahead, but the path quickly swings right and continues downhill. It passes another house, called **Can Nou**, then reaches the main Ma-10 at K49.8.

The **Camí Vell** actually crosses the road to continue past a house called **Can Bispal**, but this leaves a lot of road walking back into Sóller. It is better to turn left and walk up

the main road to K49.2, then turn right as signposted down another path for Sóller. Pine trees quickly give way to olive terraces as the old path drops downhill.

Avoid a turning to the left and keep straight ahead. The path joins a narrow concrete lane called the **Camí de Costa d'en Flassada**, which leads down to a road. Turn left along the road and keep left at a junction to walk alongside the **football ground** again. Simply keep walking straight ahead to follow the **Carrer de la Victòria 11 Maig** back into **Sóller.**

Olive terrace on the gradual ascent from Sóller to the Mirador de ses Barques

Sóller – Mirador de ses Barques	2hr
Mirador de ses Barques – Sóller	1hr 30min

45 Mirador de ses Barques and Sa Costera

Sa Costera is an isolated property in a delightful situation on a headland overlooking a bay near Cala Tuent, from where it can also be reached as described in Walk 46. With arranged transport it is enjoyable to walk all the way from Sóller to Sa Calobra, or an overnight stop could be made at Bàlitx d'Avall. This is a 300-year-old house with a round defensive tower much older than the main buildings. Under the *agroturismo* scheme it offers dinner, bed and breakfast. If you are only out for the day from the Mirador de ses Barques, you can still call in for a glass of freshly squeezed orange juice, and a glimpse of the interior with antique farm tools on display.

Hardened walkers who enjoy a challenge may like to reach the old Torre de na Seca by branching off left from near the Coll de Biniamar then descending on the north side towards Sa Costera. The way is rough, with much thorny scrub, and having done it once the author recommends spending extra time enjoying the scenery at Sa Costera!

See sketch map 19.

Starting Point	Mirador de Ses Barques at K44.8 on Ma-10
Time	5hr 15min
Distance	16km
Highest Point	424m
Height Climbed	780m
Grade	B
Maps	Alpina Tramuntana Central, Alpina C or MTN25 Sóller

Type of Walk
Mainly easy, on good paths and tracks, but quite long.

Park at the **Mirador de ses Barques**, or reach it using the summer bus service or a taxi from Sóller. Follow the path leading north up **stone steps**, signposted 'Bàlitx' and 'Sa Costera'. It rises over a small hill to reach the end of a concrete track. Walk straight ahead along a track that narrows to a path, going down through a gate to join a dirt road among olives.

Keep right to walk gently downhill and approach a farm called **Bàlitx de Dalt**. Just before reaching the farm turn right through a large gateway, or use the pedestrian gate to the right. Continue along the dirt road as far as a sharp left bend

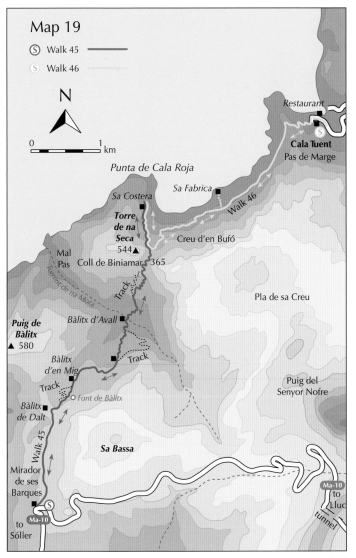

Map 19

Ⓢ Walk 45 ————————

Ⓢ Walk 46 ····················

N

0 ——————— 1 km

Restaurant

Ⓢ **Cala Tuent**
Pas de Marge

Punta de Cala Roja

Sa Costera ■

Sa Fabrica ■

Walk 46

Torre de na Seca
544 ▲

Creu d'en Bufó

Mal Pas

Coll de Biniamar 365

Torrent de na Mola

Track

Pla de sa Creu

Puig de Bàlitx
▲ 580

Bàlitx d'Avall ■

Bàlitx d'en Mig ■ Track

Track

Puig del Senyor Nofre

Bàlitx de Dalt ■

○ Font de Bàlitx

Walk 45

Sa Bassa

Mirador de ses Barques ■

Ⓢ

Ma-10 to Sóller

Ma-10 to Lluc tunnel

On the way a spring of beautiful clear water is passed, the **Font de Bàlitx**, believed to date from 1567.

at a junction. Leave the road here and go down the old **stone steps** straight ahead. ◄ The cobbled path leads to **Bàlitx d'en Mig**, once a fine house but now in ruins.

Roughly 15 minutes after the ruined farm, after crossing a cattle-grid, a branch track runs left to a building. A continuation of the old path is signposted from this track, avoiding the very bendy course taken by the dirt road down to **Bàlitx d'Avall**.

After the not-to-be-missed orange-juice stop, in a museum-like setting at the farm, the track continues further, and has been widened in connection with the construction of a pipeline taking water from Sa Costera to Palma. There is no need to use the new track, however, as an old mule track has been restored and is much more enjoyable.

Leave **Bàlitx d'Avall**, cross the streambed, keep left at a track junction, then turn right up the old mule track as signposted 'Sa Costera'. The mule track rejoins the new track some 10 minutes or so before reaching the **Coll de Biniamar**. The col is at 365m and trees largely obscure a view of the sea.

The interior of the ancient farmhouse at Bàlitx d'Avall is like a museum

Start descending the other side, but in less than 5 minutes turn left as waymarked, through an old **gateway**, along a narrow stretch of the old mule track. At the next waymark, although it points right back onto the main track, turn left instead along a much narrower path.

Although narrow and a little overgrown with *càrritx*, this path is easy to follow, and the old house at **Sa Costera** is soon in view and is reached in less than half an hour. There are places to picnic and enjoy the scenery before the long walk back to the **Mirador de ses Barques**.

On the return journey through the **Bàlitx** valley you could sample the gentler gradients of the vehicle track rather than the steeper gradients of the mule track.

Mirador de ses Barques – Bàlitx d'Avall	1hr 30min
Bàlitx d'Avall – Sa Costera	1hr
Sa Costera – Mirador de ses Barques	2hr 45min

46 Cala Tuent and Sa Costera

Cala Tuent is a small bay that was the objective of an abortive 'urbanisation' project, of which little is to be seen except a few isolated houses. Thankfully, further plans have been abandoned, and although the winding road to the bay destroyed a traditional old mule track, it has its uses in leading to the start of this attractive walk. The road branches off from the spectacular Sa Calobra road and crosses a pass on which stands the 13th-century chapel of Sant Llorenç. The path is part of a long-established route from Sóller to Sa Calobra, which is not easy to complete unless transport can be organised at the beginning and end.

The walk described here goes along a very pleasant path overlooking the sea between two rocky headlands. The destination is a large house at Sa Costera, where the terraces make perfect picnic places, and a spring is hidden in a tunnel behind the house.

See sketch map 19.

Starting Point	Cala Tuent
Time	4hr 40min
Distance	10km
Highest Point	300m
Height Climbed	370m
Grade	C+
Maps	Alpina Tramuntana Central, Alpina D or MTN25 Sóller and Port de Sa Calobra

Drive down the road towards **Cala Tuent** and turn left as signposted for a bar–restaurant. The road crosses a **bridge** over a riverbed. Park beside the road, then continue

Type of Walk
Originally a
well-made mule
track, still in good
condition, but the
branch path to Sa
Costera is more
overgrown.

walking along it towards the restaurant, which is closed in winter.

There is a turning on the left, on the wooded slope above the beach, signposted 'Sa Costera'. This road, or track, climbs in loops and waymark posts show which bends may be short cut. The old, cobbled mule track eventually leaves the vehicle track on the right before the **last house**.

Follow the path up to a gap in a **drystone wall**, at which point a splendid view of the coast and the way ahead opens up, leading the eye to the isolated building at Sa Costera. The path descends at first then keeps fairly level in parts, going through a couple more gaps in drystone walls.

At one point a green lawn and a small building are seen down by the sea. This is signposted for Sa Fàbrica and **Font des Verger**, and the way down and back up would make a fine alternative walk. The remains of an abandoned **hydro-electric plant** can be seen there. The way ahead is signposted for Bàlitx d'Avall, Fornalutx and Sóller, all places far beyond today's walk. Keep following the path, which later climbs as a rugged track leading towards the **Coll de Biniamar**. There are more signposts and waymark posts.

Before the winding track reaches the col, one short stretch of the **old mule track** is waymarked on the right, around 300m. Be sure to take this turn, then turn right again along a narrower path. This leads out of the woods and there is a view ahead of terraces and the isolated building at **Sa Costera**. The path, though narrow and a little overgrown with *càrritx*, is obviously well used and leads through a gap in a wall, to continue down through forest onto the old cultivation terraces.

Enjoy the views of the cliff coast from the old buildings, but take care around some of the more ruinous parts, which are in danger of collapse. Return to **Cala Tuent** the same way (the views are quite different in the opposite direction).

Cala Tuent – Sa Costera	2hr 25min
Sa Costera – Cala Tuent	2hr 15min

Note Routes from Sóller to the Mirador de ses Barques, and from the Mirador de ses Barques to Sa Costera are described in Walk 44 and Walk 45. With transport available, the walk from Sóller to Cala Tuent, or even onwards to Sa Calobra, makes an excellent cross-country route.

Walkers make their way along an easy path from Cala Tuent to Sa Costera (photo: Jaume Tort)

47 Puig de Bàlitx from Port de Sóller

Although only 580m high, Puig de Bàlitx is an impressive mountain with two rocky ridges, one extending to the north and the other to the southwest. Together these ridges form a continuous wall of crags overlooking the sea and the little island of Sa Illeta. Ominous leaning towers of rock hang dramatically at Penyal Bernat. The south face too has some steep crags overlooking the valley of Sa Figuera, and there are not many ways to the summit that can be reached without some rock-climbing experience.

This ascent from the Coll d'en Marquès is the easiest route to the top and is therefore recommended to ordinary walkers, bearing in mind that the higher parts are very rugged and some scrambling is required on an exposed ridge.

See sketch map 20.

Starting Point	Tram terminus at Port de Sóller
Time	5hr 45min
Distance	15km
Highest Point	580m
Height Climbed	580m
Grade	B+
Maps	Alpina Tramuntana Central, Alpina C or MTN25 Sóller

Type of Walk
An easy, gradual climb on roads and tracks, followed by steep and rocky slopes.

Starting from the bus station or tram terminus in **Port de Sóller**, head inland from the seafront along **Carrer Antoni Montis**, which is signposted for Sa Figuera. Note that this road runs on either side of the streambed of the **Torrent de sa Figuera**, and you need to be on the right-hand side heading upstream, passing the entrance to the **Hotel Es Port**. The road passes orange groves as it climbs from **Sa Figuera**, and zigzags uphill to reach a junction at K1.7 on the **Coll d'en Marquès** around 190m.

Turn left up the narrow lane from the col and follow it uphill past some restored houses around **Can Bascós**. The dirt road is private, going through gates that are normally closed but not locked (cars must not be taken up it). A clear track

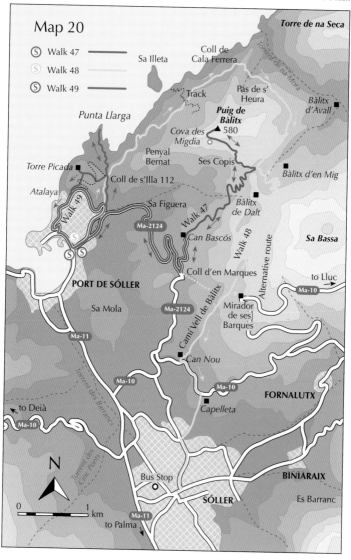

Map 20

Ⓢ Walk 47 ——————
Ⓢ Walk 48 ——————
Ⓢ Walk 49 ——————

Torre de na Seca

Sa Illeta

Coll de
Cala Ferrera

Track

Pás de s'
Heura

Bàlitx
d'Avall

Punta Llarga

**Puig de
Bàlitx**
▲ 580

Cova des
Migdia

Torre Picada

Penyal
Bernat

Ses Copis

Bàlitx d'en Mig

Atalaya

Coll de s'Illa 112

Sa Figuera

Bàlitx
de Dalt

Walk 49

Ma-2124

Walk 47

Sa Bassa

Ⓢ

Can Bascós

Walk 48

Alternative route

to Lluc
Ma-10

Ⓢ Ⓢ

PORT DE SÓLLER

Coll d'en Marques

Sa Mola

Ma-2124

Camí Vell de Bàlitx

Mirador
de ses
Barques

Ma-11

Can Nou

Torrent des Barranc

Ma-10

Ma-10

FORNALUTX

to Deià

Ma-10

Capelleta

N

Torrent des Cinc Ponts

Bus Stop

BINIARAIX

0   1
╲——————————╱ km

SÓLLER

Es Barranc

Ma-11
to Palma

227

The final rocky crest to the summit of
Bàlitx requires hands-on scrambling

continues winding uphill and leads to a **col at 397m**, south-west of Puig de Bàlitx. Do not go through the gate on the col but turn left, following a clear track to a large flat **turning area**.

Continue up a much rougher stony track for about 5 minutes, and when it bends sharply right, turn left up a rather vague stony path. Take care following this path, which isn't well trodden and is only sparsely marked with a few small cairns. It makes a rising traverse above the cliffs at **Ses Copis**, heading towards the southwest ridge of the mountain.

Before reaching the ridge, where the trees thin out noticeably, scan the rocky slopes to spot a **fig tree**. This grows from the mouth of an interesting cave called **Cova des Migdia**, because at midday the entrance is fully illuminated by the sun. Steps have been built down into it, and the space inside is enormous, filled with flowstone, stalactites and towering stalagmites.

Continue up to the rocky ridge that is very narrow and exposed, and scramble along it to reach the trig point on top of **Puig de Bàlitx** at 580m. Views along the cliff coastline are exciting, while inland lies the higher Serra de Tramuntana.

A return by the same way is recommended, as all other routes on the higher parts of the mountain are serious scrambles and rock climbs. However, there are a variety of signposted and waymarked paths and tracks beyond the isolated farm of Bàlixt de Dalt that offer descents to Sóller and Fornalutx. ▸

See Walk 48 for alternative routes to Sóller or Port de Sóller.

Port de Sóller – Col at 397m	2hr
Col at 397m – Puig de Bàlitx	1h 15min
Puig de Bàlitx – Col at 397m	1hr
Col at 397m – Port de Sóller	1hr 30min

48 Circuit of Puig de Bàlitx

A long and interesting walk with varied scenery. From the Coll de sa Figuera there is an excellent track about 100m to 200m above the sea, with panoramic views of the coast, the rocky islet Sa Illeta and an impressive

229

overhanging tower at Penyal Bernat. The return route goes inland with views of the Torre de na Seca, Coll de Biniamar, Puig Major, the Torrent de na Mora and the farmlands of Bàlitx in the valley below. From the farm of Bàlitx de Dalt, part of an old path, the Camí Vell de Bàlitx, which was the original way from Sóller to Sa Calobra, is used to reach Sóller.

See sketch map 20.

Starting Point	Port de Sóller
Finishing Point	Plaça de sa Constitució in Sóller
Time	6hr 20min
Distance	13km
Highest Point	407m
Height Climbed	655m
Grade	A+
Maps	Alpina Tramuntana Central, Alpina C or MTN25 Sóller

Type of Walk
Easy at first along a fine track, followed by rough descents and ascents involving some scrambling and route finding.

Starting from the bus station or tram terminus in **Port de Sóller**, head inland from the seafront along **Carrer Antoni Montis**, which is signposted for Sa Figuera. Continue straight along **Avinguda 11 de Maig**, which in turn gives way to **Carrer de Belgica**, climbing high above the port. When the road bends sharply left, go straight ahead instead, up a narrow lane that leads directly to the **Coll de s'Illa** at 112m.

At the col keep right to follow a narrow lane that climbs a little higher before contouring in a northeasterly direction above the coast. More height is gained in a series of bends, and some stone steps offer a chance to short cut uphill. Here, note the ominous leaning tower of rock at **Penyal Bernat**. Eventually, a high, **locked gate** is met, last seen with bars bent apart to allow walkers through!

Follow the track across the terrace beyond the gate, then zigzag down to the left and go through a **gap in a wall**. Keep right at a fork to continue straight ahead – the path is not too obvious at the beginning, but soon becomes broader and well made, being very easy to follow despite a few trees having fallen across it. (**Note** Do not be tempted, beyond the locked gate, to stay on the main track and zigzag uphill, or to

An impressive rock pillar flanks one side of the Coll de Cala Ferrera

zigzag too far downhill towards the coast. In either case steps would have to be retraced.)

The path offers good views of the little island of **Sa Illeta**, and after turning round a corner there are even more dramatic views of the cliffs ahead. The path leads past a *sitja*, and later a sign points off-route down to the left for **Font des Joncar**.

Keep right and follow the path marked by cairns along the base of the cliffs. This is known as the **Pas de na Cordellina** and is not too difficult, but the slopes are quite steep and require some care. After a slight descent the path rises in zigzags to the **Coll de Cala Ferrera**, at 225m, between an impressive rock pillar at 276m and Puig de Bàlitx.

Climb over the wall on the col and turn left to descend into a valley. There is a narrow zigzag path, marked by cairns, showing the easiest way across a **streambed**. The cairns also show the way onto a diagonal rake, where you scramble across a prominent yellow rock wall, first sloping from right to left and then back from left to right. This is the **Pas de s'Heura**.

Keep an eye on the cairns, which mark a rugged, narrow path through prickly vegetation, and more short scrambles, over a small col at 350m. The cairns continue to mark the way for another 50m, when a mule track built with stone will be found leading onto some **olive terraces**.

This area has changed almost beyond recognition with the bulldozing of a wide track in connection with a pipeline taking water from Sa Costera to Palma. The easiest thing is of course to follow the track, but walkers with eagle eyes might like to try and find the traces of the old path before it disappears entirely.

The new track goes between a **building** and a natural shelter made of large boulders. After rising slightly, go past a **locked gate** and curve right towards the valley head, where there is a **col at 397m**. Turn left at a track junction just before the col.

(**Note** To return directly to Port de Sóller, cross the col where a locked gate is passed by climbing a wall on one side. Follow a track straight ahead downhill, bending round loops and passing restored houses at Can Bascós. A narrow private road leads down to the Coll d'en Marquès, where a right turn leads along a road through the valley of Sa Figuera to return to Port de Sóller.)

After turning left, follow the track down past olive terraces into the **Bàlitx** valley. Join another track and turn right to zigzag up to a pair of tall gates near the farm of **Bàlitx de Dalt**. Turn left away from the farm and cross a cattle-grid. Leave the main track at a signposted junction.

There are a number of options available throughout the descent, and all are well signposted. For example, if you can arrange to be collected from the **Mirador de ses Barques**, then veer left as signposted and walk straight to the Ma-10. This route can also be used to continue to Sóller or Fornalutx.

To continue with the whole walk, however, turn right as signposted for the **Camí Vell de Bàlitx**. Walk down a narrow, cobbled mule track through olive terraces, passing a **small**

Walkers make slow progress over rugged terrain beyond the Pas de s'Heura

building (close all gates along the way, even if one of them is a bed!). When a narrow concrete road is reached, the **Camí de Sa Figuera** is signposted right for Port de Sóller, while the **Camí Vell** is signposted straight ahead downhill for Sóller.

(The Cami de Sa Figuera leads along a track, then heads down to the left and is clearly waymarked down narrow paths to a road junction at Coll d'en Marquès. A right turn down the main road leads through the valley of Sa Figuera and back to Port de Sóller.)

The old path is obvious and winds downhill to reach a **large house**. Cross its access road and turn left to walk through a gate. A waymark post suggests you walk straight ahead, but the path quickly swings right and continues downhill. It passes another house, called **Can Nou**, then reaches the main Ma-10 at K49.8.

The **Camí Vell** actually crosses the road to continue past a house called **Can Bispal**, but this leaves a lot of road walking back into Sóller. It is better to turn left and walk up the main road to K49.2, then turn right as signposted down another path for Sóller. Pine trees quickly give way to olive terraces as the old path drops downhill.

Avoid a turning to the left and keep straight ahead. The path joins a narrow concrete lane called the **Camí de Costa d'en Flassada**, which leads down to a road. Turn left along the road and keep left at a junction to walk alongside a **football ground**.

Simply keep walking straight ahead to follow the **Carrer de la Victòria 11 Maig** into **Sóller,** turning right to finish on the **Plaça de sa Constitució.**

Port de Sóller – Coll de sa Figuera	30min
Coll de sa Figuera – Coll de Cala Ferrera	1hr 30min
Coll de Cala Ferrera – Bàlitx de Dalt	2hr 30min
Bàlitx de Dalt – Sóller	1hr 50min

49 Ses Puntes and Torre Picada

Ses Puntes are two rocky points jutting out into the sea on the wild coastline north of Port de Sóller. There are views of impressive cliffs and the small island of Sa Illeta – an idyllic place for picnics or fishing. Torre Picada is one of the old coastal watch towers, though closed to visitors. The area surrounding it is a natural rock garden on the edge of the cliffs, with beautiful pink flowers of sage-leaved cistus, rosemary, asphodels and many other plants.

This walk may be easily extended to Torre Picada by continuing along the road from the Coll de s'Illa towards the small island of Sa Illeta and returning the same way.

See sketch map 20.

Starting Point	Tram terminus at Port de Sóller
Time	1hr 50min
Distance	6km
Highest Point	161m
Height Climbed	270m
Grade	C
Maps	Alpina Tramuntana Central, Alpina C or MTN25 Sóller

Starting from the bus station or tram terminus in **Port de Sóller**, head inland from the seafront along **Carrer Antoni Montis**, which is signposted for Sa Figuera. Continue straight along **Avinguda 11 de Maig**, which in turn gives way to **Carrer de Belgica**, climbing high above the port. When the road bends sharply left, go straight ahead instead, up a narrow lane that leads directly to the **Coll de s'Illa** at 112m.

At the col go through a gateway where two tracks diverge. Take the track to the right, which descends through woodland towards the sea. Other paths will be seen, but these simply short cut the bends on the track, and all reach the bottom of the forested slope in due course, at a little col behind the **Punta Llarga**. Explore at leisure and enjoy views of the nearby cliffs and little island of Sa Illeta.

Type of Walk
Short and easy, mainly on lanes and tracks, but the path down to the sea from the Coll de s'Illa is a little steep and stony.

Torre Picada is a well-preserved fortification on a headland above Port de Sóller

Retrace your steps up to the **Coll de s'Illa** and turn right to follow the other clear track, which leads in huge loops up to the circular **Torre Picada** at 161m. If preferred, there is a short-cut path up through the woods from the Coll de s'Illa, which rejoins the main track at a **junction** close to the tower. (**Note** Whichever approach is chosen, look out for an **old olive tree** almost in the middle of the track before reaching the tower.)

The return to Port de Sóller can be varied. One way is to go back along the track to the **junction** and turn right, to descend very gradually in big bends. Alternatively, walk only to the **old olive tree** and turn right. Cairns mark a short-cut path through the big loops of the track.

When the bottom part of the road is reached, turn right to pass a **locked gate** that keeps traffic out but allows walkers through. Turn right to follow the road down from the **Atalaya** complex, winding through the built-up parts of **Port de Sóller**, finally following the **Camí des Cingle** back to the seafront close to the tram terminus.

Port de Sóller – Coll de s'Illa	30min
Col de s'Illa – Ses Puntes	15min
Ses Puntes – Torre Picada	35min
Torre Picada – Port de Sóller	30min

50 The Lighthouse and Punta de Sóller

The aim of this excursion is to reach two spectacular viewpoints on the very edge of the cliffs near Port de Sóller, where there are excellent views of mountains and sea. Although only a short distance from the busy resort, this area is tranquil and quite wild, and in early spring there are hundreds of bright yellow-green euphorbias.

The route passes the Refugi Muleta, one of a network of huts built to provide accommodation for walkers. The *refugi* offers accommodation in dormitory rooms, has a restaurant service and a bar. (There is a central reservation number for all the *refugs*, 971–173700; the direct telephone number for the Refugi Muleta is 971–182027.)

See sketch map 21.

Starting Point	Tram terminus at Port de Sóller
Time	4hr
Distance	9km
Highest Point	132m
Height Gained	250m
Grade	C+
Maps	Alpina Tramuntana Central, Alpina B and C or MTN25 Sóller

Leave the tram terminus and walk south round the bay of **Port de Sóller**. Cross a river by using a **footbridge** and continue along the pedestrianised seafront at **Platja d'en Repic**. Follow the road that climbs steadily uphill, all the way round the bay to the lighthouse, or **Far es Cap Gros**. (This road is also signposted for the **Refugi Muleta** which, along with a restaurant, stands near the lighthouse. A narrow track begins from a stile between the lighthouse and *refugi*.)

Type of Walk
Short and easy – tarmac road to the lighthouse, then a track, and finally a rough and rocky path.

237

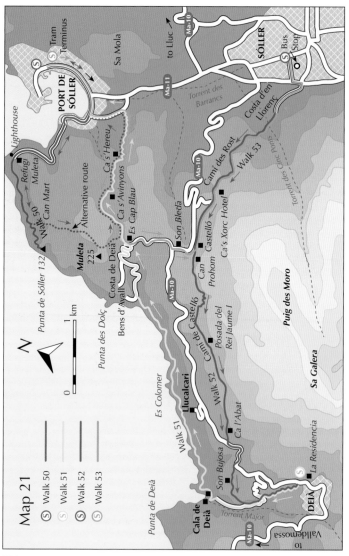

Map 21
Ⓢ Walk 50
Ⓢ Walk 51
Ⓢ Walk 52
Ⓢ Walk 53

N

km
0   1

The rugged headland of Sa Panxeta is close to the Punta de Sóller viewpoint

Follow the track gradually downhill, avoiding a path to the left. The track remains some distance from the cliff coast, and trees restrict the view of the sea towards the end. The track ends suddenly at a junction of paths. A path climbing left via **Can Mart** could be followed later, but for the time being, take the path going straight ahead.

There are a number of routes marked by cairns. Try to keep to the most well-trodden path to drop down and cross a **streambed**. Ten minutes further on the path goes through a gap in a low wall, then rises to a viewpoint on the cliff edge near an impressive overhanging rock at **Sa Panxeta**. The continuation is marked by cairns and goes up from here, partly on **rocky slabs**, to reach a higher viewpoint with good views both north and south along the coast. The end of the route is at 132m on the **Punta de Sóller**.

The return is by the same way, but it can be varied to create an alternative circular walk, as follows.

Alternative Follow the rugged path uphill via **Can Mart**, as mentioned earlier. This path is fairly well marked by cairns, eventually rising alongside a prominent wall and fence. It links with a **track,** where you turn right and cross a barrier fence, passing a few houses and a gate.

Turn left along a track before reaching a road junction near a house called **Es Cap Blau**. This allows links with the alternative routes mentioned in the last part of Walk 51, following clear tracks and mule paths back to **Port de Sóller**.

Port de Sóller – Lighthouse	45min
Lighthouse – Punta de Sóller	45min
Punta de Sóller – Port de Sóller	1hr 30min

51 Deià Coastal Walk

The stretch of coast between Cala de Deià and Alconasser is particularly attractive, with an undulating path giving lovely views of the sea. Given as a linear walk, using the bus service between Deià and Sóller or Port de Sóller, it is easy to combine with Walk 52, the Camí de Castelló, to make a much longer route.

Cala de Deià is a gem, with a cluster of old fishermen's shelters, a few boats, and a beach café in season. The village of Deià is also most photogenic, and a stroll up to the church of Sant Joan Baptista on the hill of Es Puig is recommended before starting the walk. The poet and novelist Robert Graves is buried there.

See sketch map 21.

Starting Point	Bus stop at La Residencia in Deià
Finishing Point	Tram terminus at Port de Sóller
Time	4hr 25min
Distance	12km
Height	300m
Grade	B
Maps	Alpina Tramuntana Central, Alpina B or MTN25 Sóller and Alaró

Start from the bus stop, taxi stand and car park near **La Residencia** in Deià, which is handy for exploring the historic heart of the village at the start of the walk. Leave **Deià** by walking only a few metres along the main Ma-10 in the direction of Sóller, to find a walking route signposted downhill to the left. This is the **Camí de sa Vinyeta**, and a short road leads to a stile.

Zigzag down a clear path as marked through terraces of olives. When a tarmac road is reached, the path simply slices across it, though the last stretch of road has to be followed through a parking area to reach **Cala de Deià**. Go all the way down the final ramp to find toilets on the right and a beach bar across the slipway.

The coastal path begins up a **flight of steps** about 20m from the road end (but **not** the steps leading to the toilets). Avoid a left branch after about 5 minutes, but 2 minutes later turn left where the stepped path swings right. The coastal path immediately turns right along a terrace, then crosses a **low wall** and turns left downhill at the side of this wall. One minute later it turns right again and continues to an attractive **headland** among the pine trees, overlooking the sea and the prominent white rocks of Cala de Deià.

Continue along the path, passing a *mirador* with protective railings. There are landslips and fallen trees beyond, so expect diversions. After passing a couple of stiles there are notices, forbidding camping and picnics, beside a circular **stone table** with stone seats. This is a useful landmark, indicating a fork left downhill to cross another stile.

A few minutes later, after going above a **stone-walled enclosure**, the path has fallen away and a diversion must be made up to a higher level, passing a large doorway in a wall below a house. Some **boats** are passed and the path again narrows, as it negotiates another series of diversions caused by landslips and fallen trees.

The path has to go high to avoid steep and unstable slopes, reaching an **olive terrace** well marked with cairns. At the end of this terrace watch for more cairns, as the path has to drop steeply to reach the next **stile** and follow a terrace closer to the sea.

Next, climb uphill and cross behind a headland at **Es Colomer**, among boulders and heather. Go up between olive terraces on a well-marked path. This part is very clear and

Type of Walk
Mainly easy, but care is needed where landslips have destroyed the path. Diversions will always be necessary, so look out and avoid obvious danger.

The tiny, rock-walled harbour at Cala de Deià is a charming but popular place

leads in about 15 minutes to a path that contours above a **sheer cliff** and leads to another stile. The path then dips into and out of a **streambed** and goes over another stile into a lane.

Turn left, and one minute later, when the lane ends, find the continuation of the path on the right by going up some **stone steps**, not down an adjacent flight. Five minutes later the path reaches a **concrete road** near some houses. Climb steeply uphill, but keep a sharp lookout, after 5 minutes or so, for a couple of places to cross the **streambed** running parallel. This is not obvious, but once across you will find yourself on a wide road near the **Bens d'Avall** restaurant, which is closed in winter.

Follow the bendy road uphill for 1.5km to reach a road junction at **Costa de Deià**, where a small building is painted with the words 'Urbanizacion Costa Deya'. Turn left to pass a house called **Es Cap Blau**. Turn right along a track among olives, then left at a junction to reach a cross-tracks near **Muleta de Ca s'Avinyons**, where there is a large house with a square tower.

Turn right and follow a path keeping well clear of the house, as marked, to pick up a mule track on the far side. This is well marked with GR waymark posts and leads close to the agroturismo of **Muleta de ca s'Hereu**. The mule track leads round the back of the **Rocamar Hotel**, which is derelict but still bears its name prominently.

Turn left to follow a quiet road back to **Port de Sóller** via the Platja d'en Repic, then turn right to walk round the bay to finish at either a bus stop or the tram terminus.

Deià – Cala de Deià	25min
Cala de Deià – Costa de Deià	2hr 30min
Costa de Deià – Port de Sóller	1hr 30min

Alternative Endings

One alternative ending is to turn right at the road junction at **Costa de Deià** and reach the main Ma-10, turn left for **Son Bleda**, then follow the **Camí de Castelló** back to **Sóller** as described in Walk 53.

It is also possible to follow the **Camí de Castelló** back to **Deià**, and thus create a circular walk by referring to Walk 52.

There is also a good path, well trodden, cairned and marked with paint, leading directly from **Muleta de Ca s'Avinyons** to the lighthouse, or **Far es Cap Gros**, perched above the bay at **Port de Sóller**.

52 Sóller to Deià via Camí de Castelló

Between Sóller and Deià some of the high tops of the Serra de Tramuntana are only about 2km from the sea. This linear walk explores the delightful area between the mountains and the sea, using old tracks and paths, not all of which are shown on the maps, though many have been waymarked.

There are some lovely views of the coast and there is time to look round the attractive village of Deià.

See sketch map 21.

Starting Point	Plaça d'Amèrica at Sóller
Time	3hr 30min
Distance	11km
Highest Point	300m
Height Climbed	440m
Grade	B
Maps	Alpina Tramuntana Central, Alpina B or MTN25 Sóller and Alaró

Type of Walk
Fairly easy, mainly
on good paths. For
an alternative start
see Walk 53.

This walk can be conveniently started from **Sóller** at the **Plaça d'Amèrica**, where the bus turns around. Walk straight along the road to the busy **Ma-11 bypass**, and turn left to pass a bar–restaurant and little service station. Turn right along the **Camí de sa Costa d'en Llorenç**, signposted for the Hotel Can Coll. Turn right to follow the road past the hotel, and continue straight onto a clear path signposted as a walking route to Deià via the **Camí des Rost**.

The path crosses a streambed, then rises up an impressive flight of old steps that cross over the **railway track** near a tunnel mouth. A few minutes later a branch path will be noticed on the left, signposted for Deià via the **Camí des Montreals**, but keep straight ahead on the main path.

Ten minutes later the path climbs as a patchy surfaced road for a while, then reverts to a path. Five minutes later go through a **gate**, then simply keep to the route as waymarked, avoiding turns through gates onto adjacent properties.

Cross the driveway of the **Ca's Xorc Hotel**, and continue straight ahead as signposted for Deià via the **Camí de Castelló**. The path is clearly marked and traverses along terraces, climbing gently to pass the **Castelló**, where the route is to the left of an old *ermita*. Follow the cobbled path up to the large building of **Can Prohom** and pass in front of it.

A signpost at the far corner of the building points left uphill for Deià, and the track passes a circular **threshing floor** and leads through a small gate. Continue along the narrow path next to a wall, then after about 200m enter a wood and zigzag downhill. An access road later leads to some nearby houses, but note how the restored **stone-paved path** has been built straight across it.

Walkers climb a fine mule track above Sóller to reach the Camí de Castelló

Llucalcari is a small settlement with a hotel part-way along the coast from Deià (photo: Jaume Tort)

Walk up the restored path to pass a 13th-century building called the **Posada del Rei Jaume I**. After running level for a while, the Camí de Castelló drifts gently downhill and there are glimpses of the settlement of **Llucalcari**, where there is a hotel. The path eventually reaches a private drive near **Ca l'Abat**.

Turn right down this road and watch for a short cut, towards the bottom, down to the main **Ma-10** at K60.2. Turn left along the road and walk round a bend to reach an access road at K60.7, signposted as the GR route to Deià. Walk down the road to pass the large building at **Son Bujosa** and continue down a track until it bends right. Keep straight ahead as waymarked, following a path gently downhill across **olive terraces**. A steeper stone path leads down to a road not far from a rugged cove at **Cala de Deià**, but save a visit until another day, using Walk 51.

Turn left up the road to find two waymarked paths leading up to the village of Deià. One, just across a footbridge, is the Camí des Ribassos, while the other, turning left off the road, is the **Camí de sa Vinyeta**. Use the latter path, which climbs straight up through bends in the road, then winds up through olive terraces to reach the main road in **Deià**. It reaches the village close to a bus stop, taxi stand and shops, near a hotel called **La Residencia**.

Sóller – Can Prohom	1hr 15min
Can Prohom – Deià	2hr 15min

53 Port de Sóller to Sóller
via Camí de Castelló

This delightful and undemanding walk is ideal for a hot day. It makes use of an old cobbled track to go up onto the Muleta plateau, with excellent sea views. A level, easy track leads through groves of olives and joins the Camí de Castelló track near Can Prohom. The descent by this old path gives excellent views over Sóller towards the high mountains of Puig Major, Puig de l'Ofre, Es Cornadors and Serra d'Alfàbia. A cold, refreshing drink in the square and a return to Port de Sóller by the old-fashioned tram make an attractive finish to this walk.

See sketch map 21.

Starting Point	Tram terminus at Port de Sóller
Finishing Point	Plaça d'Amèrica at Sóller
Time	3hr 45min
Distance	10km
Highest Point	260m
Height Climbed	275m
Grade	C
Maps	Alpina Tramuntana Central,
	Alpina B or MTN25 Sóller

Leave the tram terminus and walk south round the bay of **Port de Sóller**. Cross a river by using a **footbridge** and continue along the pedestrianised seafront at **Platja d'en Repic**. Turn left at the Hotel Los Geranios along a quiet road called

Type of Walk
Easy, along well-defined paths and tracks and with no steep gradients.

The circular harbour at Port de Sóller, seen above Muleta de Ca s'Hereu

Camp de sa Mar and turn right for the **Rocamar Hotel**. This is derelict but still bears its name prominently.

Turn left to walk in front of the hotel, then turn right up a mule track signposted for Deià, climbing behind the building. This is well trodden and marked with GR waymark posts, keeping well to the left of the *agroturismo* of **Muleta de ca s'Hereu**. After crossing a valley planted with olives, the mule track comes near a large house with a square tower at **Muleta de Ca s'Avinyons**.

Pass around this property as marked by signs reading Deya, and turn left to walk straight through a cross-tracks. The track now winds between olive terraces, bending left and right, and passing a junction with one track to reach a T-junction with a wider road.

Turn left here to follow the road past a house called **Son Augustinus** to reach a road junction at Costa de Deià, where a small building is painted with the words 'Urbanizacion Costa Deya'. Turn left and follow the road round to reach the main **Ma-10**. Turn left towards Sóller to reach the hotel at **Son Bleda**.

Turn right again up a dirt road opposite the hotel, leading to the large building of **Can Prohom**. This is a private road, but at the second bend on the left a public footpath leads up to an old *ermita* near the **Castelló**, where the path joins the signposted **Camí de Castelló** to Sóller.

Turn left along the path to follow it beside a wall around the Ca'n Carabasseta estate. In about 20 minutes go straight across the driveway of the **Ca's Xorc Hotel** as signposted along the **Camí des Rost**. Simply keep to the route as waymarked, avoiding turns through gates onto adjacent properties.

After going through a **gate**, one stretch of the old track has a patchy tarmac surface, but soon reverts to the old cobbled track, going down an impressive flight of old steps that cross over the **railway track** near a tunnel mouth. Continue descending to cross a streambed. Keep straight on and follow the road, turning left along the **Camí de sa Costa d'en Llorenç** to reach the busy **Ma-11 bypass**.

Either cross straight to the other side and wander along narrow streets into **Sóller**, or turn left along the main road, then right, to reach the bus stop on the **Plaça d'Amèrica**.

Port de Sóller – Castelló	1hr 45min
Castelló – Sóller	2hr

54 Punta de Sa Foradada

This is a pleasant coastal walk from near Valldemossa to a spectacular, prominent rocky peninsula, pierced with a large natural hole, at Sa Foradada. The peninsula can easily be seen from the main coastal road near Deià or from the Son Marroig *mirador*, where there is also a restaurant. Son Marroig was once the property of Archduke Lluís Salvador, and is now a museum that is worth visiting if time is available.

If possible, park a car at Son Marroig, at K65.5 on the Ma-10, then take the bus to K71.3, which is the junction with the Banyalbufar road just outside Valldemossa. It is quite feasible to do the walk using the bus from Port de Sóller or Sóller, returning from Son Marroig – even in winter there are early and late buses, but check the timetable in advance. Taking a taxi

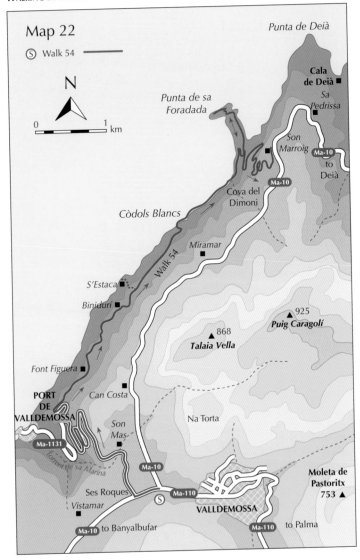

Map 22

Ⓢ Walk 54 ────

N

0 ___ 1 km

Punta de Deià

Cala de Deià ■

Punta de sa Foradada

Sa Pedrissa ■

Son Marroig ■

Ma-10 — to Deià

Còdols Blancs

Walk 54

Cova del Dimoni

Ma-10

Miramar ■

925 ▲

Puig Caragolí

868 ▲

Talaia Vella

S'Estaca ■

Binidurí ■

Font Figuera ■

Can Costa ■

Na Torta

PORT DE VALLDEMOSSA

Ma-1131

Son Mas ■

Torrent de sa Marina

Moleta de Pastoritx
753 ▲

Ses Roques

Vistamar ■

Ⓢ

Ma-110

VALLDEMOSSA

Ma-10 — to Banyalbufar

Ma-110 — to Palma

from Valldemossa to the Font Figuera gate is worth considering, and has the advantage of cutting out 4km of road walking at the start.

Another option would be to drive to Port de Valldemossa then walk to the last headland where the path disappears. Returning the same way gives a very easy walk of about 3hours. Another half day could then be spent walking down to Sa Foradada and back from Son Marroig. In this case permission should be sought at the house.

See sketch map 22.

Starting Point	K71.3 on the Ma-10 near Valldemossa
Finishing Point	K65.5 on the Ma-10 at Son Marroig
Time	5hr 10min
Distance	14km
Highest Point	370m
Height Climbed	500m
Grade	B+
Maps	Alpina Tramuntana Central, Alpina B or MTN25 Esporles and Sóller

Start at the junction of the Ma-10 and Ma-1110 just west of **Valldemossa** and walk as signposted along the road for Banyalbufar. Turn right along the Ma-1131, which is signposted for Port de Valldemossa. The road passes fine buildings at **Son Mas**, then narrows and descends in zigzags, with some entrancing views of the surrounding cliffs and the little marina far below.

Just before the **K4** marker, turn right along a good track starting at a metal gate with pedestrian access on the right. The track contours around 100m and 150m, and leads at first through pine woods, then crosses more open ground with views of the sea.

The house at **Font Figuera** is passed, then there is a locked gate with pedestrian access to the left. The track climbs above attractive buildings with ornamental parapets at **S'Estaca** (owned by the actor Michael Douglas), passing fruit trees and vines.

Type of Walk
Very easy, except for a 1km stretch near Sa Foradada. The path has been destroyed by landslips and rockfalls and care is required clambering over boulders – it is this section only that grades the walk B+, rather than C.

The curious pierced headland of the Punta de sa Foradada below Son Marroig

There is a picnic place where a stone table and seats have been built between some huge boulders.

Further on, the main track heads downhill to a chained gateway leading off-route to a quaint little harbour, also called **S'Estaca**, which is worth visiting, but the old track continues to the right, through another gateway. This narrower track leads through pine woods to a stile, then narrows greatly as it continues, passing a *sitja* and bending left to arrive at a pine-covered headland at **Còdols Blancs**. ◀

It is at this point that the old track has been destroyed by landslips. Scramble down onto the rocks near **sea level**, and then make your way along boulders and past landslips, noting the last remaining vestiges of the old track. Bear in mind that further landslips and rockfalls are inevitable, so do take care. Not for nothing is this area called the **Cova del Dimoni**!

Follow small cairns where visible, and especially watch for the point where you can climb back onto the old track, once again clear and easy to follow, to the col between **Sa Foradada** and the main cliff line. Take a short left branch path to a viewpoint, then enjoy the easy walk out to Sa Foradada.

The track crosses a narrow neck before the final climb to the rock. This is a steep but short little scramble on coarse conglomerate, and on top a path can be found leading to the **white column** above the hole. ▸

The descent to the hole involves rock climbing and should not be attempted.

Retrace steps from the headland, then follow the obvious **zigzag track** as it climbs up a forested cliff to **Son Marroig**. Cross a stile beside a metal gate at the top of the track and walk past the house and museum. (If attempting to walk downhill from Son Marroig to reach the peninsula, note the sign requesting 'Ask for permission to visit the Foradada'.)

Alongside the museum is the bar–restaurant Miradors de na Foradada, and above both are car parks and bus stops on the main Ma-10 at K65.5.

K71.3 on Ma-10 – Font Figuera gate	1hr 15min
Font Figuera gate – Còdols Blancs	1hr
Còdols Blancs – Sa Foradada path	1hr 15min
Sa Foradada path – Sa Foradada headland	40min
Sa Foradada headland – Son Marroig	1hr

55 Es Teix and Sa Galera

Es Teix is a popular mountain, easily ascended from Valldemossa, but Sa Galera is remote and rarely visited. Views are extensive and this is an interesting, but long walk.

From Es Teix the blue Mediterranean can be seen on both sides of Mallorca, with the main chain of the Serra de Tramuntana stretching out on the other side of the Coll de Sóller, and beyond it the central plain and the Serra de Llevant. Sa Galera itself is an outstanding natural *mirador*, giving almost a bird's-eye view of Deià and the coast between Deià and Port de Sóller. A high-level ridge walk, including Puig des Vent, connects Es Teix with Sa Galera.

This stony, arid area was at one time cultivated and inhabited during the summer months, with terracing, buildings that were once roofed, and there is even a threshing floor, all at an altitude of almost 1000m.

See sketch maps 23(a) and 23(b).

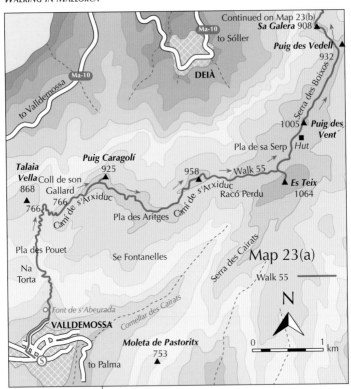

Starting Point	Plaça Campdevànol in Valldemossa
Finishing Point	Plaça d'Amèrica in Sóller
Time	8hr 15min
Distance	16km
Highest Point	1062m
Height Climbed	800m
Grade	A+
Maps	Alpina Tramuntana Central, Alpina B or MTN25 Esporles, Alaró and Sóller

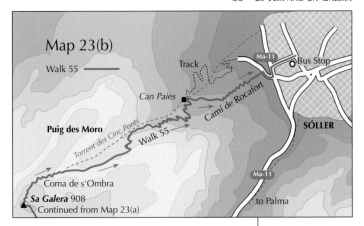

Map 23(b)

Walk 55 ——————

Track

Ma-11 Bus Stop

Can Paies

Camí de Rocafort

Puig des Moro

Torrent des Cinc Ponts

Walk 55

SÓLLER

Coma de s'Ombra

Sa Galera 908
Continued from Map 23(a)

Ma-11

to Palma

Start in **Valldemossa**, at the bus stop on **Plaça Campdevànol**, and walk away from the town centre along **Carrer Rector Joan Mir**. Turn right up **Carrer de Joan Fuster**, which runs alongside a tall-fenced sports pitch. Keep rising and turn left up **Carrer de les Oliveres**, following this road all the way to the top. Continue straight up a track, then left up a rocky path to cross a stile over a fixed gate near the **Font de s'Abeurada**.

A clear track climbs further uphill, and this is an old charcoal-burners' route zigzagging up through woods of evergreen oaks. It is quite rough and stony in places, and some of the zigzags might be short cut on the ascent.

At the top, go through a gateway in a **boundary wall**, at 685m, to reach a flattish area of fairly open ground called the **Pla des Pouet**. There is a multitude of paths and tracks in this area, where it is very easy to take the wrong one, but simply walk straight ahead into the woods to reach a polluted **well**. Three paths begin near here. One goes left to the Mirador de ses Puntes (the way of return on Walk 56). One on the right goes to the Pla d'es Aritges and is a shorter way to Es Teix, but misses out the spectacular Camí de s'Arxiduc. Take the middle way that leads up to the wooded **Coll de son Gallard**, at 766m. There is a distinctive V-shaped stone seat here.

Turn right and follow the path leading steeply up to reach the magnificent wide path, the **Camí de s'Arxiduc**, built by the Archduke Lluís Salvador. This continues along

Type of Walk
Part of the route is remote and trackless and not recommended in mist. Route finding on the descent from Sa Galera is crucial, as there only seems to be one safe way down the encircling cliffs.

View of the rugged crest of Es Teix, with Puig Major in the far distance

the very edge of the steep cliffs overlooking Deià, passing **Puig Caragolí**, a splendid viewpoint on the cliff top at 925m, continuing onto the **Pla des Aritges.**

Turn left at a prominent cairn at a junction of paths. Follow the path with care to leave the plain and gain a bit more height, where it becomes much clearer again. Pass a small *mirador* overlooking Deià, then descend to a col at 885m at **Racó Perdut**.

Turn left at another prominent cairn, leaving the Camí de s'Arxiduc. The path climbs steep and rocky at first, then in 10 minutes crosses a **boundary wall** where a fine ladder stile features a locked gate on top! Cross the high-level plain, the **Pla de sa Serp,** and walk towards a spring, the **Font de sa Serp**, where there is good drinking water in a stone trough, but there is no need to go all the way.

Teixoch, just to the east, is 1m higher, according to the latest maps.

A good path marked by cairns leads to a **small col** between Es Teix and Teixoch. Turn right to reach the top of **Es Teix**, which has a trig point at 1064m. ◀ Enjoy coast-to-coast views, then return towards the **Font de sa Serp** by the same path (the direction is north, should the clouds descend).

Follow an obvious vehicle track northeast from the **Pla de sa Serp**, but don't follow it too far down into a valley. Watch out for a cairned path off to the left, augmented by paint marks, which leads across the shoulder of a hill to reach a broad col at 965m. ▸ Climb straight up to the top of the **Puig des Vent** at 1005m. Once up on the high ground, which is very stony and arid, the way continues to be marked by paint spots and a few cairns.

There is a ruined hut here, as well as some enclosures and a threshing floor.

A slight descent leads to a **gap in a wall**, after which the ridge narrows a little and the walking becomes easier – over solid rocks instead of loose stones. Continue along the ridge of the **Serra des Boixos** until close to **Puig des Vedell** at 932m. The marker cairns turn left before this point to lead walkers onto a subsidiary ridge leading northwest. The cairns mark the way to the trig point on **Sa Galera** at 908m. (**Note** the directional arrow painted on the trig point, revealing a path running northeast, before making the next move!)

The descent from the summit starts by following a narrow path that becomes steep and stony as it runs northeast down into the tree-filled valley of the **Coma de S'Ombra**. The path is marked by cairns and is the only safe way to start the descent. Follow it down to a wall on a slight col around 780m, between Sa Galera and **Puig des Moro**. There is a fenced-off gateway in this wall, and on the other side there is a good view down to the coast.

(**Note** It is possible to descend roughly northwards from this gateway, down a steep and rugged zigzag path, then follow a long and winding vehicle track to Can Prohom. However, this passes through a woodland used for hunting, and ends at a tall, locked gate marked private, but in an emergency this path and track may offer the quickest means of descent.)

To continue the descent to Sóller, turn right on the col and go down into the wooded **Coma de S'Ombra**, on a poorly defined path with a few cairns. About 10 minutes after leaving the col a *sitja* and a ruined building will be reached. Turn left to continue down a better path for a further 5 minutes to reach a much larger *sitja* and three old shelters.

From this point a well-made but overgrown track leads down the valley on the right-hand side of the **Torrent des Cinc Ponts**. Follow this track carefully and watch for it zigzagging left down into the valley later. One path branches

Mist swirls around the steep northern cliffs of the Serra des Boixos

left, but don't follow it. Another path later branches left, and you follow this one, even though it appears to terminate abruptly. Look carefully to spot its continuation steeply downhill, which is marked by cairns and painted red arrows.

Zigzag almost down to the **streambed**, but do not cross. Instead, turn right and walk as marked along the base of an overhanging cliff, leaving the valley to link with a clear vehicle track sandwiched between impressive cliffs. Turn right to walk to a gate and stile. Follow the dirt road and go steeply downhill, zigzagging as it turns to concrete during the descent. The road runs down through terraces of olives, and a couple of curious buildings will be seen further down, made from **hollowed-out boulders**.

Either follow the road all the way down towards Sóller, bearing in mind that is is very bendy and seems to last forever, or turn right when you notice wooden waymark posts near a house called **Can Paies**. Turning right here leads, after about 10 minutes, to a signposted path junction where you turn left down an old stepped path, the **Camí de Rocafort**. This crosses the railway line twice, first using a **footbridge**, then by crossing the actual line to join a **tarmac road**.

Walk straight down the road and turn right at the bottom, then left, to reach the busy **Ma-11 bypass** on the outskirts of **Sóller**. Either cross the main road to work through winding streets into the town centre, or turn left along the main road, then right, to reach the **Plaça d'Amèrica** and the bus stop.

Valldemossa – Pla des Pouet	1hr 15min
Pla des Pouet – Es Teix	2hr 30min
Es Teix – Sa Galera	1hr 30min
Sa Galera – Vehicle track	1hr 40min
Vehicle track – Sóller	1hr 20min

56 Es Teix and the Camí de s'Arxiduc

The Archduke Lluís Salvador (Ludwig Salvator is the original form of his name) of Habsburgo-Lorena visited Mallorca in 1867 and liked it so much he later came to live here, settling at the *finca* of Miramar, near Valldemossa.

He was a great benefactor to the island and an early conservationist – he restored old buildings, and did not allow trees and shrubs to be cut down on his properties. He made a marvellous garden at Miramar with native Mallorquín plants, and wrote a treatise on the island that dealt with almost every aspect, including natural history, economy, language and folklore. One of his properties was Son Moragues, which was bought by the state in 1979 and turned over to public use. It is a centre for nature conservation and very carefully managed, with strict rules to protect plants and animals and guard against fire.

One of the archduke's achievements that is of great benefit to walkers is the construction of excellent paths on the Son Moragues estate, in spectacular situations along the edges of high cliffs looking down to Deià and the coast. Lluís Salvador had these built so that he could walk or ride here and enjoy the views without danger or difficulty. To follow in his footsteps is an enjoyable and exhilarating experience and provides one of the best walks on the island.

The route described here is quite long and strenuous, but it could easily be split into two or even three shorter walks to allow more time for appreciation of the scenery. One suggestion is to spend a day on the ascent of Es Teix via the Serra des Cairats, and devote another day to the Camí de s'Arxiduc, excluding Es Teix.

IBANAT has provided an attractive picnic place at the Font des Poll, with wooden tables and seats. A little higher up is a *refugi* equipped with tables and benches, with an enormous fireplace across one corner. This hut was originally the living quarters of the *nevaters*, or snow collectors. The snowpit nearby is an enormous 24m x 8m, but was built too low on the mountain.

Incidentally, the name *Teix* means 'yew' in Catalan, and there are a number of yews, quite rare today in Mallorca, growing on the slopes of the mountain.

See sketch map 24.

Starting Point	Plaça Campdevànol in Valldemossa
Time	6hr 20min
Distance	16km
Highest Point	1064m
Height Climbed	880m
Grade	B+
Maps	Alpina Tramuntana Central, Alpina B or MTN25 Esporles and Alaró

Type of Walk
A long but relatively straightforward walk along good mountain paths.

Start in **Valldemossa**, either at the bus stop on **Plaça Campdevànol**, or at the car parks nearby on the main Ma-1110. Walk up the main road and turn left at a children's play park, up the **Carrer de na Mas**. Turn right along **Carrer de Son Gual**, passing the big stone house of Son Gual to continue straight along the **Carrer Lluís Vives**. This road gives way to **Carrer Toscana**, but when this leads into **Carrer Xesc Forteza**, branch left through a gateway to follow a clear track into a valley.

The valley is the **Comellar des Cairats**, and the track is later joined by another track from Sa Coma after crossing a **cattle-grid** over the main streambed. Further up the valley the track bends right and left as it climbs (avoid the track running straight ahead at the first bend.)

The Son Moragues estate is entered at a **gateway** with a stone step-stile alongside. There is an information board,

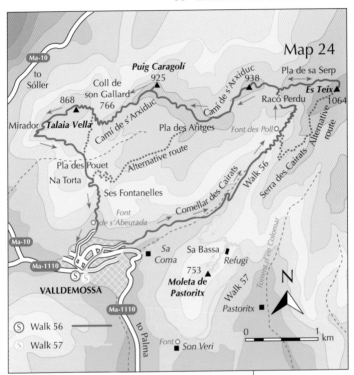

then the track rises quite steeply, with several concrete bends, before reaching a picnic area at the **Font des Poll**. (**Note** A path on the right is signposted for the Serra des Cairats – see Alternative Ascent below.)

Ten minutes further uphill the main track reaches a *refugi* hut and toilet. The road ends at a nearby **snowpit** and the walk then continues along the archduke's path, or **Camí de s'Arxiduc**. After climbing for 20 minutes the path levels out near a col at 885m. A **large cairn** marks the point where the path for Es Teix leaves on the right.

Follow this path for 10 minutes and cross a **boundary wall** using a ladder stile with a locked gate on top! It leads easily in another 10 minutes up to a small plain, the **Pla de**

The Camí de s'Arxiduc is a remarkably scenic 19th-century mountain path

sa Serp, where there is a spring. Before reaching the spring a branch path slants up to the right to the col between Es Teix and Teixoch, then to the top of **Es Teix** with its trig point at 1064m. Enjoy the views, then return to the **Camí de s'Arxiduc** to continue the walk.

Follow the clear path as it zigzags gently uphill, then the next point of interest is a small *mirador* on the edge of the cliffs overlooking Deià. The path passes some rocky pinnacles, then becomes a little indistinct as it crosses a flat area, the **Pla des Aritges** (aritges is smilax, the plant with vicious, backward-pointing thorns).

Some 40 minutes from the junction with the Es Teix path there is a path junction marked by a **large cairn** beside a clump of shady pines. (**Note** A branch path to the left could be followed over Fontanelles and down to **Pla des Pouet** to shorten the walk.) The main path, to the right, becomes especially attractive. It swings towards **Puig des Caragolí,** a high point at 925m with its own spur path leading up to it, and an excellent viewpoint. A plaque on top commemorates the Archduke Lluís Salvador. After this the path continues southwest along the edge of the cliffs to reach another fine top at 889m.

Take care on the descent towards a wooded pass – path on the left descends directly to **Pla des Pouet**, and it is easy to shorten the walk inadvertently here. Keep a watch to spot the path leading to the **Coll de son Gallard** at 766m. ▸

There is a path leading down to Deià on the right, while on the left a path descends to Pla des Pouet. If intending to climb **Talaia Vella**, then be sure to cross the col and find the path leading uphill. The main path misses the 868m summit, but another trodden path leads there.

Reach an old stone shelter near the top, called **Es Refugi** – another of Lluís Salvador's works. From the top continue along the wooded ridge, passing a trig point at 856m. This path is another of the archduke's routes, and is easy to follow in spite of being somewhat overgrown by trees. Follow it to the **Mirador de ses Puntes**, another impressive viewpoint on the edge of a 400m drop down to the flat plain of Valldemossa.

From the *mirador* turn left along a path that passes an old bread oven and several sitges on the way down to **Pla des Pouet**. Go straight on past the polluted **well** here, and in 5 minutes a clearing on level ground will be reached. Go straight on through a gap in a **stone wall** at 685m. Either follow a rough and stony track winding downhill, or look for short cuts to descend more rapidly. The route is an old charcoal-burners' track at a reasonable gradient, and many *sitges* will be noticed in the forest.

The last part of the track leads left over a stile at a fixed gate beside the **Font de s'Abeurada**. Continue downhill along the **Carrer de les Oliveres**. A right turn at the end leads down a road beside a tall-fenced sports pitch. Turn left to head into **Valldemossa** as soon as the monastery can be seen along one of the roads. This road, **Carrer Rector Joan Mir**, leads straight back to the bus stop on **Plaça Campdevànol**. A left turn up the main road leads back to the car parks.

There is a stone seat here in the form of a V and plentiful signs of the thrush-hunter's activities.

Valldemossa – *Refugi*	1hr 10min
Refugi – Es Teix	1hr
Es Teix – Coll de son Gallard	2hr
Coll de son Gallard – Talaia Vella	20min
Talaia Vella – Mirador de ses Puntes	30min
Mirador de ses Puntes – Es Pouet	20min
Es Pouet – Valldemossa	1hr

Steep cliffs rise towards Es Teix in this view from the Serra des Cairats

Alternative Ascent –
Es Teix via the Serra des Cairats
This alternative route up Es Teix is highly recommended.
It begins at the **Font des Polls** and is signposted 'Serra des
Cairats'. A wide and well-made track leads up into a steep
and narrow **wooded valley**, which is surmounted in zigzags.
Take a left turn where the main track goes straight on about
20 minutes from the *font*. In a further 20 minutes the track
ends at a *sitja*. After this a trodden path marked by **small
cairns** leads up through the wood in a northerly direction
to reach a **wall**.

Cross at a broken fence at a gap in the wall. Continue
straight uphill, and when the trees thin out, walk up the ridge
on **bare rock**. Cairns show the way past another **wall**, and
when this is reached the top of **Es Teix**, with its trig point at
1064m, can be seen and is easily gained.

To descend, follow the cairned and well-trodden **rocky
path** northwards to the **Pla de sa Serp**. Follow the path across
the plain, crossing a faint vehicle track, then cross over a
slight rise before descending to a **wall**. This is crossed using a
ladder stile with a locked gate on top! In a further 10 minutes
the **Camí de s'Arxiduc** is joined at a **large cairn**.

Turn left to zigzag down to the snowpit and *refugi*
in about 20 minutes. A further 10 minutes and the track
reaches the **Font des Polls** at the head of the valley called the
Comellar des Cairats.

Valldemossa – Font des Polls	1hr
Font des Polls – Es Teix	1hr 15min
Es Teix – Camí de s'Arxiduc	30min
Camí de s'Arxiduc – Valldemossa	1hr

57 Sa Moleta de Pastoritx

This steep-sided, wooded hill lies to the east of Valldemossa, and is of particular interest for the abundance of sites used by charcoal burners. These include *sitges*, some of them very large and prominent, because of the bright-green moss growing in a perfect circle, and there are at least three bread ovens in excellent repair.

Although there are some panoramic views of Valldemossa and the peaceful valley of Pastoritx, these are only seen occasionally because of the trees. The walk includes a complete circuit of the hill as well as an ascent, and is an excellent choice when shelter is required.

See sketch map 24.

Starting Point	Plaça Campdevànol in Valldemossa
Time	4hr
Distance	10km
Highest Point	753m
Height Climbed	400m
Grade	B
Maps	Alpina Tramuntana Central, Alpina B or MTN25 Esporles

Type of Walk
Country lanes and tracks, easy woodland paths, and a descent of a steep and stony old track. Attention must be paid to route finding as trees frequently obscure views.

Start in **Valldemossa**, either at the bus stop on **Plaça Campdevànol** or at the car parks nearby on the main Ma-1110. Walk up the main road and turn left at a children's play park, up the **Carrer de na Mas**. Turn right along **Carrer de Son Gual**, passing the big stone house of Son Gual to continue straight along **Carrer Lluís Vives**. This road leads onto **Carrer Xesc Forteza**. Walk along it, then branch left through a gateway to follow a clear track into a valley, the **Comellar des Cairats**. This track is later joined by another track from Sa Coma after crossing a **cattle-grid** over the main streambed.

The track passes a small **derelict building**, then approximately 150m afterwards, turn right along another track. Follow this track for a little over 600m then turn left at a **junction** along another track. Almost immediately leave the

Touching the top olive terraces above the old farmstead of Pastoritx

wide track and swing sharp right up a kind of mossy track through old terraces. When a wall is seen, swing left and look for a **small gap** that may be obscured by trees.

Turn left along yet another track, which leads to a simple **hunter's cabin**. Keep to the right of this to follow a narrow path above the top terraces, on a slope of oaks. Go through a **gap in a wall** and zigzag up the steep, wooded slope. Climb a wall at the top, using the sticks inserted into the stonework, to reach a wooded col at 629m.

Turn right along the cliff-edge path, then almost immediately fork left to reach the location known as **Sa Bassa**, where there is a water tank, a *sitja*, and a *refugi* building used by hunters. (**Note** This is a significant reference point for the descent.)

Follow the path from here, rising slightly to reach in 15 minutes or so a large *sitja* and a **ruined shelter**. Follow the path up left from here to reach the escarpment forming the summit ridge. ◄ Continue along the ridge to the right to reach the rather indefinite tree-screened top of **Moleta de Pastoritx** at 753m, noting the route carefully so you can retrace your steps.

> At this point there are thrush-hunting structures with impressive views down to Pastoritx.

Return to the *refugi* at **Sa Bassa**. Follow the track northeast, through a shallow, wooded valley, passing a *sitja* and avoiding a path branching left for the **Serra des Cairats**. Reach a prominent bread oven and another sitja, where the track bends sharp right and starts to descend a **steep gully** in a series of tight bends, followed by wider swings left and right. Avoid a turning to the left, and eventually reach a gap in a wall that separates the woodland from the olive terraces of **Pastoritx**.

There is no need to go down onto the olive terraces. Turn right and follow a rather vague trodden path, awkward at first, on a rising traverse. A clear track soon evolves that passes sitges, a large limekiln and a bread oven. Less than 10 minutes later go over a **stile** consisting of branches across a wire-netting fence on top of a wall.

The continuation of the track is not too apparent, but descend and swing right to discover a pleasant woodland path that reaches a fence and a **rickety stile**. Cross over and turn right to reach the **Font de Son Verí**, built in 1591, but now sadly collapsed – carved stonework scattered around gives some indication of what a fine structure it used to be.

The path descends alongside the fence and crosses another **rickety stile** to reach a narrow road by the gates of

Predio Son Veri. Turn right and follow the concrete road to the large house of **Sa Coma**, and walk down round a **hairpin bend** to reach a bend on the busy Ma-1110.

Turn right up towards **Valldemossa**, or avoid the road by going down steps on the left to follow the narrow tarmac **Camí de sa Coma** – this leads into the stone-paved **Plaça de na Búger**. Walk down **Carrer del Pare Castanyeda**, then turn right up past the church of Sant Bartolome, following the **Carrer de la Constitució**. Turn left up **Carrer Rosa**, then fork left up **Carrer Uetam**, with the large monastery rising to the left. Walking straight ahead along **Via Blanquerna**, however, leads back to the **Plaça Campdevànol**, where the walk started.

Valldemossa – Sa Bassa	1hr 20min
Sa Bassa – Moleta de Pastoritx	25min
Moleta de Pastoritx – Sa Bassa	20min
Sa Bassa – Font de Son Verí	1hr 10min
Font de Son Verí – Valldemossa	45min

Early morning sunlight catches the historic parts of Valldemossa

AREA 3

ANDRATX AND THE SOUTH

58 Banyalbufar and Port des Canonge

Port des Canonge is a small village on the coast northeast of Banyalbufar, which can be reached by driving down a steep and narrow winding road. There is not much there apart from a few boats, an abandoned urbanisation project and a restaurant that has a good reputation, Toni Moreno's.

This circular walk from Banyalbufar is extremely attractive, with views of typical countryside as well as the sea. The best time for the walk is February, when sugar-pink and white almond blossom enhances the views.

See sketch map 25.

Starting Point	Plaça de la Vila in Banyalbufar
Time	4hr 30min
Distance	14km
Highest Point	385m
Height Climbed	550m
Grade	C+
Maps	Alpina Tramuntana Sud, Alpina B or MTN25 Esporles

Type of Walk

Mostly very easy on narrow roads and wide tracks and paths. There is some objective danger where the route passes below an unstable cliff.

Start in the **Plaça de la Vila** in the centre of **Banyalbufar** and walk up the narrow, twisting road called **Carrer Jeroni Albertí**. This is later signposted as the GR route to Esporles, and its name changes to **Carrer de la Font de la Vila** as it climbs further uphill (you occasionally see the spring that gives the road its name). The ascent continues until the tarmac surface ends at the gates of **Son Sanutges**.

Follow the unsurfaced dirt road to the left, roughly contouring around 350m across forested slopes. Take care when the dirt road drops down onto the main **Ma-10**, as it lands on a bad bend. Cross with care, turn right and walk along the road facing oncoming traffic. (There is a chance to avoid

Olive terraces lead the eye to the stout manorial house of Son Bunyola

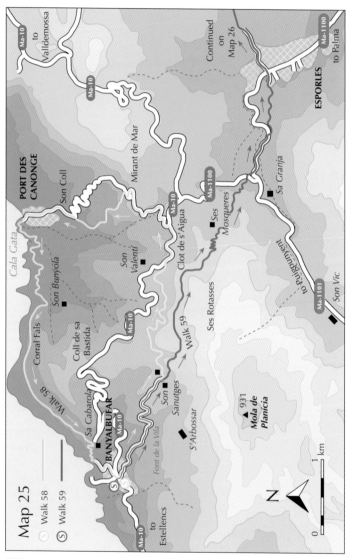

Map 25

Ⓢ Walk 58
Ⓢ Walk 59

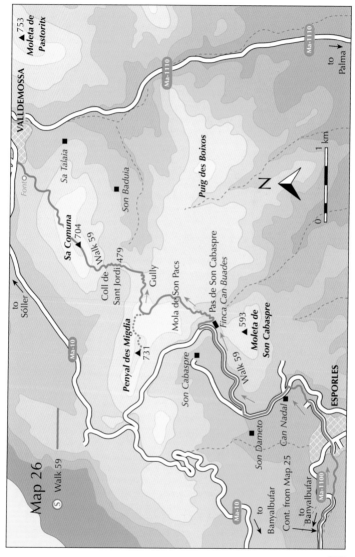

Map 26

Ⓢ Walk 59

Moleta de Pastoritx ▲ 753

VALDEMOSSA

to Sóller

to Palma

Ma-1110

Ma-10

Ma-1110

Sa Talaia ■

Font ○

Sa Comuna ▲ 704
Walk 59

Son Baduia ■

Puig des Boixos

Coll de Sant Jordi 479

Gully

Mola de Son Pacs

Penyal des Migdia ▲ 731

Pas de Son Cabaspre
Finca Can Buades

Moleta de Son Cabaspre ▲ 593

Walk 59

Son Cabaspre ■

Son Dameto ■

Can Nadal ■

ESPORLES

Ma-1100

to Banyalbufar

Cont. from Map 25

to Banyalbufar

Ma-10

N

0   1 km

some of the road walking by looking out for a vague track running parallel later, just below the road.)

Turn left at the **K80** marker, down the road signposted for Port des Canonge. This descends in tight loops and is followed for over 1km. Watch out for a path coming down onto the road from the right, from **Mirant de Mar**. Follow the road round a couple more tight bends, then turn left as indicated by a marker post down a **clear path** on the forested slope.

The path lands on a dirt road lined with old lamp posts, and another marker post is found just to the left. Continue down the path and turn right along a track to reach a road bend. Walk down the road, the **Carrer es Port des Canonge**, leading down to a couple of small restaurants in **Port des Canonge**.

Turn left to explore the little headland and cross a worn, grassy area with pine trees, then cross a streambed at **Cala Gata**. Walk over another little headland to reach another **streambed** and head inland. The streambed is actually a track, leading up to a junction where a right turn is made.

Follow a broad, clear, well-built reddish track climbing steadily away from the cliffs up a forested slope. There is a view of a cultivated valley from a gap, then a few minutes later a view of the manorial **Son Bunyola** above neat terraces. Keep right to follow the track as it winds up to a cross-tracks. Turn right here as signposted for Banyalbufar.

A narrower and stonier track leads up to the base of a high overhanging cliff at **Corral Fals**, and continues past it for about 5 minutes (**this is not a place to linger**, as a glance at the large fallen rocks below will confirm.) Once safely beyond the cliffs a wide and pleasant track contours around 100m, and then rises gently through the woods on the sloping hillside for about 2km to reach a **gate** at 150m. The gate should be open, but there is a ladder stile alongside that you can use if it's closed.

Keep on the main track until it bends sharp left at a house called **Sa Cabarola**. Immediately before the house turn right on a narrow path descending a wooded slope. About 5 minutes down the path, drop more steeply to avoid an overgrown stretch, aiming for some buildings at the bottom of the slope. Turn left to follow a narrow road.

Turn right at a little cemetery to follow the **Carrer Marina** and continue along the **Carrer Major** to return to the **Plaça de la Vila** in **Banyalbufar**.

Banyalbufar – Son Sanutges	40min
Son Sanutges – K80 on the Ma-10	1hr
K80 on the Ma-10 – Port des Canonge	1hr
Port des Canonge – Banyalbufar	1hr 50min

59 Banyalbufar to Valldemossa

The countryside between Banyalbufar and Valldemossa has no really high mountains, but is a pleasant area with many quiet roads, forest tracks and paths.

During this linear cross-country walk a short diversion can be made onto Penyal des Migdia, the highest point on the Mola de Son Pacs, at 731m – the top is on a high, rocky ridge, partly hidden in woodland. The walk can be done using a morning bus to Banyalbufar and an afternoon bus back from Valldemossa, and can be shortened by starting or finishing in Esporles. It can also be included as a stage in a long walk from Andratx to Sóller, and on through the Serra de Tramuntana to Pollença.

See sketch maps 25 and 26.

Starting Point	Plaça de la Vila in Banyalbufar
Finishing Point	Plaça Campdevànol in Valldemossa
Time	6hr 30min
Distance	19km
Highest Point	731m
Height Climbed	1040m
Grade	B
Maps	Alpina Tramuntana Sud and Central, Alpina B or MTN25 Esporles

Leave **Banyalbufar** from the Plaça de la Vila and climb up the narrow Carrer Jeroni Albertí. This is quite bendy and when it turns right its name changes to Carrer de la Font de la Vila as it climbs further uphill. It is signposted as the GR221. The road climbs relentlessly past terraces of fruit and vegetables, dipping a little to cross the Torrent de Son Roig. The tarmac eventually ends at the gateway to **Son Sanutges**, out of sight

Type of Walk
Mainly on good paths, the first half is well waymarked as the GR221 but careful route-finding is needed later on.

275

to the right. Follow the GR221 signpost straight ahead uphill, where a narrow tarmac and concrete track quickly gives way to a stony path.

The **Camí des Correu**, or post path, is rough and stony as it climbs a wooded slope past old terraces. Pine trees are passed then the path goes through a gap in a wall to enter holm oak woodlands. Pass another wall where the path broadens and rises as a well-buttressed, boulder-paved track to the gentle **Coll des Pí** at 454m (1490ft).

An easier stretch of track runs gently downhill, with brief views of mountains ahead. A limekiln stands to the left and a *sitja* is less obvious to the right. Keep straight ahead where the path is cut by a forest track. Continue down through the woods and swing left across a stream-bed, passing other *sitges*. The track rises broad and clear, passing a gap in a wall, and then descends in a series of tight zigzags, rough and rocky underfoot. Keep straight ahead at a junction then keep to the right of a drystone wall. Spurn a track dropping down left to a house at **Ses Mosqueres**. Go through a small gate in the wall and follow the boulder-paved path further downhill. Keep to the clearest path at all times. Go through another small gate and later swing left to reach the **Ma-1100 road** at a rocky cutting. Cross the road using specially constructed stone ramps then walk parallel to the road and pass a junction near **La Granja**.

The path then runs along the top of a stone buttress high above the **Ma-1100 road** and follows a concrete watercourse for a while before dropping to cross an old road bridge. Soon afterwards, cross the road and climb up a track on a wooded slope. Pass through a couple of gates, following a track between fields until stone steps lead downhill and then a narrow road, the Costa de Sant Pere, takes you in past a church to reach the Plaça d'Espanya in **Esporles**.

From the Plaça d'Espanya, cross the main road to walk away from the church along the Carrer Nou de Sant Pere. Cross a bridge and walk through the little Plaçeta des Pla, heading right to continue along Carrer de Mateu Font. Turn right to cross a bridge onto the Plaçeta de sa Taulera, then turn left to continue up a road out of the village.

The road suddenly turns left and is marked *sin salida* (no exit), so instead walk straight ahead up a track. This swings left as a narrower path, then right as a clear track leading up to a

road. Turn left to walk along the road and keep straight ahead at a junction to pass a house called **Can Nadal**. Later, the fine old house of **Son Dameto** can be seen well away to the left. Follow the road until it runs between stone gate pillars marked for Son Cabaspre. (The 'private' notices apply to cars.)

Looking across country to Mola de Planícia from above the village of Esporles

Turn right along the Camí des Bosc and climb up this road, eventually catching a glimpse of the mansion of **Son Cabaspre**. The roads swings left round the head of the valley, passing a solitary house called **Finca Can Buades**. Turn right to pass a low gateway marked as 'private' and follow the Camí de sa Coma Llobera. This broken concrete track levels out at the **Coll de sa Basseta** at 455m (1493ft). Turn left up another track, but after only a few paces turn right up a vague, cairned path marked for Valldemossa.

The path climbs up a stony slope covered in holm oak woodland, passing a *sitja* and crossing a buttress using a crude stone stile. Turn left to follow a cairned path, but spare a moment to step left onto a limestone pavement for a fine view back through valley to Son Dameto, with Puig de Galatzó beyond and Mola de Planícia to the right.

The path swings to the right and becomes clearer as it passes a *sitja* in a shallow valley, soon climbing to another *sitja* and reaching a track where a wall can be seen through the trees. Turn left along the track, walking roughly parallel to the wall, and after a couple of minutes turn left along another track. Keep to the clearest track through the woods, avoiding others to left and right. Pass a stone igloo-like bread oven and a *sitja* and later, also on your left, another bread oven, *sitges*, a covered *cisterna* and a **stone shelter**.

It is worth stepping to the left for a view over a cliff edge.

Keep right to follow the track away from the stone shelter, and right again at another junction soon afterwards, passing more *sitjas* to reach a wall. ◄

Turn right to follow the path, first alongside the wall, then drifting further away from it. The path is vague in places but after a few minutes watch for a significant left turn. Be sure to spot this turn as the path runs down into a rocky **cleft** which is one of the few breaches in the cliffs surrounding the Mola de Son Pacs. At the foot of this breach, drift left across a wooded slope, then follow a wall and fence down to the **Coll de Sant Jordi** at 479m (1572ft). There is a solitary GR221 marker here, pointing left through a metal gate.

Go through the gate and turn right to climb up a broad, clear path flanked at first by a wall and a fence. This narrows to zigzag up a steep and rocky slope. Keep to the clearest path. There are odd views down to the Hotel Vistamar and back to Mola de Son Pacs, as well as in the other direction to Palma, Es Pla, Randa and the distant Serra de Llevant. There are no views from the wooded top of **Sa Comuna**, at 704m (2310ft).

Pass a couple of low stone huts and cross a wall. Take care following the rugged path through brutally trimmed holm oak woodland where thrush-hunters operate. Pass a *sitja* and the path becomes much clearer, zigzagging down a steep and rocky slope. Early on, there are glimpses of Valldemossa below. Continue straight downhill and the path swings right across a rocky, mossy, wooded slope. Go through a metal gate in a wall and follow the path to a covered *cisterna* beside a ruined building. The GR221 is signposted straight downhill for Valldemossa. Go through a gateway in a wall and follow a steep, winding path.

Drop downhill alongside a wall to reach a house beside the **Font de na Llambies**. Go through a gate and keep left at a couple of path junctions. Drop down a short, steep and rocky slope to join a road beside another windmill at Es Molinet, now converted to a dwelling. Walk straight ahead along a concrete road then turn left along the Carrer de Uruguay to reach the main road and bus stop in **Valldemossa**, around 400m (1310ft).

There are plenty of bar–restaurants, and the Real Cartuja de Valldemossa, founded in 1399, can be visited if there is time to spare.

Banyalbufar – Esporles	2hr 30min
Esporles – Pas de Son Cabaspre	1hr 20min
Pas de Son Cabaspre – Coll de Sant Jordi	1hr 20min
Coll de Sant Jordi – Valldemossa	1hr 20min

60 Puntals de Son Fortesa from Banyalbufar

The Puntals de Son Fortesa is a high top of 893m on a long, narrow ridge between Galatzó and Mola de Planícia. Views from the escarpment edge and from the top are very fine, and although there are steep cliffs on both sides, the ridge is not narrow enough to cause any problems.

The ridge is easily reached from Banyalbufar because the area was once a highly developed centre for the production of charcoal, and good tracks were needed to take the product down the mountain. Although charcoal has long been replaced by butane gas there are still good tracks as high as 800m, which give fine, easy walking, although they have deteriorated in places.

There are still numerous examples of the charcoal workers' activities, such as *sitges, barrancas* and bread ovens, a cluster of which are found at Ses Aljubets. An *aljub* is a covered water cistern where rainwater was stored for all purposes – cooking, drinking, washing and for animals to drink. There is a double one at Ses Aljubets, with one rounded and one rectangular opening, making a distinctive landmark. When charcoal burning was taking place the fires required constant attention, so the *carboners* and their families lived up here for months at a time.

Few of the paths used are marked on published maps, which means route finding is not all that easy, the author and friends making several attempts at this route before succeeding. However, the following route description shows how easy it is to reach the top of the mountains once you know which paths and tracks to use.

Starting Point	Plaça de la Vila in Banyalbufar
Time	5hr 50min
Distance	18km
Highest Point	893m
Height Climbed	880m
Grade	B
Maps	Alpina Tramuntana Sud, Alpina B or MTN25 Esporles and Sa Vileta

Type of Walk
Mainly easy walking on tracks and paths on densely wooded slopes.

Start in the **Plaça de la Vila** in the centre of **Banyalbufar** and walk up the narrow, twisting road called **Carrer Jeroni Albertí**. This is later signposted as the GR route to Esporles, and its name changes to **Carrer de la Font de la Vila** as it climbs further uphill (you occasionally see the spring that gives the road its name). The ascent continues until the tarmac surface ends at the gates of **Son Sanutges**, a former cement works.

Turn right to go through the gateway and pass ruined buildings. The track turns sharp left downhill, then swings round a steep-sided valley to go through another **gateway**. If the gate is shut, it should not actually be locked, and the track leads to a property called **S'Arbossar**.

After passing S'Arbossar, the track forks, so keep left and walk uphill. Turn left at a junction to follow another track steeply uphill. Go through an old **gateway** in a stone wall

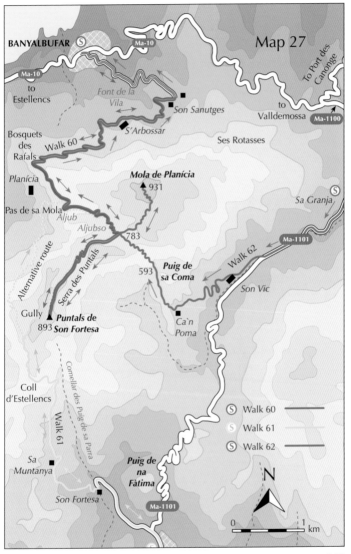

Map 27

BANYALBUFAR (S)

Ma-10

Ma-10
to
Estellencs

To Port des
Canonge

Font de la
Vila

Son Sanutges

to
Valldemossa

Ma-1100

S'Arbossar

Bosquets
des
Rafals

Walk 60

Ses Rotasses

Planícia

Mola de Planícia
▲ 931

Sa Granja (S)

Pas de sa Mola

Aljub

Ma-1101

Walk 62

Aljubso

783

Alternative route

Serra des Puntals

Puig de
sa Coma

593

Son Vic

Gully

▲ Puntals de
893 Son Fortesa

Ca`n
Poma

Coll
d'Estellencs

Comellar des Puig de sa Para

Walk 61

(S) Walk 60 ———
(S) Walk 61 ———
(S) Walk 62 ———

Sa
Muntanya

Puig de
na
Fàtima

N

Son Fortesa

Ma-1101

0   1
└─────┴─────┘ km

Looking from Puntals de Son Fortesa along the crest of Serra des Puntals

and later turn right at a triangular junction. Turn left further uphill, then simply keep following the clearest track onwards and upwards, avoiding all other tracks and paths on the steep wooded slopes.

The track rises gradually with a few short zigzags, and there are only occasional glimpses of the coast or nearby mountains. Pass a straggly old fence on a little col at **Bosquet des Rafals** and walk round into a high valley. ▶ A limekiln, ruined building, *aljub* and bread oven are passed at the head of the valley.

Look to the right to spot a narrow path climbing from the finca at Planícia, used on Walk 61.

The track climbs over a ridge and reaches the head of another valley, where there are distinctive twin aljubs at **Ses Aljubets**. Progress seems to be blocked by a wall of rock, but look carefully to spot the track making tight zigzags up through a breach, levelling out on a broad, wooded **col at 780m**.

Routes meet on the col and it is worth taking note of them for future reference. The main track swings left towards Mola de Planícia, while a cairned path straight ahead leads down towards Son Vic, Sa Granja and Esporles. Our route for the moment is to the right, where a line of cairns needs to be spotted among the trees, leading fairly quickly onto a clear track. This track avoids the crest of **Serra des Puntals**, and later zigzags gently down to a **col**, where it ends abruptly.

To continue, simply pick a way up and along the forested ridge to reach the 893m summit of **Puntals de Son Fortesa**, which is a fine viewpoint. (For future reference, you may wish to walk towards a lower top, then let a line of small cairns lead you to the right to reach the top of a rocky chimney – this is the location of the scramble referred to in Walk 61.) Simply retrace your steps back down the mountain to return to **Banyalbufar**.

If you need detailed directions for the descent, see Walk 62. If you would like to climb Mola de Planícia instead of, or in addition to Puntals de Son Fortesa, see Walk 62 for a description of the ascent from the col at 780m.

Banyalbufar – Son Sanutges	40min
Son Sanutges – Col at 780m	1hr 30min
Col at 780m – Puntals de Son Fortesa	1hr
Puntals de Son Fortesa – Col at 780m	50min
Col at 780m – Son Sanutges	1hr 15min
Son Sanutges – Banyalbufar	35min

61 Puntals de Son Fortesa
from Puigpunyent

This route could be used as part of a long walk from Andratx to Valldemossa, although it does involve a steep scramble up a chimney, which not everyone would like. The only alternative available involves a considerable detour.
See sketch map 27.

Starting Point	Puigpunyent
Time	4hr 45min
Distance	11km
Highest Point	893m
Height Climbed	680m
Grade	A+ (or B omitting scramble)
Maps	Alpina Tramuntana Sud, Alpina A or MTN25 Sa Vileta

Type of Walk
Without the final 10-minute scramble the walk makes a pleasant, moderate day-walk to a rocky viewpoint, returning the same way.

Leave the village of **Puigpunyent** by following the Ma-1101 for Esporles. When the road makes a sudden right turn near the **K1 marker**, keep straight ahead along what appears to be a broad, stony track. Go through a **gateway**, where the gate should be kept closed, to continue along a good tarmac road. The road crosses a gentle crest and later turns left up alongside the high wall of **Son Fortesa**, a large manorial house.

Just before reaching the house, turn right along a track signposted as the **Camí Vell d'Estellencs**. Go through a gate, zigzag a short way uphill, then go through a gate made from a bedstead. Join a track and turn right to follow it, as indicated by a waymark post. Another waymark post at a higher level indicates a short cut along an **old mule track**, avoiding a broad bend on the track. The track continues below the farmstead of **Sa Muntanya**.

Turn right at a junction of tracks to walk away from the farmstead, crossing a slight rise, then keeping straight ahead along the clearest track as marked. The track goes through a **gap in a wall**. Turn right to walk parallel to the wall until a signposted junction is reached. Turn left and follow a track steeply uphill, crossing a gentle, wooded shoulder at **Coll d'Estellencs**, a flat wooded area on the main ridge between Galatzó and Puntals de Son Fortesa, at 652m.

Watch carefully, on the highest part of this track, to spot a narrow path heading off to the right, marked by a **cairn** and a red paint mark (note that if you follow the track to a metal gate in a tall boundary wall, you have gone too far). The narrow path leads up to an **old gateway** in the wall at a higher level. On the other side of the wall the narrow path contours or rises slightly across the western slopes of Puntals de Son Fortesa for about 20 minutes. After a brief descent, look out for a key landmark, where **three old shelters** are clustered round a *sitja*.

A series of small cairns shows the way uphill, zigzagging and passing a large rocky outcrop on the left. Continue up steep ground to the foot of the only feasible way to the top. (This is a **scramble**, which although easy, is steep enough to deter walkers unused to this activity.) A dead tree chokes the direct line, which is rather loose, so avoid this by going to the right and then back left over firm rock – faint paint marks above confirm you are on the right route – and be sure that you are going to be able to reverse all your moves on the descent! (Those who do not fancy the scramble can more easily bear right to gain a rocky viewpoint without too much difficulty.)

Emerging from the top of the chimney, **small cairns** show the way across a slight depression, and a very short climb leads to the 893m summit of **Puntals de Son Fortesa**. Enjoy the view and return the same way to **Puigpunyent**.

If you do not feel confident about reversing the scramble in the chimney, see Route Avoiding Chimney, below.

Another way down is to follow the route to Banyalbufar, see Walk 62.

Puigpunyent – Son Fortesa	30min
Son Fortesa – Coll d'Estellencs	1hr 20min
Coll d'Estellencs – Puntals de Son Fortesa	45min
Puntals de Son Fortesa – Coll d'Estellencs	35min
Coll d'Estellencs – Puigpunyent	1hr 35min

Route Avoiding Chimney
Be aware that by avoiding the chimney you are committing yourself to a 7km detour, including 300m of descent and

*Snow-covered track used on the lengthy route
avoiding the chimney scramble*

450m of ascent, all of which needs to be reversed afterwards, making for a very long day. Allow as much as 5 hours extra just for this diversion there and back.

Coming from the **Coll d'Estellencs**, instead of climbing from the **three old shelters** to the chimney, keep left along the path across the slope, then turn left down a broader **track**. Watch carefully to follow this downhill, as there are a couple of fallen trees across it. Pass *sitges* and shelters, then reach a T junction where you see a **wall** ahead. Turn right and follow the track through a **gateway** in another part of the wall. Again, keep to the clearest track heading downhill, noting a concrete *cisterna* off to the left.

Go down between some big **boulders**, then when a junction is reached at an **abandoned car**, turn right and walk more or less on the level – the track later winds downhill past sitges and a **limekiln**. Turn right along another track and follow this to a corner of a wall and fence, around 450m, near the finca of **Planícia**. Turn right up another winding track, but watch for a yellow arrow on a **boulder**, pointing left up a narrow, cairned path.

The cairns and paint marks on trees show the way to the narrow cleft of the **Pas de sa Mola** in the cliffs, where the path climbs in tight zigzags. Continue climbing up through the steep, wooded valley to reach a clear **track** around 600m. Turn right to reach a limekiln, ruined building, *aljub* and bread oven at the head of a valley.

The track climbs over a ridge and reaches the head of another valley, where there are distinctive twin aljubs at **Ses Aljubets**. Progress seems to be blocked by a wall of rock, but look carefully to spot the track making tight zigzags up through a breach, levelling out on a broad wooded **col** at over 780m.

Routes meet on the col and need care. Look to the right, where a line of cairns needs to be spotted among the trees, leading fairly quickly onto a clear track (do not follow another line of cairns down into a valley). This track avoids the crest of **Serra des Puntals**, and later zigzags gently down to a col, where it ends abruptly.

To continue, simply pick a way up and along the forested ridge to reach the 893m summit of **Puntals de Son Fortesa**. Reverse the whole route to return to **Puigpunyent**.

62 Sa Granja to Banyalbufar

This walk is linear and makes use of the buses that run between Esporles and Banyalbufar – get off the bus outside Esporles at the junction with the road to Sa Granja.

The route crosses the Serra des Puntals using paths exploiting rocky breaches in the range. Either Puntals de Son Fortesa or Mola de Planícia can be climbed as a diversion from the high, wooded col in the middle of the range.

See sketch map 27.

Starting Point	Sa Granja at the junction of the Ma-1100 and Ma-1101
Time	4hr 20min
Distance	14km
Highest Point	780m
Height Climbed	690m
Grade	B+
Maps	Alpina Tramuntana Sud, Alpina A and B or MTN25 Sa Vileta and Esporles

Type of Walk
Mainly on good tracks, but some rough paths.

From **Sa Granja** walk 2km along the **Ma-1101** in the direction of Puigpunyent. Just after passing the **K8** marker, turn right to cross a stile next to the gates of **Son Vic** (a nearby stone gives its full name, 'Son Vich de Superna'). When the palatial building is close to hand, turn right between some **outbuildings** and go through a gate to find a clear track climbing uphill. Keep to this track as it climbs in bends up the wooded hillside.

Just before reaching the isolated house of **Ca'n Poma**, turn right up a short track marked by cairns, then cross a field to reach a prominent **wall** on the other side. Turn right and walk up to a little col where there is a **threshing circle**.

Go through a narrow **gateway**, from which there is a view into a high upper valley, and of the large house of Son Balaguer. The path is now rough and rocky, and continues steeply upwards on the right-hand side of this valley, on the

slopes of **Puig de sa Coma**, crossing a wide track twice. After going through a narrow gap in a stone **wall**, turn left and follow a narrow and overgrown path up through the wood to reach the **Coll del Pujol de Sa Coma** at 593m.

The palatial residence of Son Vic, near Sa Granja, seen in a rare mantle of snow

Although a wide track crosses the col, your route crosses it by turning right and descending very slightly, then turning left along a **narrow path** leading up into a narrow valley. At first the path is overgrown, but soon improves and is easy to follow – look out for cairns marking the way.

The path zigzags steeply uphill and squeezes up through a **breach** in the cliff face. At the top it levels out on a wide and confusing area of woodland on a **broad col** at 783m, which lies between Mola de Planícia and Puntals de Son Fortesa. Follow the **cairned path** straight ahead to reach a **track**, then there is a choice to be made – you can either climb Puntals de Son Fortesa, which is to the left, or Mola de Planícia, which is to the right, or climb neither and head onwards to descend to Banyalbufar.

Ascent of Puntals de Son Fortesa

Turn left, not along the track, but along a line of **cairns** stretching through the woodland. These lead to another **track**, which is clear and easy to follow. This track avoids the

Trig point on the 931m summit of Mola de Planícia after a recent fall of snow

crest of **Serra des Puntals**, and later zigzags gently down to a **col**, where it ends abruptly. To continue, simply pick a way up and along the forested ridge to reach the 893m summit of **Puntals de Son Fortesa**, which is a fine viewpoint. Retrace your steps to the **col at 780m.**

This ascent adds 2km, 140m of ascent and 1 hour to the day's walk.

Ascent of Mola de Planícia

Turn right to follow the clear track, which winds about through dense woodlands, but generally heads northeast. It passes an igloo-like *aljub* before gradually petering out near the summit. Pick a way uphill by following small cairns to reach the trig point on **Mola de Planícia** at 931m, but note that there are other summits, including one at 933m, and one with a **small hut** offering a bird's-eye view down on Banyalbufar. Obviously there is no way to descend directly to Banyalbufar, so return to the **col at 780m.**

This ascent adds 4km, 160m of ascent and almost 2 hours to the day's walk.

Descent to Banyalbufar

From the col at 780m, turn left along the clear track, which soon zigzags down through a rocky breach to reach the distinctive twin *aljubs* at **Ses Aljubets**. The track continues across a ridge and descends to a valley head, where there is a ruin, *aljub*, bread oven and limekiln. Continue following the track across and gently down the wooded slope to pass a straggly old fence on a little col at the **Bosquets des Rafals**.

There are only occasional glimpses of the coast or nearby mountains as the track descends and makes a few zigzags on a steep, wooded slope. Keep following the clearest track downhill, avoiding all other paths and tracks. Turn left at a triangular junction and walk steeply downhill through an old **gateway** in a stone wall.

Turn right at a junction with a broader, clearer track and follow this downhill to pass the prominent property of **S'Arbossar**. The access track runs through a **gateway**, and if the gate is shut, it should not actually be locked. Continue along the track, which swings round a steep-sided valley, climbs and turns sharp right. After passing ruined buildings at **Son Sanutges**, go through a gateway and turn left down a narrow tarmac road. The road is waymarked as a GR route and is called the **Carrer de la Font de la Vila**.

As you follow the road downhill, twisting and turning, you occasionally see the spring that gives its name. At the bottom the road is called the **Carrer Jeroni Albertí** as it enters the **Plaça de la Vila** in the centre of **Banyalbufar**.

Sa Granja – Ca'n Poma	1hr 30min
Ca'n Poma – Col at 780m	1hr
Col at 780m – Son Sanutges	1hr 15min
Son Sanutges – Banyalbufar	35min

63 Galatzó via Pas des Cossi

Galatzó is the highest peak in the southwestern mountains. It is the only one over 1000m in this area, and because of its position commands some outstanding views. It is seen as a prominent pyramid from many parts of the island, and can be climbed using a variety of signposted, waymarked routes, but all combine for the final ascent.

The way described here, via the Pas des Cossi, has been restored and signposted. It is an interesting route, especially when combined with another restored path on the eastern and northern flanks of the mountain, allowing a circular walk to be enjoyed. On the way up there is a picnic site by a *sitja*, along with a reconstruction of a charcoal-worker's shelter, roofed with *càrritx* grass in the traditional manner.

The nearest large car park is at the Restaurante Es Grau, at K98 on the Ma-10, which can also be reached by occasional buses from Peguera, but check the timetable as this is a limited service.

See sketch map 28.

Starting Point	Son Fortuny gate at K97 on the Ma-10
Time	5hr 30min
Distance	11km
Highest Point	1027m
Height Climbed	850m
Grade	B+
Maps	Alpina Tramuntana Sud, Alpina A or MTN25 Galatzó and Sa Vileta

Type of Walk
Strenuous and rough.

Parking is available near the **Restaurante Es Grau** on the Ma-10. Take a look at the view from the *mirador* perched above the nearby road tunnel, then walk through the tunnel and continue for 1km to reach the **K97** marker. Turn right up a wide, stony track, passing a noticeboard bearing the name **Son Fortuny**, an estate belonging to the government and designated as a recreational area.

After 10 to 15 minutes uphill, turn left at a track junction (the track to the right leads to S'Esclop and is used on Walk

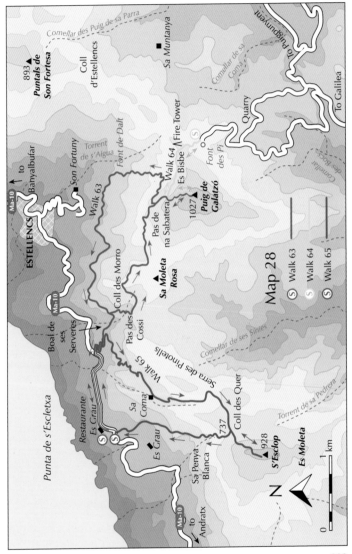

Looking back down the Pas des Cossi on the way towards Coll des Morro
(photo: Alan Parker)

65). A picnic site is reached at around 400m at **Boal de ses Serveres**, where there is a reconstruction of a *carboner*'s hut.

There is a **signpost** beside stone gateposts and a choice of routes, straight on or to the right. Both ways lead to Galatzó, and in the following route description the ascent is via Pas des Cossi and the descent is via Font de Dalt.

Turn right to follow the **restored path** signposted for Pas des Cossi. Though steep, the path is easy to follow and there are impressive views of nearby cliffs. At the top of the pas, reached in about 15 minutes, is another **signpost** indicating a left turn for Galatzó (a right turn here offers a more arduous approach to S'Esclop than Walk 65.)

Turn left and follow the path, which rises at an easy gradient across slopes of *càrritx*, passing a **well** and swinging round towards the valley head to cross the **Coll des Morro** at 610m. The path proceeds easily, then dips into a **streambed** before rising again.

An important path junction is reached on the **Pas de na Sabatera**, at around 700m (the way straight ahead is the way used for the descent). Turn right uphill to reach the foundation of a **ruined shelter**, previously a prominent landmark around 800m. (Avoid the path left, which comes from Font des Pi on Walk 64.) Keep right to follow the well-trodden and cairned path climbing higher.

At first, easy ground leads to the foot of a **rocky staircase**. The angle eases at the top of this, but the path continues to rise up to a natural **rock shelter**. A little rock scramble, which is quite steep but not difficult, leads to the top of **Puig de Galatzó**, where there is a trig point at 1027m. Enjoy the splendid views.

To descend, return to the path junction at the **ruined shelter** and keep left. Continue down to the path junction at the **Pas de na Sabatera** and turn right. The path descends a slope of *càrritx* and heather, but gradually drops down into a devastated area of **woodland** that has been cleared, leaving chopped logs.

There are plenty of waymark posts and occasional signposts, but route finding is generally a case of staying on the clearest track. ▶ Pass a **ruined building** and later keep straight ahead at a **junction of tracks**, bearing in mind that there is no permitted descent to the village of **Estellencs**. A clear path traverses around 450m at the base of some cliffs,

There is a turning on the right for **Font de Dalt**, but if you visit it, return afterwards.

later dropping as low as 400m. The path later climbs uphill and passes a *mirador* on the way back to the picnic site at **Boal de ses Serveres**.

Simply retrace your earlier steps of the day, down the track and along the road to **Es Grau** to finish.

Es Grau – Boal de ses Serveres	45min
Boal de ses Serveres – Puig de Galatzó	2hr 15min
Puig de Galatzó – Boal de ses Serveres	2hr
Boal de ses Serveres – Es Grau	30min

64 Galatzó from Puigpunyent

Puigpunyent is a delightful mountain village to the east of Galatzó, reached by narrow, winding roads either from Sa Granja, near Esporles, to the north, or from Capdella and Galilea to the south. Although only short, this is a highly recommended route, with splendid distant views and impressive rock scenery nearer at hand. The most difficult part of the route is finding the way to the starting point from the village.

To reach the starting point, take the road west from Puigpunyent as sign-posted for La Reserva, a kind of country park with many amenities, well worth visiting on an off-day. Keep following the signs for La Reserva until, after many twists and turns, and some 3km from Puigpunyent, you come to a wide road junction on a col around 400m at Sa Boal. At this point, instead of going left, turn right and follow the road uphill. Turn right again about 1km after passing an old quarry. Keep climbing steadily, then the road levels out. The surfaced road ends at a turning place with two minor roads going off to the right. Park here near Font des Pi, bearing in mind that you don't actually see the *font*, which is both hidden and dry.

See sketch map 28.

Starting Point	Road end near Font des Pi
Time	2hr 45min
Distance	6km
Highest Point	1027m
Height Climbed	530m
Grade	B+
Maps	Alpina Tramuntana Sud, Alpina A or MTN25 Sa Vileta

A good path leaves the road end near **Font des Pi**, and there is a right turn after only a few minutes, followed shortly by a left turn. A reasonably good path continues to zigzag upwards with markers, but still needs care. A prominent tall **fire tower** is passed on a ridge, where a path begins a rising traverse across the impressive northeast face of Galatzó.

Follow the marked path and do not attempt a direct ascent, either from the ridge or up the face of the mountain. Cross scree and pass below the rock tower of **Es Bisbe** ('the Bishop'), then rise to reach the foundation of a **ruined shelter**, the same one passed on the ascent or descent from Boal de ses Serveres in Walk 63.

Turn left to follow the well-trodden and cairned path climbing higher. At first, easy ground leads to the foot of a **rocky staircase**, then the angle eases at the top of this, but

Type of Walk
Easy path through woodland where there are many fallen trees, then open ground. A good traverse path runs below crags, then a well-marked route goes up steep and rocky ground to the top.

The sprawling village of Galilea huddles on the lower slopes of mighty Galatzo (photo: Jaume Tort)

the path continues to rise up to a natural **rock shelter**. A little rock scramble, which is quite steep but not difficult, leads to the top of the **Puig de Galatzó**, where there is a trig point at 1027m. Enjoy the splendid views, then return the same way to the parking space near **Font des Pi**.

Font des Pi – Ruined shelter	1hr
Ruined shelter – Puig de Galatzó	30min
Puig de Galatzó – Font des Pi	1hr 15min

65 S'Esclop

S'Esclop (the name means 'the Clog') is at the southernmost end of the Serra de Tramuntana. Although under 1000m it is wild and rough, and the ascent should not be undertaken lightly. Near the summit are the ruins of a stone hut where the scientist Francesc Aragó lived while making a triangulation to measure the meridian in 1808.

The route used for the ascent was for a long time barred to walkers, but the isolated property of Sa Coma is being converted into a *refugi*, and its access road offers a splendid approach to the mountain, linking with a cairned path to the top.

There is a car park at the Restaurante Es Grau at K98 on the Ma-10, which can also be reached by bus from Peguera from Monday to Friday (but check the timetable as this is a limited service).

See sketch map 28.

Starting Point	Restaurante Es Grau at K98 on the Ma-10
Time	4hr 55min
Distance	8km
Highest Point	928m
Height Climbed	650m
Grade	B+
Maps	Alpina Tramuntana Sud, Alpina A or MTN25 Galatzó

Parking is available near the **Restaurante Es Grau** on the Ma-10. Take a look at the view from the *mirador* perched above the nearby road tunnel, then walk through the tunnel and continue for 1km to reach the **K97** marker. Turn right up a wide, stony track, passing a noticeboard bearing the name **Son Fortuny**, an estate belonging to the government and now designated as a recreational area. After 10 to 15 minutes uphill, turn right at a track junction close to a circular **water tank**. ▸

The stony track winds steeply uphill through a couple of **gates**, then runs more gently uphill in a high valley. It passes the isolated property of **Sa Coma**, or Coma d'en Vidal, which is to serve as a *refugi* for walkers. Keep following the track, which is now mostly grassy, until it narrows and finally expires on a **col at 652m**.

There is a wall with a fence on top, and as the fence has been peeled back to make an obvious gap, the wall is easily

Type of Walk
An easy start on a good track, giving way to rough and rocky paths.

The signposted track to the left leads to Galatzó and is used on Walk 63.

View of the rugged slopes of S'Esclop from the equally rugged slopes of Galatzo (photo: Alan Parker)

crossed at that point. On the other side turn right to follow the **cairned path** uphill, passing a threshing floor on a higher col, around 724m. Five minutes later the **Coll des Quer** is reached at 737m.

From this point the path climbs straight uphill, and is usually clearly trodden and cairned. It climbs up sloping grassy ledges and rises steeply, finally reaching a **high shoulder**. There is another old threshing floor on this shoulder with a ruined building alongside it. Simply follow the cairns to the trig point on top of **S'Esclop** at 928m.

Retrace steps from the summit of S'Esclop to the Restaurante Es Grau. However, note that it is now possible to follow a waymarked route down from the col at 652m, through the Comellar de ses Sinies, to the Finca Galatzó and the village of Es Capdella. This was all private property during earlier editions of this guidebook, but the area was recently purchased and dedicated for public use.

Es Grau – Water tank	30min
Water tank – Coll des Quer	1hr
Coll des Quer – S'Esclop	45min
S'Esclop – Coll des Quer	40min
Coll des Quer – Es Grau	2hr

66 La Trapa from S'Arracó

The area lying to the northwest of Andratx is wild and unspoilt, being devoid of the encroaching *urbanizacions* that flourish elsewhere in the south of the island.

There are two high points of interest on this walk – one is a really magnificent viewpoint, the Mirador d'en Josep Sastre, overlooking the sea and Sa Dragonera, the other is La Trapa, an abandoned Trappist monastery, now preserved and protected by GOB.

When the work on the monastery is completed, it will offer accommodation, food and drink for birdwatchers and walkers. There are impressively built terrace walls, parts of an old irrigation system, and an old mill that still has some machinery inside. A disastrous fire in 1994 set back the restoration programme, but it is now progressing again. The system of water channels, which made possible the growing of crops in this arid region, is also being repaired. On the edge of the cliffs is a large circular area, a popular picnic place now, which was once a threshing floor.

See sketch map 29.

Starting Point	The roundabout at S'Arracó
Time	5hr
Distance	15km
Highest Point	450m
Height Climbed	670m
Grade	B
Maps	Alpina Tramuntana Sud, Alpina A or MTN25 Andratx and Galatzó

The village of **S'Arracó**, between Andratx and Sant Elm, is a good starting point for many walks and it can be reached by bus. From the bus stop, walk round the **roundabout** as if entering S'Arracó, but turn left along the **Camí des Castellas**, which leads to a **sports complex**. If arriving by car there is a little parking along this road.

Beyond the sports complex the road narrows and is unsurfaced, but keep following it straight ahead and gradually uphill. Turn left at a sign saying 'Camí des Castellas del 15 al 31'. After this the track bends right, runs straight through a **cross-tracks**, then swings left.

Look out for a point where paths intersect. Turn right along a **narrow path** flanked by low walls and tight hedgerows, with groves of almond trees on either side. Keep walking straight ahead along this path, which rises a little through a **pine wood**. When a wide track is met at a corner, turn left and follow it uphill, rounding a few bends. After passing a restored caseta with a garden, called **Can Corso**, turn left along another track.

The track climbs clearly across the southern slopes of **Puig d'en Guida**, crossing the little col of **Pas d'en Guida**. It swings right and zigzags uphill to run easily along to the right-hand side of a broad valley, the **Comellar des Sabaters**.

Type of Walk
Moderately strenuous, but on well-defined paths.

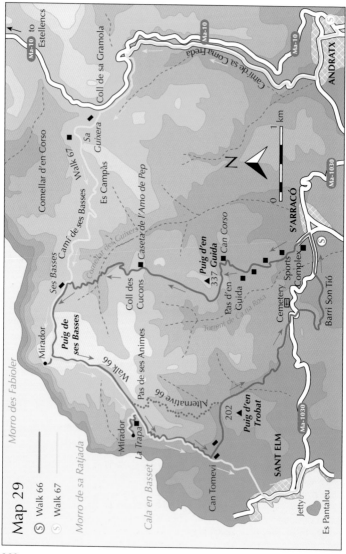

Map 29

Ⓢ Walk 66
Ⓢ Walk 67

A couple of little casetas will be noticed up to the left. A few minutes later the lone, ruined **Caseta de l'Amo de Pep** stands to the right of the path near a few pine trees.

The path levels off around 320m on the **Coll des Cucons**, then contours into and out of a streambed. Descend into the valley of **Comellar des Guixers**, which runs south to S'Arracó. On reaching a dam in the valley floor, climb up a winding track and turn left along a higher track to reach the casetas around 380m at **Ses Basses**.

Turn left and follow the good path that contours round the north side of **Puig de ses Basses**. There are outstanding views northeast along the coast, with S'Esclop dominating the scene inland, and Puig Major far beyond. As the path rounds a headland, a large cairn marks a short diversion to a *mirador* overlooking Sa Dragonera.

Continuing onwards, the path contours and then descends through open ground. ▶ Some 30 minutes from the *mirador* a wide track is met at a bend. The way uphill to the left is signposted for S'Arracó and Sant Elm, but turn right downhill to reach **La Trapa** in about 10 minutes.

After exploring the area, follow the wide track back uphill from the main building to the first sharp bend left, where there is a signpost pointing the way to Sant Elm. (You could of course follow the track all the way uphill, then walk down through a valley on the other side of the hill to link with the main route.) The path slopes gently up to a high shoulder around 300m, and then descends some **rocky ground** by a choice of routes. Keeping too far left leads to some difficult scrambling, while the more obvious route on the right is a little easier.

Once this bit is negotiated an easy path swings round the head of a side valley, crosses a spur and swings round another corner before descending a **forested slope**. This can be a confusing area, so stick to the winding path, which is well trodden and abundantly cairned. (Avoid other paths to left and right, many of which have been blocked by stones or branches to keep walkers on course.)

When a clear track is reached, with **two concrete gateposts** on the right, continue straight ahead down the path to reach another track junction beside the derelict house of **Can Tomeví**. Take a moment to study signposts around this junction, and bear in mind that by walking

A devastating fire in 1994 destroyed all the pines on these slopes, leaving charred and splintered trunks littering the ground.

303

Near the monastic site at La Trapa, an old mill still contains pieces of machinery

straight ahead you could quickly reach the village of **Sant Elm** (see Walk 67).

To continue the walk, however, turn left to follow the clear track that is later signposted as the **Camí Punta de sa Galera**. Keep right at a couple of track junctions to reach another cross-tracks bearing abundant signposts. (Straight ahead is the clear track that is used by most people visiting La Trapa.)

Turn right, as signposted for S'Arracó, along **the Camí sa Font dels Morers**. This clear track leads over a low col beside **Puig d'en Trobat**, and later passes a junction with the Camí de Can Bolei. Keep left to follow the main track gently uphill to reach the **Ma-1030**, and keep left again to follow the road round a bend almost to a **cemetery**.

To avoid walking down the main road, turn right along the track signposted as the **Barri Son Tió**. This leads to a quiet road where a left turn leads down a winding road and crosses gentle farmland. It rejoins the main road where a right turn leads quickly to the **roundabout** and bus stop just outside **S'Arracó**.

Walk past the roundabout if you wish to go into the village for food and drink at one of the bar–restaurants.

S'Arracó – Ses Basses	1hr 40min
Ses Basses – La Trapa	1hr 20min
La Trapa – S'Arracó	2hr

67 La Trapa via Coll de sa Gramola

This walk does not make a complete circuit and use is made of the buses running between Sant Elm and Andratx. Be sure to carry current timetables, as buses out of Sant Elm are quite limited in winter.
See sketch map 29.

Starting Point	Bus station in Andratx
Finishing point	Sant Elm
Time	5hr 20min
Distance	14km
Highest Point	450m
Height Climbed	600m
Grade	B
Maps	Alpina Tramuntana Sud, Alpina A or MTN25 Andratx and Galatzó

Type of Walk
Easy up to Coll de sa Gramola on an old tarmac road, then an easy track to Ses Basses, followed by narrow paths to La Trapa and Sant Elm.

Leave the tiny bus station in **Andratx**, cross the main road and follow the short **Carrer Son Estiva**. Turn right up the **Avenida Juan Carlos I** (still written in Castilian, but if it changes to Catalan it will read Avinguda Joan Carles I) to reach the tiny **Plaça des Pou** just below the church.

Turn left to follow the **Carrer General Bernat Riera**, which is signposted for S'Arracó and Sant Elm. Simply walk straight ahead and gradually downhill to reach the edge of town, then turn right up the **Carrer Barcelona**. This road has a smooth tarmac surface at first and continues uphill as the **Camí de sa Coma Freda**. Keep to the right-hand side of the valley, avoiding turnings, and note that the road surface is rougher later.

When the road bends sharp right to reach the main **Ma-10**, keep straight ahead along a track and swing left instead. The track narrows, then broadens and climbs to a bend on the main road on the **Coll de Sa Gramola** at K106. There is a parking space to the left of the road, and the **Camí des Campàs** is signposted both left and right. Keep right, as signposted for Ses Basses, La Trapa and Sant Elm.

The route is a well-known and popular walk. Cars are prevented from using the track further along, and it offers very pleasant walking, on earth rather than stones, contouring with only a few ups and downs at about 400m. Be careful to follow the main track, which is drivable to the casetas at **Ses Basses**, and avoid any turnings leading downhill.

From Ses Basses, follow the route description in Walk 66 to **Can Tomei**. From Can Tomei, simply walk straight ahead along a track, which joins a road on the outskirts of **Sant Elm**. Alternatively, walk from **Can Tomei**, using the

The old monastic site at La Trapa is being converted into a refugi for walkers

description in Walk 66, to finish at **S'Arracó**, for a longer walk.

Andratx – Coll de sa Gramola	1hr 40min
Coll de sa Gramola – Ses Basses	1hr 10min
Ses Basses – La Trapa	1hr 20min
La Trapa – Sant Elm	1hr 10min

68 Sant Elm to Port d'Andratx

There is a hinterland of rough country between Sant Elm and Port d'Andratx that provides some satisfying walks. The tops named on maps as Es Tres Picons have a long, curving ridge, and a trig point stands at 321m at the west end on Penyal Vermell. There are steep cliffs on the north side, breached by a good ledge path, the Pas Vermell, which is the key to linking the resorts of Sant Elm and Port d'Andratx on foot. There are excellent views of S'Esclop and the Sa Dragonera from the top.

Two walks are described, the other being Walk 69, and other variations can be worked out.

See sketch map 30.

Starting Point	Sant Elm
Finishing Point	The marina at Port d'Andratx
Time	3hr 15min
Distance	9km
Highest Point	321m
Height Climbed	350m
Grade	B
Maps	Alpina Tramuntana Sud, Alpina A or MTN25 Andratx

Type of Walk
Mainly easy on good paths, but one steepish section near the top.

Begin at the bus stop at the start of the Avinguda Jaume I at **Sant Elm**. Follow the **Carrer Cala es Conills**, which runs parallel to the coast, giving way to the **Camí de sa Torre**, which ends at a fine *mirador* overlooking a rocky cove and Sa Dragonera. Pass seawards of the **last house**, scrambling up rocks to turn inland up a narrow, cairned path on a forested slope.

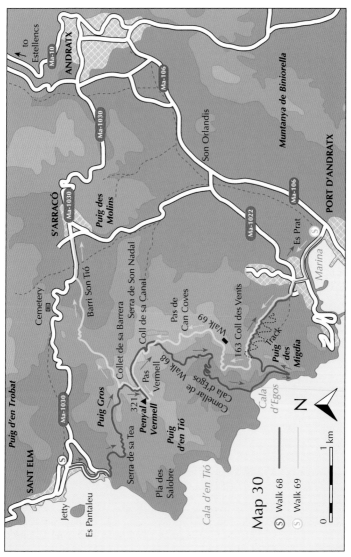

Map 30

Ⓢ Walk 68
Ⓢ Walk 69

0 1 km

A fine track leads up from the coast at Sant Elm, giving way to good hill paths

When a clear vehicle track is reached, turn right and follow it up through a **gateway**. When the track levels out briefly as it turns around a little valley, turn left up another narrow, cairned path on **Serra de sa Tea**. Follow this until another track is reached, which rises to **Collet de sa Barrera**, where there is a circular water tank.

Fork right along a narrow but obvious path that begins to zigzag steeply uphill and leads to an attractive **ledge path** at the foot of cliffs. Go through the breach of **Pas Vermell** to join a clear track on the other side. Turn right and follow this to the trig point at 321m on **Penyal Vermell** and enjoy the full-length view of the Sa Dragonera.

To continue, return along the track and continue straight past the branch path from the Pas Vermell. The way to Port d'Andratx is easy to follow. Simply stay on the good, wide track, keeping to a high level. Avoid the steep track on the right, which descends to Cala d'Egos, but turn right at a cross track later, on the **Pas de Can Coves**.

Descend past a couple of buildings to reach **Coll des Vent** at 163m. Either turn left and follow the main track down the valley to reach a surfaced road, or short cut from bend to bend using a steep, stony path marked with cairns. The track leads onto a road, **Carrer de Cala d'Egos**, which is followed to the left at a junction.

Turn right at a crossroads to walk down **Carretera Aldea Blanca** to reach the marina at **Port d'Andratx**. Turn left to find a bus stop, or continue alongside the marina to enter the resort and reach its shops and bar–restaurants.

Sant Elm – Penyal Vermell	2hr
Penyal Vermell – Port d'Andratx	1hr 15min

69 Port d'Andratx to S'Arracó

This route includes a visit to Cala d'Egos, a small, attractive bay with no access for vehicles, so it is unspoilt and quiet. It also crosses the ridge of Es Tres Picons, taking in the splendid view from the trig point on Penyal Vermell.

Tracks and paths used on this walk can be combined with those on Walk 68 to create a longer route.

See sketch map 30.

Starting Point	The marina in Port d'Andratx
Finishing Point	Roundabout at S'Arracó
Time	4hr
Distance	10km
Highest Point	321m
Height Climbed	490m
Grade	B
Maps	Alpina Tramuntana Sud, Alpina A or MTN25 Andratx

Type of Walk
Easy, but with some steep sections.

Start at the bus stop at the far side of the marina at **Port d'Andratx**, and turn right up the **Carretera Aldea Blanca**. Turn left at a crossroads along the **Carrer de Cala d'Egos**. The road forks right, then becomes a track, which later has a gate across to stop cars. You could follow the broad bends of the track as it climbs up the forested slope, or look out for the path short cutting from bend to bend, marked with cairns and a couple of signs nailed to trees. Either way, reach **Coll des Vent** at 163m.

At the col descend towards **Cala d'Egos** by turning left at the first junction. (The track to the right could be followed to give a longer but easier route to the beach, but would also involve some backtracking. Follow the track down to the left and then back to the right until it ends. A narrow path continues in the same direction to reach the rocky cove at Cala d'Egos, getting steeper at the end.)

To continue the walk from the beach, go up a track roughly following a streambed. A series of big bends later

leads up to join the other track coming from Coll d'es Vent. Turn left and about 15 minutes later turn left again. The track climbs fairly steeply to reach a higher track, also coming from Coll des Vent, just below the top of **Puig d'en Ric**. Turn left and continue to the very end of this track to reach the trig point at 321m on **Penyal Vermell**. Enjoy the full-length view of Sa Dragonera.

Return along the track for about 5 minutes and turn left along the narrow footpath leading over a breach in the ridge, the **Pas Vermell**. A good **ledge path** slopes down easily below a cliff and then zigzags down to a wider track and circular water tank on **Collet de sa Barrera**. At this point you could turn left to go down to **Sant Elm**, which is Walk 68 in reverse, but for the descent to S'Arracó turn right and after about 20 minutes fork right down a narrow surfaced road. (The left fork leads to the main road near a cemetery.)

Both the road to the right and the fork to the left are known as **Barri Son Tió**, and are signposted as such from the main **Ma-1030**. Turn right along the main road to reach the bus stop at a roundabout just before **S'Arracó**.

The Pas Vermell slices easily across a cliff-face to allow a descent to S'Arracó

313

This walk could also be structured as a circular walk from **Port d'Andratx** to the **Penyal Vermell**, returning as in Walk 66(a).

Port d'Andratx – Cala d'Egos	1hr 15min
Cala d'Egos – Penyal Vermell	1hr 30min
Penyal Vermell – S'Arracó	1hr 15min

70 Sa Dragonera

Sa Dragonera lies off the extreme west coast of Mallorca opposite the small resort of Sant Elm. The highest point is Na Pòpia at 349m, which is crowned with an abandoned lighthouse. There are two other lighthouses at the north and south of the island. On the west side vertical cliffs plunge straight down to the sea, and are one of the sites where Eleanora's falcons can be observed, giving superb flying displays as they prepare to head off to Madagascar for the winter.

Sa Dragonera was bought by the government in 1988 in order to protect it from development – plans for a deluxe urbanisation had been put forward in 1974. Approval for *parc natural* status was given in 1995 and it is in the care of GOB, the important bird and conservation organisation. There is a landing fee of one euro per person, collected with the ferry fare, for those between the ages of 13 and 65, though this is waived on Saturdays and for school groups.

The island is very arid and only a small area was ever cultivated, with a few olives, almonds, figs and other fruits. The vegetation is typically Mediterranean, with lentisc, rosemary, *Erica multiflora*, pink and white cistus and wild olive. There are more than 20 endemic Balearic plants, incuding *Limonium dragonericum*. Goats have been eliminated so that all the plants are flourishing. Besides birds there is little wildlife except for the millions of tiny indigenous lizards, known as *sargantana* in Mallorquí.

The island is reached by a regular ferry service from Sant Elm. Follow signposts along Avinguda Jaume I for 'Parc Natural de sa Dragonera' to find a jetty below a couple of restaurants. The Margarita sails from about 10.15 every day except Sunday, when it runs only in the afternoon, then plies back and forth between Sant Elm to the island, landing at Cala Lladó. A full day is recommended.

Note The boat will not go out in bad weather conditions. Check sailings in advance on 639–617545 or 696–423933.

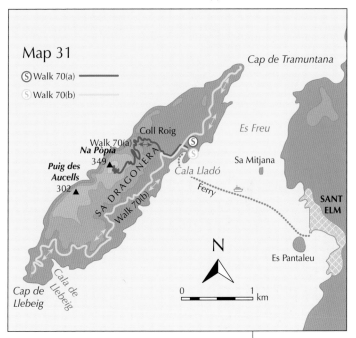

70(a) Na Pòpia

Sa Dragonera can be fully explored in a day. There and back to the northern lighthouse takes about an hour, and to the southern lighthouse two hours, in each case along a narrow lane with no traffic, encroached on both sides by flowering shrubs. The walk up to the top, Na Pòpia, takes a little longer and three hours should be allowed.

This route uses a good, wide path built during the 19th century by prisoners during the construction of the lighthouse. The light ceased functioning in 1910, but the path has since been restored.

See sketch map 31.

Starting point	Boat landing at Cala Lladó
Time	3hr
Distance	6km
Highest Point	349m
Height Climbed	350m
Grade	C+
Maps	Alpina Tramuntana Sud, Alpina A or MTN25 Galatzó

Type of Walk
A good track and path on a steep and rugged slope.

For this route set off from **Cala Lladó** and turn left at the cross-track above the boat landing, as if heading for the Cap de Llebeig. After about 250m turn right, where the main track bends left. The path heads almost north up a shallow valley, the **Comellar des Coll Roig**.

After passing a stone building the route goes up terraces towards **Coll Roig** before turning south, then winds uphill in two series of tight bends linked by a level traverse.

Enjoy views from the 349m summit of **Na Pòpia** and return the same way to **Cala Lladó**.

Sa Dragonera and its highest point, Na Pòpia, as seen from close to Sant Elm

Cala Lladó – Na Pòpia	1hr 45min
Na Pòpia – Cala Lladó	1hr 15min

70(b) Sa Dragonera

This is a satisfying mini-expedition – the route traverses Sa Dragonera from one lighthouse to the other, following a clear track throughout. For maximum time ashore, choose the first and last ferry crossings.

See sketch map 31.

Starting Point	Boat landing at Cala Lladó
Time	3hr
Distance	13km
Highest Point	100m
Height Climbed	340m
Grade	C
Maps	Alpina Tramuntana Sud, Alpina A or MTN25 Galatzó and Andratx

From the boat landing at **Cala Lladó**, walk uphill and turn right to take the gravel road to the lighthouse on **Cap de Tramuntana.**

Retrace steps along the gravel road, passing the junction for **Cala Lladó**. Follow the gravel road onwards, and if you have all day to spare, then climb **Na Pòpia**, as described in Walk 70(a).

The gravel road twists and turns, rises and falls, and eventually reaches the lighthouse at the **Cap de Llebeig**.

Allow a good hour for the walk back along the gravel road to the boat landing a Cala Lladó.

Type of Walk
Easy, along good tracks and paths.

Cala Lladó – Cap de Tramuntana	30min
Cap de Tramuntana – Cap de Llebeig	1hr 30min
Cap de Llebeig – Cala Lladó	1hr

71 Puig d'en Garrafa

Puig d'en Garrafa is a low hill to the east of Andratx. It consists of a long ridge running almost north–south, and has several rocky tops known as *geps*. There are impressive cliffs on both sides, but a path provides an easy walk along the ridge that is partly wooded. The top is clear of trees and is an excellent viewpoint, especially of S'Esclop and Galatzó.

Note A few street names in Andratx are still written in Castilian, but should they change in future, Catalan spellings are also given in brackets.

See sketch map 32.

Starting Point	Bus station in Andratx
Time	3hr 25min
Distance	7km
Highest Point	462m
Height Climbed	420m
Grade	B
Maps	Alpina Tramuntana Sud, Alpina A or MTN25 Andratx

Type of Walk
The ascent is quite steep and the path very rocky. Easy walking along a well-trodden path along the ridge is followed by an easy descent on a wide track.

If arriving in Andratx by car, park near the tiny bus station just off the main road through town. If arriving by bus, you can ask to be dropped at the *gasolinera* and avoid having to walk back out of town.

Walk out of **Andratx** along the main road towards Palma. This involves walking down the **Avenida Juan Carlos I** (Avinguda Joan Carles I), then up the **Avenida de Luis Alemany** (Avinguda Lluís Alemany), as signposted for Palma and Peguera. The road passes the Repsol **petrol station**.

(**Note** If considering an ascent via the alternative route outlined below, then check to see if the gates are open. If not, then switch to the main route. If you are considering a descent via the alternative route, it is prudent to check that the gates are open before proceeding further.)

After passing the Repsol **petrol station** keep following the main **Ma-1** and walk on the left-hand side to face oncoming traffic. This road is busy and unpleasant for over

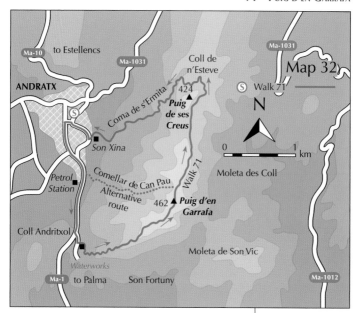

500m, but the only way to avoid it is to walk through an almond grove, which is undoubtedly private.

Pass a **slip road** with care, then thankfully turn left along the course of the old road, reached just before the **Coll Andritxol**. This quiet road is the **Camí Coll Andritxol**, and in about 2 minutes there are locked gates on the left – the construction of a **waterworks** has barred one of the paths formerly used to climb Puig d'en Garrafa.

Look for a path running behind the waterworks buildings, level with the rooftops. This well-trodden and **cairned path** winds uphill, crossing a few fallen trees. Watch carefully at a higher level for its continuation up steeper, rocky, open slopes, still marked by cairns. The path runs close to the **cliff tops** on the southern side of the hill.

Eventually the path levels out on the **stony crest** and there is a glimpse of the main summit ahead. One final pull leads to a fire tower, hut and trig point, at 462m on top of **Puig d'en Garrafa**.

The summit of Puig d'en Garrafa, at 462m, bears a prominent fire tower

Continue north along the path, which first descends in a couple of minutes to a **col** where a cairn indicates the alternative way up or down (a tree has fallen across the path at the junction so it is not too obvious). The main path runs almost north along the ridge, passing geps of 422m and 427m, largely unseen because of trees. After about half an hour the path descends on the eastern side of the ridge at **Puig de ses Creus**, then swings back left (west) to go through a **gap in a wall** and reach the small, grassy **Coll de n'Esteve** among pine trees.

From this point a clear track begins to descend into a cultivated valley, the **Coma de S'Ermita**. Step down onto a narrow path when the track passes a caseta, then rejoin the main track, which winds downhill in a succession of bends.

The track finally reaches a tall, **locked gate**, marked as private, but having a gap at the side to allow walkers to pass. Turn left to follow a tarmac road, the **Camí de Son Simó**, downhill to reach a junction at **Son Xina**. Turn left, then join a wider road, the **Via Joan Riera**, then walk uphill towards a school.

Turn right along the **Carrer de Son Moner** to reach the tiny bus station in **Andratx**.

Andratx – Coll Andritxol	20min
Coll Andritxol – Puig d'en Garrafa	1hr 10min
Puig d'en Garrafa – Coll de n'Esteve	45min
Coll de n'Esteve – Andratx	1hr 10min

Alternative Ascent

This alternative ascent, which takes about one hour from **Andratx,** starts just before the Repsol **petrol station**, with a left turn up a track. Go through a wide **gate** and turn right. The track runs beside a tall wall around a field full of almond trees. After passing a property called **Sidi Fennuch** the track turns sharp left downhill, so leave it to walk towards a **rocky gully**.

A fine path supported by a monumental stone buttress leads to a **gate**, which may be locked, in the mouth of the gully. When open, the path leads straight uphill through the forested valley of **Comellar de Can Pau**, reaching a col on the crest of the hill. Turn right to follow a clear, stony path to the top of **Puig d'en Garrafa** at 462m.

Follow the route description from Puig d'en Garrafa, above, to return to Andratx.

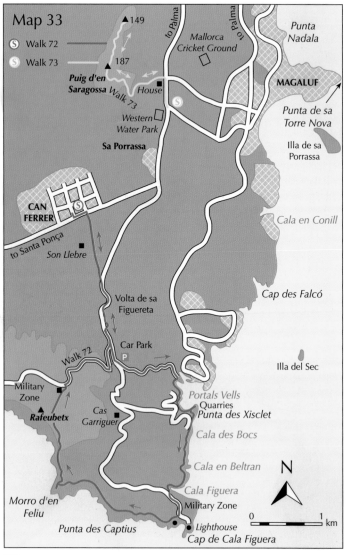

Map 33

Ⓢ Walk 72 ─────
Ⓢ Walk 73 ─────

▲149
▲ 187
Puig d'en Saragossa
Walk 73
House
Western Water Park
Sa Porrassa

to Palma
to Palma

Mallorca Cricket Ground
Ⓢ

Punta Nadala

MAGALUF

Punta de sa Torre Nova

Illa de sa Porrassa

CAN FERRER
Ⓢ
to Santa Ponça
Son Llebre

Cala en Conill

Volta de sa Figuereta

Cap des Falcó

Car Park
P

Walk 72

Illa del Sec

Military Zone
Rafeubetx ▲
Cas Garriguer

Portals Vells
Quarries
Punta des Xisclet

Cala des Bocs

Cala en Beltran

N

Cala Figuera
Military Zone

Morro d'en Feliu

0   1 km

Punta des Captius

Lighthouse
Cap de Cala Figuera

Portals Vells is a quiet, attractive little bay with a small sandy beach protected by encircling rocks. Its most remarkable feature is a series of caverns to the south, where the stone used for building Palma Cathedral was quarried out of the rock. These are best appreciated from within – there is no difficulty and no torch is required. On a tiny peninsula below the quarry is a small square room cut out of the rock. It was used as a fort to protect the quarrymen from attack by pirates.

Cap de Cala Figuera is the southern tip of the Calvià peninsula. An old watch tower on the edge of the cliffs looks across a small bay to a lighthouse on the point. Nearby is a military installation, with four cannon making an interesting object of exploration, on the occasions when it is unoccupied. Machinery for raising shells up to the gun emplacements is still intact.

But the best part of this walk is still to come, along the edge of the cliffs in the only truly unspoilt and undeveloped part of the Calvià coast, with views of the steep cliffs of Rafeubetx, normally only seen from the sea. Again, bear in mind that the military may restrict access to this area.

The starting point at Son Ferrer is reached by bus from Palma, Magaluf, El Toro or Peguera. (If you have a car, parking at a small car park near Portals Vells is recommended, saving around 4km. An advantage is that the track from Son Ferrer, flanked by dumped building rubble, is thereby avoided.)

See sketch map 33.

Starting Point	On the main road at Son Ferrer
Time	5hr (or 3hr 45min)
Distance	14km (or 10km)
Total Height	300m
Grade	C+
Map	MTN25 Illa del Toro y Cap de Cala Figuera

Type of Walk
Easy, along dirt tracks, metalled roads and a paint-marked path. The path at Cala Figuera requires care and some scrambling in one place.

Start at the shops beside the main road at **Son Ferrer**, where parking is available and there are nearby bus stops. Walk along the road in the direction of Palma, and turn right along a broad **dirt road** halfway between two roundabouts. This runs roughly southwards with a **golf course** on the left and

323

fields on the right around **Son Llebre**. The second half of this track is barred to vehicles, but you can walk round the gates to continue straight ahead.

When a tarmac road is reached around **Volta de sa Figuereta**, turn right to follow it. The road bends right, then as it bends left, look out for a short cut on the left, running through forest parallel to the road. Turn left along the road at a higher level and fork left at a **junction**. Turn left at a **small white building** bearing a painted sign for Portals Vells, where there is a small car park (this is the alternative starting point if you arrive by car for a shorter walk).

Walk down the wide road on to a small **promontory**, where some ruins on the left are the remains of a film set used for filming John Fowles' *The Magus* in the 1960s. Turn right and walk down to the small **sandy beach** where there is a bar. Pass in front of this and climb up some steps, then continue round the cliff coast past some wind-sculpted rocks to reach another **small bay** and bar. Continue round this along a narrow path to reach some **old quarries**.

After visiting the caverns and admiring the rock carvings, backtrack along the path, then fork left to follow a narrower path up to the cliff top at **Punta des Xisclet**. Here a track leads to a path running south along the cliffs, marked by blue paint blobs. This leads first to a small headland with a deep inlet on the right at **Cala en Beltran**.

The small path bypassing this may not be noticed at first, but will be found on returning from the headland if you overshoot – watch for a painted **blue arrow** marking the turning. This delightful path now leads south again to reach **Cala Figuera**. Here, although the descent appears a little difficult, paint spots show an easy way along quarried rock ledges down to the head of the cove. ◀

The caves noticed in the cliff opposite are said to have been inhabited 2000 years ago.

Cross the narrow shingle beach and paint marks will be found showing a path up the cliffs, with **little steps** cut out of the rock in places. Turn left along the lighthouse road at the cliff top, which leads past a barrier and some derelict **military buildings**, then turn right and follow a track to the **old stone tower** on the cliff top near **Cap de Cala Figuera**. (**Note** When the military are in occupation, there is a guard posted on the barrier and another way must be used. The alternative route is a rough path beginning some 20m from the boundary fence, and leading through scrub

and old walls in a rather confusing way to reach the old watch tower outside the fenced area.)

Quarries cut into cliffs at Punta des Xisclet yielded stone for Palma Cathedral

To continue the walk, set off in a westerly direction along the edge of the cliffs. Easy paths, sometimes marked by **cairns**, occasionally turn inland a little to avoid dense clusters of pines growing right up to the edge. At the **Punta des Captius** the direction becomes northwest, then curves around the next bay to reach a headland called **Morro d'en Feliu**, which is a superb viewpoint. On the way there, a wide track is followed for a while.

To continue, backtrack northeast at first, then pick up a branch path on the left. Watch for other paths, some leading only to the cliff edge for splendid views around **Cala Rafeubetx**, while others gradually rise towards **Rafeubetx** itself. It is not possible to reach the 162m summit, which is in a military zone. When you come to the boundary fence, turn right to follow it, meeting a good track beyond a white building known as **Es Fort**.

Turn left through a gateway, then immediately right to follow a **battered road** away from the military zone. This leads down to a junction near the little car park by the **small white building** passed earlier in the day's walk. If you parked there, then short cut down the forested slope to finish, otherwise, turn left at the road junction and retrace your steps back through the forest to **Son Ferrer**.

Son Ferrer – Small white building	40min
Small white building – Cala Figuera	1hr 30min
Cala Figuera – Rafeubetx	1hr 40min
Rafeubetx – Son Ferrer	1hr 10min

73 Puig d'en Saragossa

This low hill in the southwest of the island is a natural garden of flowering shrubs. In February there are brilliant yellow splashes of thorny broom and the air is fragrant with dense spikes of lavender. It is an outstanding viewpoint, with the peaks of S'Esclop and Galatzó to the north and the sea nearly all round. It is best to shut one's eyes to the unsightly resorts along the coast, but it provides a pleasant half-day out for anyone finding themselves in this area.

On the main summit is a bunker dating from the civil war and also the remains of earlier fortifications. The lower top overlooks Coll de sa Batalla, where an historic battle took place in 1229, when the Moors were defeated by Jaime I of Aragon.

See sketch map 33.

Starting Point	Western Water Park at Sa Porrassa near Magaluf
Time	2hr 30min
Distance	5km
Highest Point	188m
Height Climbed	280m
Grade	B
Map	MTN25 Sant Agustí

Start at the popular **Western Water Park** at Sa Porrassa outside Magaluf, where there is a car park, bus stops and the Restaurante Ca'n Bernat. Walk along a broad **footpath and cycleway** beside the main road, away from a roundabout, as signposted for Palma and Andratx.

In 400m another roundabout is reached, where a left turn leads to a **gateway**. A metal gate at this point is usually locked and bears a notice reading 'No passing'. As this edition went to press, it was reported that the gate had been strengthened and may not be easy to climb. In any case, avoid turning left on the track, which leads to the farm, and keep straight ahead towards the forested hillside. ▸

Continue up the track, which becomes somewhat steeper, then rises more gradually through a profusion of flowering shrubs. There is no mistaking the way to the main summit of **Puig d'en Saragossa**, which bears an underground bunker and a trig point at 188m.

To reach the lower top, follow a very faint path along the ridge, which vanishes in thorny scrub before you reach a saddle at **Sa Selleta**. Climb up another scrubby slope to the summit at 150m, on which is a ruined *talaiot*, or **tower**. There is no real path and a good deal of thorny vegetation, so if this does not appeal you can spend longer on the main summit admiring the views.

Type of Walk
Easy track up to the main summit, then through pathless thorny scrub to the lower top.

In a few minutes a curious building is seen on the right – an old **limekiln** converted to a small weekend retreat.

A trig point and a bouldery cairn stand on top of Puig d'en Saragossa at 188m

Retrace your steps to return to the **Western Water Park**. (There is an alternative route leading directly back to **Magaluf** via the **Mallorca Cricket Ground**, but this passes through an area of wild scrub spoiled by dumping.)

Sa Porrassa – Puig d'en Saragossa	50min
Puig d'en Saragossa – 150m summit and return	1hr
Puig d'en Saragossa – Sa Porrassa	40min

74 Circuit of Puig d'en Bou

Puig d'en Bou is the highest point on the Serra de na Burguesa, but its summit is covered in scrub and not easily attained. This walk wanders round the upper slopes and visits the fine Mirador de n'Alzamora on the end of a ridge. From the terrace outside the crumbling stone shelter there are panoramic views across the cultivated Valldurgent to S'Esclop and Galatzó.

Although near Palma, this area is very quiet and peaceful, but it is popular with hunters and mountain bikers at weekends. Among the luxuriant vegetation there is an abundance of *Arbutus unedo*, the strawberry tree.

See sketch map 34.

Starting Point	Coll des Vent at K6 on the PMV-1043 / Ma1043
Time	3hr
Distance	8km
Highest Point	490m
Height Climbed	200m
Grade	C
Map	MTN25 Sant Agustí or Alpina Tramuntana Sud

Type of Walk
Easy, on good tracks and paths.

Park at K6 at 380m on top of the Ma-1043 at **Coll des Vent** – there are a couple of small parking spaces for cars. Follow a track south through the forest and almost immediately fork

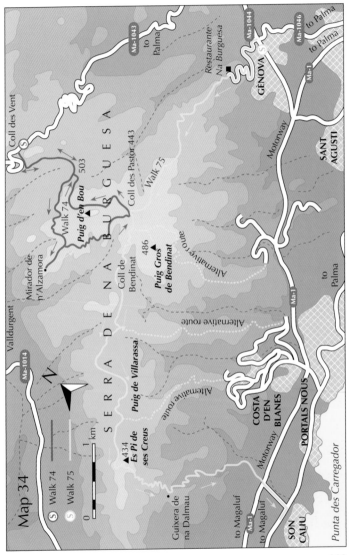

Map 34

Ⓢ Walk 74

Ⓢ Walk 75

0   1 km

N

The Mirador de n'Alzamora has the appearance of a crumbling fortification

right, walking down a path parallel to the road. Turn left gently up a clear track, passing a **water tank**. Go downhill a little and step across a chain barrier. The track sweeps round the head of the valley, **Coma de ses Corbateres**, rising very slightly to where another track joins it from the left.

Keep straight on, but a couple of minutes later, turn right along another track. This track rises gently, then descends towards a streambed where there is a **limekiln**. After climbing up again as a narrower stony path on the other side of the stream, it continues to rise to a path junction marked by a **cairn** on the ridge. (Take note of this point before turning right, in anticipation of your return.) The **Mirador de n'Alzamora**, which has the appearance of a crumbling fortification at 430m, is reached in less than 10 minutes from here, and offers fine views over Valldurgent and Calvià.

To complete the circuit around Puig d'en Bou, walk back to the path junction and **cairn** and turn right. Keep on the clear and obvious path, which becomes rough and rocky where it descends into a **gully**. Cimb uphill and keep left at junctions with two tracks to reach a complex track junction on the **Coll des Pastor**.

Again, keep left to walk up the clearest track, passing close to the forested, scrub-covered summit of **Puig d'en Bou,** at 503m. The track descends and rejoins the route used at the start of the day. Simply retrace your earlier steps to return to **Coll des Vent**.

An optional extension to this walk is to include the ascent of Puig Gros de Bendinat. Do this by turning right along a track before reaching **Coll des Pastor**, then turn left at another track junction. Pass a **tall gate** and turn right up a clear, stony path.

This quickly leads to the 486m summit of **Puig Gros de Bendinat**, which offers fine views from Palma and the Serra de na Burguesa to the high Serra de Tramuntana.

Retrace your steps for the return, or for a longer walk, link with Walk 75, to finish at Gènova or Son Caliu.

Coll des Vent – Mirador de n'Alzamora	1hr
Mirador de n'Alzamora – Coll des Vent	2hr
Puig Gros de Bendinat return trip	30min

75 Serra de na Burguesa

Although close to Palma and many resorts along the south coast, the Serra de na Burguesa is not well known. This low range of hills is a world away from the crowded coastal resorts, and some quiet and pleasant walks can be found. Although devastated by forest fires in recent years, flowering shrubs have quickly recovered and new trees have been planted. Since these serious fires, access tracks have been cleared and a fire tower has been built on Es Pi de ses Creus.

Important archaeological discoveries have been made in hidden caves in these hills. Although crossed by some wide and easy tracks, there are deep, steep-sided valleys filled with almost impenetrable scrub and chaotic rocks. This walk makes use of a major track running along the ridge from a conspicuous statue above Gènova to the television and radio masts near Es Pi de ses Creus to the west. To reach the starting point, take the No4 EMT bus from Palma to Gènova.

Variations of this walk can easily be found – for example there are clear tracks leading to the ridge from Cas Català, Costa d'en Blanes or Portals Nous.

See sketch map 34.

Starting Point	Crossroads on the Ma-1044 at Gènova
Finishing Point	Son Caliu
Time	4hr 15min
Distance	12km
Highest Point	450m
Height Climbed	500m
Grade	C
Map	MTN25 Sant Agustí

Type of Walk
Very easy, except that the descent path is a little rough and stony in places.

Start at the crossroads and bus stops at the top of the Ma-1044 in the village of **Gènova**. Take the road uphill, as signposted 'Na Burguesa', passing the **Méson Ca'n Pedro** and its car park. Take the next road on the right, also signposted 'Na Burguesa'.

This surfaced road zigzags quite steeply uphill to a conspicuous statue where there is the **Restaurante Na Burguesa**. A short distance above the restaurant the road is private, so turn right along a track that leads up on to the ridge between fences, passing communication masts. The track follows the crest of the ridge at first and then keeps on the north side, rising gently before contouring to **Coll des Pastor** at 443m.

Turn sharp left on the col, and in a couple of minutes the track from the Mirador de n'Alzamora (Walk 74) comes in on the right, so keep left. About 200m further on turn right. (The track straight on reaches a col where there is a gate and noticeboard, then descends to Bendinat as the Camí de Bendinat. A diversion could be made, turning right beyond the gate, up a stony path to the 486m summit of Puig Gros de Bendinat.)

The track we are following descends to **Coll de Bendinat** in less than 1km. From this point, at 375m, it makes a wide sweep around to the south side of an unnamed hill, making a left bend at a junction.

Turn right after another 100m (a left turn leads down a ridge to Portals Nous). Keep on the main track, which now runs west, for about 600m. After swinging south the track turns west again at **Puig de Vilarrassa**, and later reaches a junction with a well-used track from Costa d'en Blanes. Turn right and follow this track towards the communication masts, but on reaching the crest, turn left towards the fire tower on **Es Pi de ses Creus**.

You can go all the way to the tower at 434m for the view, but note a right turn marked by **cairns**, where a rough path is used for the descent. The narrow, rugged path weaves steadily downhill, zigzagging on a broad ridge, passing an **old well** to link with a well-made **mule track**. This in turn zigzags downhill into a valley, passing below a steep crag to reach a ruined building with a well at **Guixeria de na Dalmau**.

Just below this ruin there is a conspicuous pylon. Turn sharp left before it and continue downhill to join a narrow, surfaced road by a ruined building near the gates of **Finca s'Hostalet**. Turn right and go under the **motorway**, crossing rungs set into a tall barrier gate.

Later, turn right at a roundabout and follow the main road to reach the bus stops at the **Restaurante Méson Son Caliu**.

Fine tracks are followed along the entire crest of the Serra de Burguesa

Gènova – Coll des Pastor	1hr 30min
Coll des Pastor – Es Pi de ses Creus	1hr 30min
Es Pi de ses Creus – Son Caliu	1hr 15min

AREA 4

SERRA DE LLEVANT AND RANDA

76 Talaia de son Jaumell

The old tower of Talaia de son Jaumell is a superb viewpoint at 273m, on a headland between two bays of pure white sand, Cala Agulla and Cala Mesquida. The area is protected, with attractive pine woods and dunes, and in autumn carpeted with meadow saffron. Although the *talaia* is ruinous, the near views of the coast and the distant views that extend to Formentor make it a fine excursion. The jewel-like colours of the sea on a sparkling winter day, jade and turquoise, have to be seen to be believed. The beach at Cala Agulla is perfect for swimming on a hot day, but likely to be crowded in summer.

For a shorter, easier walk, going over the Coll de Marina to Cala Mesquida and back takes about one hour each way.

To reach the starting point, simply follow signs from Cala Rajada to Cala Agulla. A taxi can be hired for the short run from the Plaça dels Pins to the end of Carrer l'Agulla, and there are summer buses, or you could walk there in half an hour.

See sketch map 35.

Starting Point	Cala Agulla near Cala Rajada
Time	2hr 50min
Distance	8km
Highest Point	273m
Height Climbed	360m
Grade	B
Map	Alpina G or MTN25 Artà

Type of Walk
Mainly easy tracks and well-trodden mountain paths, but the last pull up on to the ridge is quite steep.

Start at the turning point at the end of **Carrer l'Agulla**. Walk to the north end of the sandy **Platja de Cala Agulla**, where there is a white building on the neck of a narrow rocky peninsula, **Punta des Gulló**. Walk straight past the building

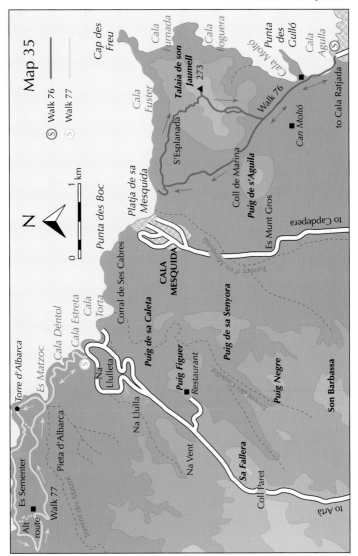

Map 35

Ⓢ Walk 76
Ⓢ Walk 77

N

0   1 km

The crumbling remains of the Talaia de son Jaumell on a hilltop at 273m

to follow a track past the rocky inlet of **Cala Moltó** and go through a gateway. Three minutes later take a left fork, then keep right. Next comes a junction marked with a **large cairn** and signpost. Keep left as signposted for Cala Mesquida (the other way is the return route from Talaia de son Jaumell).

The wide track continues over **Coll de Marina**, passing a limekiln at 84m. On the descent towards Cala Mesquida turn right at a track junction and almost immediately fork left. Continue on the right-hand side of a **drystone wall** to reach a gap, where the path turns left and descends to the beach. There is access to food and drink at **Cala Mesquida** if required.

To continue, walk back uphill from the beach and look for a **narrow path** liberally spotted with blue paint, at first roughly parallel to the coast. After passing some scattered pine trees at **S'Esplanada**, the path rises towards the ridge on the right-hand side of a shallow gully. The ruined tower, or *talaia*, is clearly visible all the way.

Near the top the path veers left into the gully where it becomes rather steep. When the ridge is reached the **Talaia de son Jaumell** is about 100m away to the left, on top of the hill at 273m.

From the tower follow the path back along the ridge and continue past the point of ascent. At the end of the ridge there are two main variants, both of which are quite easy to follow. They meet lower down and then rejoin the main track to Coll de Marina, beyond a prominent **limekiln**.

Turn left downhill to follow the outward route back to the start at **Cala Agulla**.

Cala Agulla – Cala Mesquida	1hr
Cala Mesquida – Talaia de son Jaumell	55min
Talaia de son Jaumell – Cala Agulla	55min

77 Torre d'Albarca

This is one of the best coastal walks on the island, with views of the colourful sea all the way. The old watch tower on Morro d'Albarca is in a fine state of preservation, and there is a spiral staircase, a little precarious, leading to a large circular viewing platform on top, on which is an old cannon barrel. The walk continues to the Platja de sa Font Celada, a small sandy bay between rocky points where the sea is a pale turquoise; in winter this can be enjoyed in solitude.

The walk begins at Cala Estreta, which is reached by following signposts for Cala Torta, just outside Artà on the road to Cala Rajada. The road is badly potholed for most of its 10km. In 2005 a barrier was erected, closing the road to all but local traffic at Coll Paret, and taxi drivers from Artà were unwilling to use the road. Repairs should be made, as the beaches at the end of the road are very popular.

See sketch map 35.

Starting Point	Cala Estreta at the end of a road from Artà
Time	3hr
Distance	9km
Highest Point	80m
Height Climbed	300m
Grade	C+
Map	Alpina G or MTN25 Betlem

Type of Walk
Moderately easy on coastal paths, but a little rough in places.

Leave the road and cross the streambed at the head of **Cala Estreta**. Pick up a narrow path heading round the low cliff coast. This goes through a **gateway** in a fence on a headland and then turns round the inlet of **Cala Déntol**. Further on there is a fine view from the headland Na Brotada to **Es Matzoc**. Follow the path down to the beach and cross to the other side, where a continuing path leads up a rocky ridge to the **Torre d'Albarca**.

To continue, follow the track southwest from the tower, and after about 350m look for a cairn among the trees that shows the start of a path that descends almost to the sea and then rises again to the next headland at **Es Seulonar**. On

this headland the path goes through a **gateway** in a fence. Continue along a low, rocky path to the sandy beach of **Platja de sa Font Celada**.

View along the coast from the Torre d'Albarca to the distant Talaia de Morei

Although it is probably more rewarding in terms of scenery to return the same way, the walk can at first be varied by an inland route. From the western side of the beach follow a **track** inland, swinging sharp left and rising to reach a **small ruin** at a sharp bend right. (Alternatively, you could take a short cut to this point directly from the east side of the beach.)

Five minutes later turn sharp left at a **cross-track** and follow this eastwards. After about 1km a **gate** in a fence can be circumvented on the right if locked. Either keep on the main track back to the **Torre d'Albarca** and retrace your steps from there, which is the most attractive alternative, or take a right turn down through the woods to the cove at **Es Matzoc** and pick up the outward route at that point. (Don't be tempted inland along any other paths and tracks from the cove, as these ultimately lead to locked gates.)

The coastal path is the best way to return to the road at **Cala Estreta**.

Cala Estreta – Torre d'Albarca	50min
Torre d'Albarca – Platja de sa Font Celada	45min
Platja de sa Font Celada – Es Matzoc	50min
Es Matzoc – Cala Estreta	35min

78 Bec de Ferrutx and Ermita de Betlem

The mountains of Artà are the highest of the Serra de Llevant, the discontinuous chain of mountains bounding the central plain of Mallorca on the east. Although only of the order of 500m, they have many of the characteristics of the higher Serra de Tramuntana, and are certainly wild and unfrequented. Bec de Ferrutx is not the highest of these hills, Puig Morei being 561m, but it is certainly the most spectacular.

The mountain tops are all very stony and arid, with a *garriga*-type vegetation – many asphodels, flat-topped thistles, sparse clumps of *càrritx* and some dwarf fan palms. There are wide and dramatic views across the bay of Alcúdia to the Serra de Tramuntana.

The walk can easily be split into two shorter walks if required. From Betlem to the *ermita* and return is short and easy – allow 3 hours including an ascent of Sa Coassa. There is a narrow but adequate driveable road from Artà to the *ermita*, best avoided at weekends, enabling an easier walk to Bec de Ferrutx and back. The way through the narrow streets of Artà to the *ermita* is reasonably well signposted.

See sketch map 36.

Starting Point	Cases de Betlem
Time	5hr 20min
Distance	15km
Highest Point	528m
Height Climbed	770m
Grade	B
Maps	Alpina G or MTN25 Colònia de Sant Pere and MTN25 Artà

Type of Walk
Not strenuous, with few route-finding difficulties. Mainly along tracks and paths and all fairly easy walking.

To reach the start of the walk, drive past Colònia de Sant Pere straight towards **Betlem**. A track on the right is signposted as the GR route to the Ermita de Betlem. (If you miss the

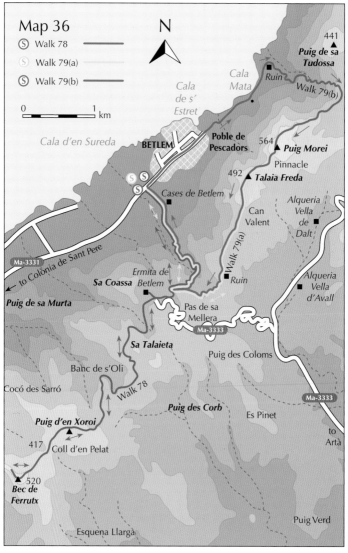

Map 36
Ⓢ Walk 78
Ⓢ Walk 79(a)
Ⓢ Walk 79(b)

N

0 — 1 km

441
Puig de sa Tudossa

Cala de s' Estret

Cala Mata

Ruin

Walk 79(b)

Cala d'en Sureda

BETLEM

Poble de Pescadors

564
Puig Morei

Pinnacle

492
Talaia Freda

Cases de Betlem

Alqueria Vella de Dalt

Can Valent

Ermita de Betlem

Sa Coassa

Walk 79(a)

Ruin

Alqueria Vella d'Avall

Ma-3331

to Colònia de Sant Pere

Puig de sa Murta

Pas de sa Mellera

Ma-3333

Sa Talaieta

Puig des Coloms

Banc de s'Oli

Cocó des Sarró

Walk 78

Puig des Corb

Es Pinet

Ma-3333

to Artà

Puig d'en Xoroi

417
Coll d'en Pelat

520
Bec de Ferrutx

Esquena Llargà

Puig Verd

Bec de Ferrutx is a splendid viewpoint surrounded on most sides by sheer cliffs

start and reach a roundabout, turn round and drive back for 300m.) The track veers right at some old farm buildings at the **Cases de Betlem**.

About 5 minutes after passing the farm a path leaves the track and is signposted uphill to the left, passing some carob trees on terraces. Follow the well-marked path uphill at a moderate gradient, zigzagging up to the left of a steep **head wall** to reach a wide upper valley.

After going through a gap in a wall, the path continues up towards a field shelter made out of a boulder. Before reaching this, it crosses the stream to join a wide track and rises towards the *ermita*. When a **stone gateway** is seen, do not go through it, but follow the track left to reach a **spring**. There is a grotto and a picnic table by the clear water of the *font*, which is roofed over and provided with a chained iron ladle.

Follow the track from here to the gates of the **Ermita de Betlem**, 5 minutes from the spring. It is here that the surfaced road from Artà ends, and where there is some parking space for those who choose to start the walk here, at 280m.

Those making the short walk will have plenty of time to visit the chapel and go up to the hill behind it, Sa Coassa, at 322m, where there are panoramic views of land and sea. There is an old, semi-roofless building offering some shelter here. The Ermita de Betlem does not offer food, drink or accommodation, but the Refugi s'Alqueria Vella does, having been established off the winding road from Artà to serve walkers following the waymarked GR route through the Serra de Llevant.

To continue the main walk, take the track beginning at the gates of the *ermita*, following the boundary wall. This leads southwest then south into a shallow valley, crossing the bed of the **Torrent de sa Jonquera**, then climbing round the shoulder of **Sa Talaieta**. The old narrow track descends into another valley and becomes a wider track, which is easily followed.

About 40 minutes from the *ermita* a wire fence across the track can be lowered and easily stepped over. The track swings downhill, then uphill on the **Banc de s'Oli**. When a junction is met, turn right and follow the track round a gently sloping upper valley, until it ends near the southeast extremity of **Puig d'en Xoroi**. A path climbs across the slopes, passes a large overhanging rock and crosses the crest of the hill at 487m.

Continue southwest down to **Coll d'en Pelat** at 417m, and walk uphill in the same direction to the trig point on top of **Bec de Ferrutx** at 520m – there is a vague, cairned path over stony ground between clumps of *càrritx*.

To fully appreciate this spectacular mountain, continue to the end of the northwest ridge, which is the true mountain top at 528m, falling sheer on almost all sides.

Retrace your steps afterwards to the **Ermita de Betlem**, if you parked there, or the **Cases de Betlem** far below.

Cases de Betlem – Ermita de Betlem	1hr
Ermita de Betlem – Puig d'en Xoroi	1hr 10min
Puig d'en Xoroi – Bec de Ferrutx	40min
Bec de Ferrutx – Ermita de Betlem	1hr 45min
Ermita de Betlem – Cases de Betlem	45min

79 Puig Morei

At 561m Puig Morei is the highest point on the Artà peninsula. On a good day the views are outstanding, and it is almost like being on an island, with sea to the west, north and east. Although not high, it is the culminating point of a long escarpment of imposing cliffs on which are some good scrambling routes. The hinterland is rough and stony ground, scattered with ruined buildings and tumbled terraced walls, evidence of cultivation in times gone by.

The starting point is the same as for Walk 78, the Cases de Betlem.

Routes 79(a) and 79(b) are on sketch map 36.

79(a) Linear walk

Starting Point	Cases de Betlem
Time	4hr 30min
Distance	12km
Highest Point	564m
Height Climbed	590m
Grade	B+
Maps	Alpina G or MTN25 Colònia de Sant Pere, MTN25 Artà and MTN25 Betlem

Start from the **Cases de Betlem** by walking up the track used to approach the **Ermita de Betlem**, as in Walk 78. Just before reaching the *font* and grotto, a good path traverses back left, signposted as the GR route to S'Alqueria Vella and Albarca. This path goes across the valley head, zigzags uphill and goes through two **gateways** in stone walls. Veer left towards a prominent **ruin**, and head roughly northwards to find a vague path heading towards the main ridge at a sudden **escarpment**.

Follow the escarpment edge roughly northwards to reach the top of **Talaia Freda** at 492m, on which is a prominent metal cross. Descend to a col at 450m in about 10 minutes, then traverse round the right-hand side of a **large pinnacle** and ascend to reach the escarpment edge at a higher col. Continue up quite steep but easy ground to reach the trig point at 564m on top of **Puig Morei**.

To return, go back the same way to the 450m col, then continue towards the escarpment edge, bypassing **Talaia Freda** and its cross. A line of cairns can be picked up, and followed back directly to join the route of ascent just below the prominent **ruin**, to return towards the *ermita*, and so continue back down to the **Cases de Betlem**.

Type of Walk
Mainly pathless and rough or stony ground, or overgrown paths, but no real difficulties.

Looking northwards towards Puig Morei from near the Ermita de Betlem

Cases de Betlem – Ermita de Betlem	1hr
Ermita de Betlem – Talaia Freda	1hr 15min
Talaia Freda – Puig Morei	15min
Puig Morei – Ermita de Betlem	1hr 15min
Ermita de Betlem – Cases de Betlem	45min

79(b) Circular walk

Starting Point	Cases de Betlem
Time	5hr
Distance	10km
Highest Point	564m
Height Climbed	605m
Grade	A+
Maps	Alpina G or MTN25 Colònia de Sant Pere, MTN25 Artà and MTN25 Betlem

Type of Walk
Tricky route finding and easy scrambling make this a route for the adventurous.

Start from the **Cases de Betlem** and walk along the road straight through the roundabout at **Betlem**, though the **Poble de Pescadors**. When the surfaced road ends, continue along the rough track that leads towards Es Calo. After about 1km, turn right along a wide track towards a **ruined building** and go past this to climb to the end of the track.

At this point there is not much of a path, but keep going upwards by the best way you can find to reach the base of the **layered cliff** at the head of the valley. There is no mistaking this point, as on either side there are steep and broken cliffs seamed by gullies, some of which can be climbed, but are loose and not recommended. In contrast, the layers of this **head wall**, which average about 1m thick or less, are easy to surmount by following various ledges between the layers, the way sometimes marked by cairns.

At the top is a col at almost 330m, between **Puig de sa Tudossa**, crowned with communication masts on the north side, and our objective, **Puig Morei**, to the southwest. Turn right and follow the escarpment edge to reach the summit trig point at 564m.

A dramatic gap on the rugged crest between Puig Morei and Talaia Freda

The descent is by the same way as in Walk 79(a). Those who have already made the ascent by this route will find it much easier than those who have not! Head roughly south-west down a steep and stony slope to reach a col at over 450m. Keep left to pass a **large pinnacle** and cross another col at 447m. Climb over **Talaia Freda**, whose 492m summit bears a metal cross.

Look carefully to spot a sparse line of cairns marking a vague path that sometimes runs near the edge of the escarpment. Look ahead to spot a prominent **ruin** and head towards it. Veer right to follow a path downhill, swinging left to traverse round a valley head, passing through two **gateways** in stone walls and zigzagging downhill a little. The path joins a clearer track close to a *font* and grotto near the **Ermita de Betlem**.

Either turn left to visit the *ermita*, or right to follow the clear, waymarked path as it zigzags down through a wild valley to pass the **Cases de Betlem** and finish back on the road where the walk started.

Cases de Betlem – Ruined building	1hr 15min
Ruined building – Puig Morei	1hr 45min
Puig Morei – Ermita de Betlem	1hr 15min
Ermita de Betlem – Cases de Betlem	45min

80 Randa

This flat-topped hill in the centre of the Mallorcan plain is known as the Holy Mountain, and there are three monasteries here, the oldest of which, the Santuari de Nostra Senyora de Cura, was founded in 1275. The great Mallorcan scholar Ramon Llull lived there for about 10 years while writing the first of more than 250 books in Catalan. The library holds collections of old music books, missals and medieval manuscripts.

Cura is right at the top of the hill and the church is open at all times. A museum is open to visitors and a donation is requested. A bar–restaurant is open throughout the year, but closed on Mondays. From the large terraces there are panoramic views, and it is said that 32 towns and villages can be seen on a clear day.

The Santuari de Sant Honorat is another monastery with an attached church, 1.5km below the top. The third monastery, the 15th-century Santuari de Gràcia, is built under an impressive overhanging cliff on the southern slopes of the hill.

Although there is a drivable road to the top, this easy walk from Randa village takes advantage of a number of obvious short cuts, making a pleasant half day.

See sketch map 37.

Starting Point	Randa village
Time	2hr 15min
Distance	6km
Highest Point	556m
Height Climbed	220m
Grade	C
Map	MTN25 Algaida

Take the Ma-5018 uphill from **Randa**, signposted for Cura. Go through a metal gate at a **hairpin bend** and follow the path until it rejoins the road near the entrance gate of the **Santuari de Gràcia**. Go through the gateway and follow the road in front of the Santuari, where there is a drinks machine. Continue to the end of the terrace to find a *mirador*, and enjoy views across the plains to the Serra de Llevant.

(There used to be a splendid path running round the base of the overhanging cliffs, later linking with a path leading to the hilltop near Cura, but this is now fenced off due to the ever-present danger of rockfall. Note the wire mesh holding the cliffs in place.)

Walk back along the road to the **entrance gate** and turn right. Almost immediately, leave the road and follow a narrow stony path uphill, missing another hairpin bend on the road, to reach the **Santuari de Sant Honorat**. The *ermita* can be visited, but the rest of the site is reserved for the monastic community.

Type of Walk
Easy, along a road and narrow paths.

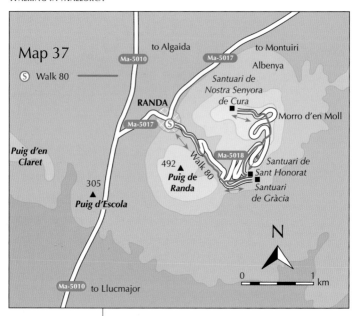

Map 37

Ⓢ Walk 80 ———

to Algaida
to Montuiri
Ma-5010
Ma-5017
Albenya

Santuari de
Nostra Senyora
de Cura

RANDA

Ma-5017
Ⓢ
Morro d'en Moll

Puig d'en
Claret

Ma-5018
Santuari de
Sant Honorat

492 ▲
Walk 80
Puig de
Randa
Santuari
de Gràcia

305
▲
Puig d'Escola

N

0   1 km

Ma-5010   to Llucmajor

Walk down the access road and turn right to walk up the main road as far as another **hairpin bend**. A stony path climbs up to a higher stretch of road, then continues away to the left on the other side of the road, becoming a good **mule track**.

Cross the road again and follow the narrow path towards a prominent **radome** and masts. Turn left to follow the road to its end at the **Santuari de Nostra Senyora de Cura**.

After exploring the site, which offers food, drink and accommodation, simply retrace your steps to **Randa**.

Randa – Santuari de Gràcia	30min
Santuari de Gràcia – Santuari de Cura	45min
Santuari de Cura – Randa	1hr

Cliffs lean dangerously over the Santuari de Gràcia, and have been stabilised

APPENDIX 1

HIGH LEVEL WALK FROM ANDRATX TO POLLENÇA

Every year Mallorquín walkers organise a very tough three-day walk from Andratx to Pollença. This is usually only attempted by the young and the superfit, and even then very few actually complete the rather gruelling course. The walk from Andratx to Pollença described here in note form has been devised for those who indulge in walking for pleasure rather than as a challenge. Even so, it is quite a strenuous undertaking, requiring skills in route finding and some easy scrambling. (**Refer to the individual walk descriptions for detailed directions.**)

The route takes in several mountains over 1000m. It can be done in six days with overnight stops at Puigpunyent, Banyalbufar, Valldemossa, Sóller and Lluc. However, the section from Sóller to Lluc is very long, and could be done in two stages by providing for an overnight bivvy at an attractive spring, the Font des Prat, or moving off-route to the Refugi des Tossals Verds.

The route only touches surfaced roads when it has to, around Puigpunyent, for example, and for short distances at Sóller, Cúber, Lluc and Pollença. Otherwise it takes the walker through wild country, reaching the tops of Puig de Galatzó, Puntals de Son Fortesa, Es Teix, Sa Galera, Puig de l'Ofre, Puig de sa Rateta, Puig de Massanella, Puig Tomir, Puig de Ca and Cuculla de Fartàritx. Naturally, there is spectacular scenery.

In part it follows ancient tracks once used by pilgrims travelling on foot from Sóller to Lluc Monastery.

Day 1
(Refer to Walk 64 and Walk 63)

Use the bus from Peguera or Andratx to reach the Restaurante Es Grau on the Ma-10. Walk down the road for 1km to the K97 marker, then follow the track uphill past a noticeboard bearing the name Son Fortuny. Turn left at a track junction to reach a picnic site at Boal de ses Serveres. Use the signposted and waymarked route via the Pas des Cossi and Pas de na Sabatera to ascend Puig de Galatzó, reaching the trig point at 1027m.

To descend, retrace your steps to the first signposted path junction and turn right, using a path across steep and rugged slopes, passing below the prominent rock tower of Es Bisbe. Pass a fire tower and follow a path down to Font des Pi. At this point navigate along a network of minor roads to Puigpunyent. It is unlikely that accommodation will be found in the village, but there are buses to and from Palma.

Day 2
(Refer to Walk 61 and Walk 62)

Walk out of Puigpunyent as if following the road to Esporles, but follow the access road to Son Fortesa instead. A signposted and waymarked route, the Camí Vell d'Estellencs, can be followed along a series of good tracks and paths. Pass the isolated farmstead of Muntanya on the way up to the broad wooded Coll d'Estellencs.

Use a narrow path to climb towards the cliffs of Puntals de Son Fortesa, the idea being to climb the mountain via a scramble up a chimney. Some walkers would not like this, but a detour to avoid it involves dropping down almost to the finca of Planícia before another breach in the cliffs can be located at the Pas de sa Mola.

From the 893m summit of Puntals de Son Fortesa, follow the ridge to a wooded col and pick up an old track leading to another broad wooded col at 780m. At this point a left turn along a clearer track leads down to Ses Aljubets, continuing around and down the wooded slopes of Planícia to reach vehicle tracks.

Turn right to pass a house at S'Arbossar and continue to Son Sanutges, where a left turn leads down a quiet road into the centre of Banyalbufar. Accommodation is recommended at the Mar i Vent Hotel.

Day 3
(Refer to Walk 59)

Walk back up the road to Ses Sanutges, then continue along a signposted and way-marked path called the Camí des Correu. This traverses wooded slopes and links with other paths and tracks to descend to Sa Granja – the route has been kept off roads as much as possible on the way to Esporles.

Walk through the village and use roads and tracks to reach the old estate of Son Cabaspre, where the Pas de Son Cabaspre is the key to getting back into the hills. Careful navigation is required across the wooded plateau of Mola de son Pacs, and there is an option to climb onto the 731m top of Penyal des Migdia.

A narrow, rocky gully has to be located on the descent to Coll de Sant Jordi, then reasonably good paths and tracks lead over the top of Sa Comuna on the way to Valldemossa.

Day 4
(Refer to Walk 55 and Walk 56)

Leave Valldemossa and head up into the Comellar des Cairats to reach the Font des Poll. A path on the right is signposted for the Serra des Cairats, rising through woodland and eventually up a rocky ridge onto Es Teix at 1064m. A short, easy descent leads onto the Pla de sa Serp.

The route rises over Puig des Vent at 1005m and follows the crest of the ridge, over bare rock, with superb views towards Puig Major and the peaks of the Serra de Tramuntana. The ridge runs northeast, and before a final top a left turn is made to Sa Galera, at 908m.

The descent begins by going down to a col between Sa Galera and Puig des Moro. Route finding is complex, but walk down into a valley to reach a *sitja* and a ruined building. An old track leads down the right-hand side of the valley, and the second left turn allows a descent almost to the streambed. Don't cross the streambed, but traverse below the base of a cliff to find a good vehicle track. Turn right to pass a gate and stile, then follow the track steeply downhill, passing a couple of houses made out of hollowed-out boulders.

The track could be followed all the way down to Sóller, but it is better to turn right along a waymarked route, then left at a signposted junction of paths, and follow an old, stepped path called the Camí de Rocafort downhill. This crosses the railway twice before roads are followed into Sóller. The Hotel El Guia is recommended.

Day 5a
(Refer to Walk 40, Walk 32 and Walk 31)

If you are capable of walking all the way from Sóller to Lluc over the mountains, then good luck, otherwise aim to split the distance over two days.

Walk along roads from Sóller to the village of Biniaraix. Follow the signposted path up the beautiful gorge of Es Barranc – the cobbled and stepped path climbs enchantingly up terraces of olive trees into the ever-narrowing valley below the towering cliffs of Es Cornadors.

Before reaching the Cases de l'Ofre the path heads left and is clearly signposted. Either follow a track or a waymarked path up to the Coll de l'Ofre, then turn right along a track contouring round the south side of Puig de l'Ofre.

Just after going through a gap in a wall, turn left to follow a rugged path to the top of Puig de l'Ofre. From here there is a delightful walk along the ridge and over Puig de na Franquesa to Puig de sa Rateta. To the left there are views over the Cúber reservoir to Puig Major, and to the right across the Comasema valley to the striking sugar-loaf peaks of Puig de s'Alcadena and Puig d'Alaró.

From the top of Puig de sa Rateta the way down to the Cúber dam is roughly northeast (steep crags prevent any wandering astray). A cairn shows the entrance to a hidden valley with a cairned path leading downwards. Lower down, watch for cairns showing the point at which to strike left, crossing a scree gully, then going through an old fence to reach easier ground.

From the reservoir dam, walk to the main road and turn right. Walk only to Font des Noguer, then follow a large, open *canaleta* for about 2km – the path then runs over the Coll des Coloms and on to the Font des Prat. This is a possible bivouac site if the distance to Lluc is being covered over two days. An alternative would be to follow a clear, waymarked path traversing round the mountainside to the Refugi des Tossals Verds.

Day 5b
(Refer to Walk 27)

From the Font des Prat a waymarked path leads up attractive and uninhabited Comellar des Prat, all the way to the Coll des Prat and down over the other side to Comafreda – this is the way once used by pilgrims travelling from Sóller to Lluc, and it is quite pleasant and easy to follow. However, the ascent of Puig de Massanella is one of the highlights of this walk and should not be missed.

Before the col is reached there is a way round to the right and up to another col between Massanella and Puig de Ses Bassetes. There is a vague path, but to reach the col it is necessary to scramble up a little rock wall. There is nothing difficult about it, but it does involve trusting sloping holds with nothing much for the hands, until, after a couple of steps up, a good 'jug handle' can be gripped with the right hand.

Once this little rock scramble is negotiated, make a rising traverse across scree to the foot of a rocky spur, and go up until a way can be found leading back left to the ridge. There are some cairns, but it is best to rely on your own judgement to pick out the best way. Once on the ridge it is easy walking to the top of Puig de Massanella at 1367m.

There are two means of descent, which will no doubt be familiar to those who have climbed the mountain previously. Newcomers should follow the waymarked path directly down to the Coll de sa Línia, rather than via the Font de s'Avenc. Either way, head down to the col and turn left to continue the descent.

Look out for a painted boulder on the right, showing the way down through woods to Comafreda. The farm track leads to a gate, then continues down to the Ma-2130 at Coll de sa Batalla. From a nearby road junction, a quiet road barred to traffic leads down to Lluc Monastery, which offers accommodation and meals, though there is also the nearby Refugi Son Amer.

Day 6
(Refer to Walks 19, 20, 21 and 24)

To leave Lluc Monastery you need to find the football pitch off the road, then follow a clear track rising away from it. This is the Camí Vell de Pollença, which leads up to the main Ma-10 , then runs up a minor road past Menut and Binifaldó. The Camí Vell could be used as an easy, low-level walk to Pollença from Binifaldó, but this route aims to stay high in the mountains.

A path leaves the Binifaldó bottling plant to climb Puig Tomir – the way is well trodden and easy to follow, despite being steep and rocky. The summit of Puig Tomir is at 1104m, from where you go down past a snowpit. Continue down to a col to face the cliffs of Puig de Ca. Follow a track down to the right from the col, then turn left up an obvious breach in the cliffs to climb the mountain. The summit rises to 876m, but there are other tops close to that height.

Walk on down the ridge towards the Coll de Miner, coming down on the north side of the wall that crosses this col, as there is a high, locked gate later. Walk down a track, then branch off to the right when the track bends left. Pick up the old track that contours along the high, cultivated area of Fartàritx. There is still the option of climbing Cuculla de Fartàritx, either by way of a scramble up a chimney, or up an easier breach in the cliffs to reach the summit at 711m.

Options for the final descent are as follows. Walk along the delightful old mule track from Fartàritx Gran to Vall d'en Marc, passing near a house called Can Huguet. If Cuculla de Fartàritx is climbed, however, then a descent by way of a high farmhouse called L'Assarell means that a road through Vall de Colonya could be used.

355

Either way, the final destination is the town of Pollença, heading for the Plaça Major, where welcome refreshment may be had. Rooms are usually available at the Hotel Juma on the square.

APPENDIX 2

ALPHABETICAL REFERENCE SECTION

Accommodation

For the benefit of those who prefer to travel independently, here are the names and telephone numbers of some selected hotels. This information has been taken from tourist publications and websites and has not all been personally verified.

H = hotel, HS = *hostal*, HA = hotel apartments, HR = *residencia*, which is a hotel without a restaurant.

Hotel Name	Grade	Open	Telephone
Cala de Sant Vicenç			
Molins	H****	May–Oct	971–530200
Cala de Sant Vicenç	H****	Feb–Nov	971–530250
Don Pedro	H***	Apr–Oct	971–530050
Simar	HA***	May–Oct	971–534464
Niu	H***	Apr–Oct	971–530100
Mayol	HS**	Apr–Oct	971–530440
Oriola	HS**	Mar–Oct	971–531998
Los Pinos	HS**	May–Oct	971–531210
La Moraleja	HR*****	Apr–Oct	971–534010
Port de Pollença			
Daina	H***	Apr–Nov	971–866250
Illa D'Or	H***	Feb–Nov	971–865100
Pollensa Park	H***	Apr–Oct	971–865350
Pollentia	H***	Apr–Oct	971–865200
Ses Pins	HR***	Apr–Oct	971–867050
Uyal	H***	Apr–Sep	971–865500
Pollença			
Juma	H*	Mar–Oct	971–535002
Port de Sóller			
Los Geranios	H**	All Year	971–631440
Marina	H**	Feb–Nov	971–631461
Eden	H****		971–631600
Eden Park	H***		971–633656
Miramar	H*		971–631350
Hotel Es Port	H***	Feb–Nov	971–631650

Sóller

| El Guia | H* | Apr–Oct | 971–630227 |
| Nadal | HR** | All Year | 971–631180 |

BANKS

Most of the main resorts have several banks, and opening hours are 08.30 to 14.00. Changing money is simple, using travellers' cheques or Eurocheques. Passports must be shown and they may want to know where you are staying. The exchange rate is usually more favourable in banks than in hotels and travel agencies.

BOATS

There are several regular boat services running in summer which can be very useful to walkers. The following services operate in summer only, and exactly when summer begins and ends may depend on the weather. Times may vary from year to year, so it is advisable to check the noticeboards displayed in the ports and pick up current timetables.

> Port de Pollença – Formentor (daily except Sunday)
> Port de Sóller – Sa Calobra (daily)
> Port de Sóller – Cala Tuent (Saturday only)
> Port de Sóller – Deià (Tuesday only)
> Sant Elm – Sa Dragonera (daily)

BUS TRAVEL

Although walkers may find it useful to hire a car for getting to the start of walks, public transport can often be used. This edition of the book was updated entirely by using public transport.

The best place to get hold of timetables is at the new Estació Intermodal in Palma, although some tourist offices and hotels have copies or display them – times are posted on the brightly coloured bus stops too.

Although there are several bus companies, they all operate under the aegis of Transport de les Illes Balears, or TIB, and most vehicles are painted in the same red-and-yellow livery, regardless of operating company.

The following services are given in brief outline, and timetables are published to cover the summer season, from April to September, and the winter, from October to March.

Walkers who wish to make extensive use of buses should base themselves centrally in Palma (the Hostal Terminus is the most central budget accommodation option).

Buses run from early until late, although some remote villages have few buses and at limited hours. The summer bus service over the mountains between Port de Pollença and Port de Sóller is particularly useful for reaching some of the more remote walks.

Airport – Palma

Those who book 'flight only' deals can use an airport bus service to reach the Plaça d'Espanya in Palma, close to both railway stations and the main bus station. Buses run fast, frequently and cheaply from early until late.

Palma – Pollença – Port de Pollença

There are only a few buses making the direct run from Palma to Pollença. Between times, go to the SFM railway station and get a *tren+bus* ticket to cover the journey, changing from the train to a waiting bus at Sa Pobla.

Pollença – Port de Pollença

There is a bus station of sorts in Pollença, near the Plaça Major. The bus stop in Port de Pollença is on the seafront beside the marina. The journey takes only 15 minutes.

Pollença – Cala de Sant Vicenç

Buses to and from Cala de Sant Vicenç are much more plentiful in the summer than in the winter.

Port de Pollença – Alcúdia – Can Picafort

This service can be used to reach Alcúdia, where a short and cheap taxi ride can access the walks on the Alcúdia peninsula. It is also a useful service enabling birdwatchers to reach the Parc Natural de s'Albufera.

Palma – Valldemossa – Deià – Port de Sóller

This bus is useful to walkers based in Sóller, but on winter Sundays there may only be three buses per day making the full journey. There is a small bus station in Port de Sóller. The bus turns around the Plaça d'Amèrica in Sóller.

Sóller – Port de Pollença

This is a very important service for walkers in the Sóller area, running daily (except Sundays) through the summer, but unfortunately not in winter. The bus can be full as it leaves Port de Sóller in good weather, in which case you would be advised to go there to catch it, rather than risk it being full when it reaches Sóller. The bus leaves the mountain road to serve the little port of Sa Calobra – useful for anyone tackling the Torrent de Pareis.

Palma – Tunel – Sóller – Port de Sóller

This is the direct bus service between Palma and Sóller – don't get on it by mistake if heading for Deià or Valldemossa! It runs through a tunnel beneath the Serra d'Alfàbia, and while good for quick travelling between the towns, it doesn't really reach many walks, bypassing even the village of Bunyola.

Palma – Andratx – Port d'Andratx
Fleets of buses run frequently west of Palma to Andratx and Port d'Andratx, passing a number of resorts. Some services are faster than others.

Palma – Banyalbufar – Estellencs
Perhaps the best service for reaching walks on this part of the island, but be sure to check the timetables if considering long or remote walks in the area.

Transport Illes Balears, or TIB, keeps up-to-date details of all buses and trains on a website at http://tib.caib.es. The site is in four languages, easy to navigate, and the timetables are clear and easy to understand.

Car Hire
Some package holidays offer 'free' or reduced car hire as part of the deal, especially during the winter months (it's not really free, because you have to pay the insurance). If this does not apply, then it is cheaper to hire locally than book a car in advance with one of the international companies. The smallest and cheapest cars are the Ford Ka and Japanese models, which are good for driving along narrow mountain roads. A current driving licence and passport must be produced when hiring a car.

Chemists
The sign for a chemist is a green cross and the name is *farmàcia*. Some medicines for which a prescription would be required in Britain, such as antibiotics, may be bought over the counter, but not tranquillisers, for example. However, these are not handed over just for the asking, and a detailed description of symptoms will be required. Staff are usually very helpful and many speak English. After normal hours, one chemist in each town is usually open until late at night. Details are posted in the windows of all chemists.

Complaints
All hotels, shops, bars, garages, and any places offering services to the public, are compelled by law to have a complaints book, or *libre de reclamaciones*. These are only for very serious complaints, and should only be resorted to after every attempt has been made to get things put right in a friendly way. If a polite approach to a manager or owner has not worked, then simply asking for the book may bring about a dramatic change of attitude, as it is a serious matter to have a complaint registered. The forms are in triplicate: one copy for the offending organisation, one to be sent to the tourist office in Palma and one copy to be retained by the complainant.

Currency
The monetary unit is the euro. Banknotes come in denominations of 500, 200, 100, 50, 20, 10 and 5 euros. Coins come in values of 2 and 1 euro, as well as 50, 20, 10,

5, 2 and 1 cents. The 1 and 2 cents may well be phased out in time. Counterfeiters tend to expend most of their energies on the larger notes, so it is wise to accept large denominations only from banks, or insist on smaller notes when you change money. ATMs are available at most banks in the towns, and even in villages and some monasteries!

DRINKS

There are very many bars where drinks are served all day, even in small villages. Bars serve coffee and soft drinks and often food as well. Supermarkets and most village shops sell wine, beer and spirits. Some good Mallorquín wines are made at Felanitx and at Binisalem by Franja Roja. Beer (*cervesa*) is generally good. Draught is *de barril* or a *presion*.

DRIVING

Getting to the start of the walks often means driving along narrow winding roads. The roads themselves are mainly good, but there can be problems when meeting coaches going in the opposite direction. The drivers are always very good, and expert at edging past with only an inch or two to spare. The worst place for this is the narrow, twisting road between Deià and Sóller, but this has been improved. Go very slowly when you know you are going to make a turn, and expect it to be a sudden one.

Driving Offences

Traffic police are very strict and on-the-spot fines are very high. It is as well to be aware of the following Spanish laws.

1   Always use the seat belts.
2   Always indicate you are pulling out when overtaking anything, including parked cars and cyclists, and allow 1m clearance at least.
3   Always dip headlights when coming up behind another vehicle as well as when approaching.
4   Pay particular attention to *ceda el paso* ('give way') signs and 'Stop' signs. Some road junctions can be confusing, but 'Stop' means 'stop', as the author was told by the policeman charging an on-the-spot fine!
5   Give way to all vehicles coming from the right.
6   Keep to the speed limit of 110km on main roads and 90km on other roads, or other speeds as shown locally.
7   Never cross an unbroken white line in the centre of the road, and 'No Overtaking' signs back up these lines.
8   Do not park facing oncoming traffic or within 3m of a corner.
9   Obey the priority signs on narrow roads and bridges. You have priority at a sign with a white arrow pointing up, and must give way at a sign with a red arrow pointing up.

10   Each car in Spain should carry a set of spare bulbs, but car hire companies do not provide these. Any fine incurred will be refunded by the hire company.

If you are stopped by the police for any offence whatsoever it is no use pleading ignorance of the law, and highly inadvisable to argue. The best course of action is to apologise: *lo siento*, or *lo siento mucho*. If it is not a serious offence then you may be let off with a warning, but it is more likely that you will be charged and have to pay a fine (*una multa*). If this is the case you will be given a slip of paper explaining what is to happen. The policeman will fill in a form describing the offence and ask you to sign it. He will sign it too and give you a copy to keep.

EMAIL (SEE INTERNET)

FLIGHTS
Budget flights allow the independent traveller to reach Mallorca for as little as £50 return, including taxes, from airports around Britain. Check flight times and prices with the following airlines: Easyjet **www.easyjet.com**, BMI Baby **www.bmibaby.com**, Globespan **www.flyglobespan.com** and others.

FOOD (SEE ALSO MARKETS AND RESTAURANTS)
Mallorquín cuisine, or *cuina mallorquina*, is not always similar to that of Catalonia on the mainland. Fish dishes are a speciality and so are *tapas*, which are wonderful titbits served with drinks in many bars. They are usually laid out behind glass on the counter and you can point to the ones you want. Small or large helpings are offered and a large one can make a substantial meal.

Food in hotels catering for English people can be rather bland, although the tendency now is for most meals to be self-service, and there is often an excellent buffet with a good selection. You may like to sample the following dishes when you have the opportunity.

angules small eels fried whole in batter
arròs brut rice soup with meat
bacallà dried codfish with tomatoes in a casserole
butifarra Catalan spiced sausage
calamars squid, served *a la romana* or deep fried, in rings
caldereta de peix fish soup with rice and slices of bread
capó a lo Rei en Jaume capon, cock or turkey stuffed with marzipan and sweet potatoes and lightly fried
cargols snails cooked in garlic mayonnaise sauce
xocolata calenta (chocolate a la taza) thick hot chocolate for dipping pastries such as *ensaimadas* or *cocas de patatas*
coca de trempó looks like a pizza without cheese

coca de patata light, round bun (looks like a potato) for dipping in chocolate

ensaimada a light, flaky, spiral bun sprinkled with icing sugar, often eaten for breakfast or on picnics

escaldums a casserole of chicken and potatoes in an almond sauce

espinagada savoury pie of eels and seasoned vegetables

frit Mallorquí a fry-up of liver, kidneys, onions and garlic

gambes prawns

gazpacho a cold soup made from tomatoes, onions, peppers, cucumber, garlic, oil and vinegar

greixonera de peix fish with vegetables and eggs

greixera mixed pressed cold meats with egg, artichokes, peas, beans and herbs

guisantes a la catalana peas fried with ham and onions

Laccao trade name for a hot or cold chocolate drink like cocoa

llangosta a la catalana lobster sautéed in wine and rum with herbs and spices

llenguat sole, usually grilled with fresh herbs

molls red mullet

musclos a la marinera mussels cooked in a spicy sauce

napolitanas like sausage rolls, but filled with chocolate or custard (*crema*)

pa amb oli bread drizzled with oil, may also be rubbed with tomato and garlic, and may be served with sliced meat

paella a classic Spanish dish, the best are cooked to order and take at least half an hour; it is a combination of rice with poultry, various seafoods and pork, plus onions, tomatoes, peppers and garlic – normally served in an iron dish straight from the oven, for a minimum of two people

paella catalana spicy sausage, pork, squid, tomato, chilli peppers and peas

paella marinera fish and seafood only

paella valenciana the traditional dish with chicken, mussels, shrimps, prawns, peas, tomatoes and garlic

panada (empanada) meat and/or vegetable pie

porcella rostida roast suckling pig (a famous speciality)

sobrassada pork-liver sausage, bright red with pimento

sopes mallorquines very filling soup, almost a stew, made from garlic, onions, vegetables in season and bread

trempó a summer salad with mixed vegetables

truita means trout or omelette in Mallorquí, hence: *truita a la navarra* – trout stuffed with bacon or smoked ham, *truita de patates (tortilla española)* – omelette with potatoes

tumbet a type of ratatouille with layers of aubergines, peppers, tomatoes and potatoes cooked in olive oil

xoriç (chorizo) a strong, spicy sausage

zarzuela a stew of various fish in a hot spicy sauce

HOLIDAYS

Visitors should note a number of religious or cultural holidays, or *fiestas* (Spanish) or *festes* (Catalan). Many businesses close and public transport operates a reduced service. The main dates are 1 and 6 January, 1 March, Good Friday, Easter Monday, 1 May, 25 July, 15 August, 12 October, 1 November, 6, 8, 25 and 26 December. Some towns and villages may have additional *festas,* but these may only affect local businesses and not public transport.

INTERNET

Internet cafes are becoming features on the streets of most towns, especially the tourist resorts, and even some villages. Many hotels also offer internet facilities to their guests.

MARKETS

Anyone self-catering will enjoy buying fresh fruit and vegetables at the open markets. There is a superb selection, even in the depths of winter, and prices are very reasonable. They are good places to buy food for packed lunches too, especially the local oranges. A visit to one of these markets is a colourful and entertaining event and highly recommended. Most of them open early in the morning and finish by lunchtime.

Alcúdia Tuesday, Sunday
Andratx Wednesday
Calvià Monday
Consell Sunday (flea market)
Inca Thursday
Santa María Sunday
Sineu Wednesday
Palma Saturday (antiques market)

MEDICAL MATTERS

When booking a holiday make sure that you have adequate insurance cover. Note that if you intend rock climbing it is often excluded from insurance cover, so that arrangements should be made, for example, with BMC Insurance. There are doctors in all towns, and hospitals at Palma and Manacor that can be reached in under two hours from the most distant parts of the island. First-class specialist and emergency treatment is available. (See also Chemists.) In emergency dial 112.

PHOTOGRAPHY

If not shooting digital, bring all the film that you are likely to need, as it is more expensive to buy in Mallorca. Colour prints can be developed within 24 hours. Kodak transparencies can be sent to Madrid and should be returned within a week. Remember that the light is very bright and it is easy to overexpose, especially near the sea or white buildings.

Police

There are three police forces and all are armed. The Policía Municipal wear blue and are attached to local councils. The Policía Nacional wear brown. The Guardia Civil, once very powerful, are often seen in rural areas and they also operate a mountain rescue service. All three police forces may be called upon if you need help and the telephone numbers are 112 or 062.

Post Offices

Post offices (*correus*) are generally open from 09.00 to 14.00 from Monday to Friday. The main post office in Palma is open all day and Saturday mornings. Stamps (*sellos*) can be bought at tobacconists, or from shops selling postcards, or from a hotel reception desk. Mailboxes are yellow. A box labelled *extranjero* is for foreign-bound mail. Mail can be sent to a post office to be collected if you do not know what your address will be. The form of address is:

> 'Mr and Mrs Smith'
> Lista de Correus
> Port de Pollença
> Mallorca
> Illes Balears
> Spain

Public Transport (*See Bus Travel and Trains*)

Public transport generally fans outwards from Palma and reaches most parts of Mallorca, but there are some bus journeys that don't run to or from Palma. The city buses, country buses and trains all operate from the new combined underground bus/train interchange, or Estació Intermodal, off the Plaça d'Espanya in Palma.

Railways (*see Trains*)

Restaurants

There is a wide choice of places to eat in every resort, and many bars serve food and most hotels offer meals to non-residents. Your own hotel will probably offer specialities at extra cost that can be ordered instead of the standard fare. Menus and prices are usually posted outside the entrance, so that you can see what is available before deciding where to eat, but it is a good plan to ask someone with local knowledge to recommend somewhere.

There is a wide range of prices, but paying more does not always mean a better meal – it may just mean a more elaborate service. In tourist places the menu is often in several languages including English. In smaller places with more authentic local cooking it pays to know some of the words that may be on the menu (see 'Food' and 'Language'). The menú del día is always good value. This is a two- or three-course meal including bread and wine at a set price. (Be aware that if you try to vary a set menu, the price increases dramatically!)

SHOPS AND SHOPPING (*SEE ALSO MARKETS*)

Shopping for food is easy everywhere on the island. Even the smallest villages have a general store and they are nearly all self-service. Hours are generally 09.00 to 13.00 and 16.00 to 20.00. Some shops stay open all day, while some close on Saturday afternoons. If you go to Palma for a day's shopping and sightseeing, remember that while the afternoon *siesta* is becoming a thing of the past, especially in winter, many businesses still close because of tradition, or for a long lunch break.

SMOKING

Smoking is prohibited on all forms of public transport. Bars and restaurants are required by law to state whether they are smoking or non-smoking – in practise, only 20% are non-smoking. Large bars and restaurants (those over 100 square metres) must have a non-smoking area. Hotels and other forms of accommodation may apply their own rules to guest rooms – clear pictorial signs offer guidance.

TAXIS

Taxis are cheaper than in Britain and can be good value for four people sharing. They are usually found in main squares or in front of hotels, or the reception desk at the hotel will call one. The green sign *Lliure/Libre* means 'free' and any taxi displaying this can be flagged down. There is usually a board near the taxi rank displaying the standard fares to nearby places, or you can ask to see a scale of charges approved by the local municipality. If you want to go on a long journey you may have to pay the fare both ways, even if you are not returning. Metered journeys average around 1 euro per kilometre after flagfall. Tips of 10% of the fare are customary. Generally, a taxi fare will cost 10 times the equivalent bus or train fare.

TELEPHONES

The telephone system is modern and all public telephones have tone dialling and can be used for international calls. They take euro coins, and any coins not used are refunded when you hang up. Some public telephones take phonecards or credit cards. Most bars have telephones. The dialling tone is a single intermittent note and the engaged sign a very rapid intermittent note. To make a call to England, first dial 0044, then omit the first '0' of the area code (e.g. 161 for Manchester, not 0161). Hotels will usually make calls for you, but there is often a surcharge. To make a personal call, ask the operator for persona a persona and to reverse the charges ask for cobro revertido. If making a call to a Mallorcan, the first word they usually say is diguim (speak to me). Mobile phone coverage is generally excellent around Mallorca, but there are plenty of places in the mountains and valleys where no signal can be obtained. Ask your supplier whether you will be able to make or receive calls in Mallorca.

Theft

In Palma and the busy resorts of the south coast it is necessary to be on guard against handbag-snatchers and pickpockets, as in many places today. Never accept a free carnation for your buttonhole – this is a ploy to gain free access to your wallet!

Car thieves operate all over the island, and it is never safe to leave valuables or anything at all in a car when you go walking for the day. Leave the car empty with the seats tipped foward to show there is nothing hidden underneath. Friends have had cars broken into and all sorts of items taken, from cameras and clothes to old trainers and a few groceries.

Toilets

There are few public toilets in Mallorca and most people use those in bars and restaurants. There are usually pictorial signs for men and women. A useful phrase to know is *Dónde está el servicio, por favor?* ('Where is the toilet, please?').

Tourist offices

Spanish National Tourist Office, 22–23 Manchester Square, London W1M 5AP. Phoning 020 7486 8077 connects to a 24-hour brochure-request service, otherwise ☎ 0906 3640 630, or visit their website at **www.tourspain. co.uk**.

Tourist offices are located in all the main resorts, where some may close in winter, as well as at the airport, which is open all year. The offices in Palma are open all year and are located centrally at the Plaça d'Espanya, ☎ 971–711527, or 971–754329, as well as on the Plaça de la Reina, ☎ 971–712216. Check the website **www. illesbalears.es**, which is available in six languages.

Tour operators

Thomson

Major tour operators such as Thomson offer winter holidays in the above resorts, **www. thomson-holidays.co.uk**.

Try Holidays

This is the new name for long-established Alternative Mallorca. They offer hundreds of apartments and hotels in lesser-known places, as well as courses in birdwatching, painting and other activities. Try Holidays, 60 Stainbeck Road, Leeds LS7 2PW, ☎ 0113–2786862, **www.tryholidays.co.uk**.

Classic Collection Holidays

Offers a choice of hotels around Mallorca in small and attractive places such as Deià, Valldemossa, Banyalbufar and Estellencs. Classic Collection Holidays, Wiston House, Wiston Avenue, Worthing, West Sussex BN14 7QL, ☎ 0870–7873377, **www.classic collection.co.uk**.

TRAINS

There are two railway lines on the island – the Serveis Ferroviaris de Mallorca, or SFM, and the Ferrocarril de Sóller. The Sóller line is of special interest to walkers, and may be used by the independent traveller going to stay in Sóller, or by walkers staying in Palma to get there for the day, but it is much more expensive than taking a bus.

In Palma the railway lines have adjacent stations on the central Plaça d'Espanya, and both stations are a short walk from the main bus station. The Sóller line was built in 1912 as a steam-hauled service, and although now electrified it still uses very old and attractive carriages with brass fittings. The rickety train ride itself is highly recommended for its own sake. The 10.50 from Palma is a special tourist train that stops at a viewpoint high above the Vall de Sóller for 10 minutes while everyone leaps out with their cameras. This train can be very crowded, especially at peak holiday times, and unless you are early at the station you may find that it is standing room only on the platforms between the carriages.

There is also an old tram, or tranvia, which runs between Sóller and Port de Sóller, and again offers an exciting and scenic ride. The busier SFM line from Palma to Inca and Sa Pobla links with a number of bus services that run towards the mountains, and all-in-one tren+bus tickets can be bought to cover journeys to places such as Mancor de la Vall, Lluc or Pollença. There is a long-term plan to extend the railway to Artà, where it used to terminate.

Tranport Illes Balears, or TIB, keeps up-to-date details of all buses and trains on a website at http://tib.caib.es, in four languages. The site is easy to navigate and the timetables are clear.

WATER

It is perfectly safe to drink the tap-water, though some say it has an unpleasant taste and prefer bottled water. There are Mallorcan brands and some walks pass bottling plants at their sources. For best value buy 5 litre bottles from supermarkets, rather than expensive small bottles from bars.

APPENDIX 3

LANGUAGE NOTES AND
TOPOGRAPHICAL GLOSSARY

Introduction

There are two official languages in Mallorca – Castilian Spanish and Catalan. Catalan is spoken all the way from Andorra to València, as well as on the Illes Balears. Mallorquí is a dialect of Catalan and includes words of French and Arabic origin. No one expects visitors to learn Catalan, let alone Mallorquí, and the Castilian 'Spanish' you may have learned before visiting the island is readily understood everywhere. Be assured that many people in the main resorts and large hotels speak English, German and other languages, although this may not be the case in small villages and in the countryside.

Catalan in its written form may be understood by anyone with a little knowledge of Spanish, but the spoken language is another matter entirely. Between themselves, most islanders speak Mallorquí, so that conversations on buses and in bars and shops may be incomprehensible to visitors. However, if you try to speak a little Spanish, you will find that people are delighted that you are making the effort and will help you all they can, and even more so if you attempt to converse in Catalan. It is well worth taking the trouble to learn a few words and phrases so as to be able to pass the time of day with local people.

One of the best ways of learning Castilian Spanish is to listen to cassettes or radio programmes such as the BBC sometimes produces, then make the effort to use the language in your travels. Castilian is pronounced exactly as it is spelled, so that once the rules are known a reasonable attempt at pronunciation can be made. Stress is on the last but one syllable unless indicated otherwise by an accent.

Opportunities to learn Catalan are limited, so it is not easily accomplished, but the book Teach Yourself Catalan, published by Hodder & Stoughton, is a good place to start.

Key to Castilian pronunciation

The following guide is given for reference and merely to introduce a few words of vocabulary. It is no substitute for listening to people talking on cassettes, radio or, best of all, in real life.

a Between 'a' in lass and in father – *adiós* = goodbye
b As in English – *banco* – bank
c Used before 'i' and 'e', like 'th' in thin – *cinco* = (thin)co five; used before anything else, as in cat – *cliente* = customer
ch As in church – *chico* – boy

d Used at beginning of word, like 'd' in dog – *dos* = two; used in other places, like 'th' in though – *verdad* = true
e As in men, but at end of word as in day – *leche* = milk
f As in English – *fácil* = easy
g Used before 'a', 'o', 'u' or consonants, as in gas – *gasolina* = petrol; used before 'e' and 'i' as 'ch' in loch – *gente* = people
gu Used before 'a', like 'gw' – *agua* ('agwa') = water
h Is always silent – *hombre* ('ombre') = man
i Between 'i' in bit and in machine – *litro* = litre
j Like 'ch' in loch – *ajo* = garlic
k As in English – *kilo* = kilo
l As in English – *libro* = book
ll Like 'lli' in million – *me llamo* = I'm called
m As in English – *mantequilla* = butter
n As in English – *naranja* = orange
ñ As 'ni' in onion – *los niños* = the children
o Between top and for – *oficina* = office
p As in English – *pan* = bread
q Like English 'k' – *quizás* = perhaps
r Pronounced slightly rolled – *el norte* = the north
rr Pronounced strongly rolled – *carretera* = main road
s Voiceless hiss, as in sin – *seis* = six
t As in English – *tienda* = shop
u As in boot – *usted* = you
v Like a soft English 'b' – *vaso* ('baso') = glass
x Used at end of word, like 'tch' – *Felanitx* (place name); used between vowels, like 'gs' – *taxi* ('tagsi') = taxi
y Like 'y' in yes – *mayor* = main
y The word 'y', as the 'i' in machine – *y* = and
z As 'th' in thick – *manzana* (man*th*ana) = apple

The three double letters 'ch', 'll' and 'rr' are considered as separate letters by the Spanish Academy, so they have separate sequences in Spanish dictionaries.

KEY TO CATALAN PRONUNCIATION
Essentially, the sounds are broadly the same as for Castilian, as above, including those pronounced as in English, but with a few notable exceptions. Mastering the rules ensures you will have no trouble with place names.

c Used before 'e' or 'i' is soft, otherwise hard, never lisped – *cinc* ('sink') = five
ç Sounds like 's' in English – *plaça* ('plassa') = square
g Used before 'e' or 'i' is soft, otherwise hard

j Is pronounced softly, the same as the French pronounce 'Jean'
ll Like 'lli' in million
l.l Sounds like 'll' in English, as in *col.laboració* = collaboration
ny Is always used in Catalan where Castilian uses 'ñ' – Bunyola/Buñola
qu Used before 'e' or 'i' like k', but before 'a' or 'o' like 'kw'
r Is pronounced rolled at the start of a word
v Used at the start of a word sounds like 'b', otherwise sounds like 'f'
z Is pronounced like an English 'z' and is never lisped

BASIC WORDS AND PHRASES

Some very basic words and phrases are included here because it can be useful to have reference to them without carrying a separate phrase book in your rucksack.
Note Question marks and exclamation marks are always used upside down at the beginning of a question or exclamation in Castilian.

Everyday Words and Expressions

English	Castilian	Catalan
Hello	*Hola*	*Hola*
Good morning	*Buenos días*	*Bon dia*
Good afternoon	*Buenas tardes*	*Bones tardes*
Goodnight	*Buenas noches*	*Bona nit*
Goodbye	*Adiós*	*Adéu*
See you tomorrow	*Hasta mañana*	*Fins demà*
See you later	*Hasta luego*	*Fins després*
Yes/no	*Sí/no*	*Si/no*
Please	*Por favor*	*Per favor*
That's all right	*De nada*	*De res*
Thank you very much	*Muchas gracias*	*Moltes gràcies*
Excuse me	*Perdón*	*Perdoni*
I'm sorry	*Lo siento*	*Ho sento*
I'm English (man)	*Soy inglés*	*Sóc anglès*
I'm English (woman)	*Soy inglesa*	*Sóc anglesa*
I don't understand	*No comprendo*	*No ho entenc*
Would you repeat please?	*¿Puede repetir, por favor?*	*Ho pot repetir, per favor?*
More slowly, please	*¿Puede hablar más despacio, por favor?*	*Pot parlar més poc a poc, per favor?*
What did you say?	*¿Qué ha dicho usted?*	*Que m'ha dit vostè?*
What is that?	*¿Qué significa ésto?*	*Què vol dir això?*
Do you speak English?	*¿Habla inglés?*	*Parla anglès?*
I don't speak Spanish	*No hablo español*	*No parlo espanyol*
I don't speak Catalan	*No hablo catalán*	*No parlo català*
There is/are, is/are there	*Hay*	*Hi ha*
Is there a bank here?	*¿Hay un banco aquí?*	*Hi ha un banc prop d'aquí?*

English	Castilian	Catalan
Where is …?	*¿Dónde está …?*	*A on és …?*
… the post office?	*¿ … la oficina de correos?*	*l'oficina de correus?*
… the toilet? –	*¿ … el servicio? …*	*el banyo?*
Men	*Señores/hombres/ caballeros*	*Homes*
Women	*Señoras/mujeres*	*Dones*
Open/closed	*Abierto/cerrado*	*Obert/tancat*
Today/tomorrow	*Hoy/mañana*	*Avui/demà*
Next week	*La próxima semana*	*La setmana que ve*
Where can I buy …?	*¿Dónde se puede comprar?*	*A on se pot comprar?*
… a newspaper/stamps	*¿ …un periódico/sellos*	*un diari/segells*
I'd like that	*Quiero eso*	*Voldria això*
I'll have this	*Me llevo ésto*	*M'en duc això*
How much?	*¿Cuánto cuesta?*	*Quant val?*

Accommodation

Do you have a room?	*¿Tiene una habitación?*	*Té alguna habitació?*
Double/single	*Doble/individual*	*Doble/individual*
Tonight	*Esta noche*	*Aquesta nit*
For two/three nights	*Para dos/tres noches*	*Per dues/tres nits*
How much is the room?	*¿Cuanto cuesta la habitación?*	*Quan val l'habitació?*
With bath/without bath	*Con baño/sin baño*	*Amb bany/sense bany*

Bar and Restaurant

Drinks	*Bebidas*	*Begudes*
Breakfast	*Desayuno*	*Berenar*
Lunch/dinner	*Comida/cena*	*Dinar/sopar*
I'd like/we'd like	*Quiero/queremos*	*Voldria/voldriem*
I'll have/we'll have	*Tomo/tomamos*	*Prendré/prendrem*
A black coffee	*Un café solo*	*Un café sol*
Two black coffees	*Dos cafés solos*	*Dos cafés sols*
White coffee	*Un café con leche*	*Un café amb llet*
Three white coffees	*Tres cafés con leches*	*Tres cafés amb llet*
Tea with milk	*Un té con leche*	*Un tè amb llet*
Tea with lemon for me	*Un té con limón para mi*	*Un tè amb llimona*
Beer	*Una cerveza*	*Una cervesa*
The house wine	*El vino de la casa*	*El vi de la casa*
A glass of red wine	*Un vaso de vino tinto*	*Un tassó de vi negre*
White wine	*Un vino blanco*	*Un vi blanc*
A dry sherry	*Un jeréz seco*	*Un xerès sec*

English	Castilian	Catalan
A bottle of water	*Una botella de agua*	*Una botella d'aigo*
Fizzy/still	*Con gas/sin gas*	*Amb gas/sense gas*
Orange juice	*Zumo de naranja*	*Suc de taronja*
Starters	*Prima plato*	*Primer plat*
Soup	*Sopa*	*Sopa*
Eggs, egg dishes	*Huevos*	*Ous*
Fish, fish dishes	*Pescados*	*Peix*
Sea food/shellfish	*Mariscos*	*Marisc*
Meat, meat dishes	*Carne*	*Carn*
Game	*Carne de caza*	*Carn de caça*
Vegetables	*Verduras/legumbres*	*Verdures/llegums*
I'm vegetarian	*Soy vegetariano, vegeteriano*	*Sóc vegetarià/vegetariana*
Cheese	*Queso*	*Formatge*
Fruit	*Fruta*	*Fruita*
Ice-cream	*Helados*	*Gelat*
Desserts	*Postres*	*Postres*
Sandwich	*Bocadillo*	*Panet*
Anything else?	*¿Algo más?*	*Qualque cosa més?*
Nothing, thank you	*Nada más, gracias*	*Res més, graciès*
The bill, please	*La cuenta, por favor*	*El compte, per favor*
Packed lunches	*Picnics*	*Picnics*
Two packed lunches	*Dos picnics*	*Dos picnics*
For tomorrow	*Para mañana*	*Per demà*

Getting About		
By car/on foot	*En coche/a pie*	*En cotxe/a peu*
How do I get to Sóller?	*¿Por dónde se va a Sóller?*	*Com es va a Sóller?*
Where is …?	*¿Dónde está…?*	*A on és …?*
… the bus station?	*…la estación de autobúses?*	*…l'estació d'autobusos?*
… the bus stop?	*…la parada de autobús?*	*…la parada d'autobús?*
… for Pollença?	*…para Pollença?*	*…per Pollença?*
How much is the fare?	*¿Cuánto vale el billete?*	*Quan val el bitllet?*
Return	*Ida y vuelta*	*D'anada i tornada*
Single	*Sencillo/solamente ida*	*Només anada*
Where is the road to …?	*¿Dónde está la carretera de…?*	*A on és la carretera de…?*

Car Travel		
Where can I hire a car?	*¿Dónde se puede alquilar un coche?*	*A on se pot llogar un cotxe?*

English	Castilian	Catalan
How much is it …?	*¿Cuánto cuesta…?*	*Quan val…?*
… per day?	*¿ …por día?*	*…per día?*
… for a week?	*¿…por una semana?*	*… per una setmana?*
Petrol, standard/premium	*Gasolina normal/super*	*Benzina normal/súper*
Petrol station	*Gasolinera/estación de servicio*	*Benzinera*
Car repair shop/garage	*Taller/garaje*	*Taller de reparacions*
Fill it up please	*Lleno, por favor*	*Ple, per favor*
10, 20, 30 litres	*Diez, veinte, treinta litros*	*Deu, vint, trenta litres*
May I park here?	*¿Se puede aparcar aquí?*	*Es pot aparcar aquí?*

Especially for Walkers

English	Castilian	Catalan
Where is the footpath to. ?	*¿Dónde está el camino a. ?*	*A on és el camí…?*
May we go this way?	*¿Se puede pasar por aqui?*	*Es pot passer per aquí?*
Is it far?	*¿Está lejos?*	*Està lluny?*
How far?	*¿A qué distancia?*	*A quina distància?*
How long?	*¿Cuánto tiempo?*	*A quans minuts?*
Very near?	*¿Muy cerca?*	*Molt proper*
Left/right	*Izquierda/derecho*	*A l'esquerra/a la dreta*
Straight on	*Todo recto*	*Tot recte*
First left	*La primera a la izquierda*	*La primera a l'esquerra*
Second right	*La segunda a la derecha*	*La segona a la dreta*
In front of the church	*En frente de la iglesia*	*Davant l'església*
Behind the hotel	*Detrás del hotel*	*Darrera l'hotel*
At the end of the street	*Al final de la calle*	*Al final del carrer*
After the bridge	*Después del puente*	*Passat el pont*
Where are you going?	*¿Adónde va/van?*	*A on va/van?*
I'm going/we're going to..	*Voy a/vamos…*	*Vaig a/anam a…*
A right of way	*Derecho de paso*	*Dret de pas*
Private hunting	*Coto privado de caza*	*Àrea privada de caça*
Please close	*Cierren, por favor*	*Tancau, per favor*
Dogs on guard	*Cuidado con el perro*	*Alerta amb el ca*

Days of the Week

English	Castilian	Catalan
Monday	*Lunes*	*Dilluns*
Tuesday	*Martes*	*Dimarts*
Wednesday	*Miércoles*	*Dimecres*
Thursday	*Jueves*	*Dijous*
Friday	*Viernes*	*Divendres*
Saturday	*Sábado*	*Dissabte*
Sunday	*Domingo*	*Diumenge*

English	Castilian	Catalan
Emergencies		
Help! Fire!	*¡Socorro! ¡Fuego!*	*Ajuda! Foc!*
Police	*Policía/Guardia Civil*	*Policía/Guardia Civil*
I've had a breakdown	*Mi coche se ha estropeado*	*El meu cotxe s'ha espatllat*
There's been an accident	*Ha habido un accidente*	*Hi ha hagut un accident*
Call a doctor quickly	*Llamen a un medico, rapidamente*	*Cridin al metge, ràpidament*
It's urgent!	*Es urgente!*	*És urgent!*

Road signs

Most are international symbols, but you may also see these.

Calzada deteriorada	Bad road
Calzada estrecha	Narrow road
Ceda el paso	Give way
Cruce peligroso	Dangerous crossroads
Curva peligrosa	Dangerous bend
Cuidado	Caution

PLACE NAMES

Most places in Mallorca have had two names in the past, Castilian and Mallorquí. Since Mallorquí was given equal status with Castilian, almost all Castilian place names have vanished from signposts and street signs. In fact, only in a few tourist resorts are there any Castilian signs to be seen, and Mallorquí may be the only language in evidence in rural areas. Confusion is likely to arise if you use old maps and guidebooks, which generally offer only Castilian place names. However, even with official IGN maps, changes have been slow to appear and the process is ongoing.

Names are fairly similar as a rule, such as La Calobra/Sa Calobra or La Puebla/Sa Pobla. Some hotels and businesses insist on using Castilian forms for their addresses, so you may find your hotel is listed as being in Puerto Sóller or Puerto Pollensa, but you will have to follow road signs for Port de Sóller or Port de Pollença to get there!

Some Place Name Pronunciations

Cala de Sant Vicenç 'kah-lah de-sant vee-sens'
Lluc 'l'yook'
Mallorca 'my-orka'
Pollença 'pol-yen-sa'
Puig 'pooj' (with a soft j)
Sóller 'sole-yair'
Ternelles 'tern-ell-yes'
Valldemossa 'vall-day-moh-sah'

TOPOGRAPHICAL GLOSSARY

This glossary is given in Catalan and English only, to assist walkers who are interested in place names in order to be able to unravel their meanings. The list contains names that occur regularly on maps and throughout this guide. Some names seen frequently on signs are also included. (Where some Castilian place names might still be lingering, these are shown in brackets.)

albufera	lagoon
alzina	evergreen oak
aguila	eagle
arena	sand
avenc	deep cleft
avinguda (avenida)	avenue
badia	bay
baix	low
bassa	small pool
barranc	ravine
bini	house of (Arabic)
blanca	white
bosc	woodland
cala	small bay or cove
caleta	small bay
camí	path
camp	field
can/ca'n	house of
canaleta	open canal
cap	rocky point
capella	chapel
carrer (calle)	street
cas/casa	house
castell	castle
cavall	horse
cingle	cliff
clot	hollow/depression
cocó/cocons	very small rockpool/s
coll	mountain pass
coma	valley
comellar	small valley
comuna	communal land
corral	animal pen
costa	coast

cova/coves	cave/caves
des/d'es	of the
embassament	reservoir
ermita	hermitage
es	the
església	church
finca	farm or country estate
font	spring/fountain
forn de calç	limekiln
gorg	a pool in a gorge
gran	big
illa/illes	island/s
jardí	garden
llarga	long
lluc	personal name, Luke
major	main/big
mar	sea
migdia	midday
mirador	viewpoint
mola	tooth
moleta	mill
monestir	monastery
moro	Moor (Arab)
morro	snout
museu	museum
neu	snow
palau	palace
parc	park
pas	a 'rake' or rocky scramble
penya/penyal	steep-sided mountain
pic	peak
pla	plain/flat land
plaça (plaza)	square
platja (playa)	beach
pont	bridge
port (puerto)	port or harbour
porta	door
porxo	shelter
puig	hill or mountai
punta	rocky point
racó	hidden corner
rafal	small farm attached to finca

rei	king
roca	rock
roig	red
rota	marginal farm
salt d'aigua	waterfall
santuari	sanctuary
Sant/Santa	male/female saint
serra	mountain range
serreta	a small 'serra'
sitja/sitges	charcoal-burning site/s
talaia	watch tower
torre	tower
torrent	river
vall	valley
vell	old
vent	wind
verd	green
verger	fertile area
vinyes	vineyard

APPENDIX 4

FURTHER READING

WALKING GUIDEBOOKS

Beese, Gerhard, *Richtig wandern: Mallorca* (2nd ed., Koln, Dumont, 1990)

Crespi-Green, Valerie, *Landscapes of Mallorca: A Countryside Guide* (several editions, London, Sunflower Books)

Goetz, Rolf, *Mallorca* (Rother)

Heinrich, Herbert, *12 Classic Hikes Through Majorca* (several editions, Palma, Editorial Moll)

Llofriu, Pere, *Caminant per Mallorca* (Manuals d'introduccio a la naturalesa, 8, 2nd ed. Palma, Editorial Moll, 1989)

Palos, Benigne, *Itineraris de Muntanya: excursions a peu per la Serra de Mallorca* (2nd ed. – Manuals d'introduccio a la naturalesa, 5 – Palma, Editorial Moll, 1984)

Palos, Benigne, *Valldemossa Com a Centre D'excursions* (Mallorca, Editorial Moll, 1989)

Vallcaneras, Lluís, *20 Itineraris Alternatius per la Serra de Tramuntana (I)* (several editions, Palma)

NATURAL HISTORY BOOKS

General

Parrack, James D, *The Naturalist in Majorca* (David & Charles, Newton Abbot, 1973, out of print)

Birds

Bannerman, David & Bannerman, W Mary, *The Birds of the Balearics*, illus. by Donald Watson (Croom Helm, 1983)

Busby, John, *Birds in Mallorca* (Christopher Helm, 1988)

Hearl, G and King, J, *A Birdwatching Guide to Mallorca* (Arlequin Pubns, 1995)

Heinzel, Herman & others, *The Birds of Britain and Europe with North Africa and the Middle East* (Collins, London 1972)

Peterson, Roger, & others, *A Field Guide to the Birds of Britain and Europe* (4th ed., Collins, London, 1983)

Serra, Joan Mayol *The birds of the Balearic islands* (tr. from the Catalan by Hannah Bonner, Editorial Moll, Mallorca, 1990)

Stoba, Ken, *Birdwatching in Mallorca* (Cicerone Press, 1990)

Watkinson, Eddie, *A Guide to Birdwatching in Mallorca* (2nd ed., J.G.Sanders, Alderney, 1982)

Flowers

Beckett, Elspeth, *Wild flowers of Majorca, Minorca and Ibiza; with keys to the flora of the Balearic islands* (Balkema, Rotterdam, 1988)

Bonner, Anthony, *Plants of the Balearic islands* (Manuals d'introduccio a la naturelesa, 1, Editorial Moll, Palma, 1982)

Polunin, Oleg and Huxley, Anthony, *Flowers of the Mediterranean* (Chatto and Windus, 1972)

Polunin, Oleg, *Flowers of Europe: A Field Guide* (OUP, 1969)

Straka, Herbert, & others *Führer zur Flora von Mallorca/Guide to the Flora of Majorca* (Gustav Fischer Verlag, Stuttgart/New York 1987; in German, English, Spanish and French)

Geology

Adams, A E, *Mallorcan Geology: A Geological Excursion Guide* (Dept of Extramural Studies, University College, Cardiff, 1988)

Jenkyns, H C & others, *A Field Excursion Guide to the Geology of Mallorca* (Geologists Association Guide, ed. C J Lister, 1990)

GENERAL INTEREST

Berlitz Travel Guide, *Majorca and Minorca* (English ed. dist. by Cassell, 1982)

Facaros, Dana & Pauls, Michael, *Mediterranean Island Hopping: The Spanish Islands, A Handbook for the Independent Traveller* (Sphere Books, London, 1981)

Fenn, Patricia, *Entree to Mallorca* (Quiller Press, 1993)

Foss, Arthur, *Majorca* (Faber and Faber, 1972)

Graves, Robert and Hogarth, Paul, *Majorca Observed* (Cassell, 1965)

Lee, Phil, *Mallorca and Menorca* (Rough Guide, 1996)

Sand, George, *Winter in Majorca* (tr and annotated by Robert Graves, Valldemossa, 1956)

Thurston, Hazel, *The Travellers' Guide to the Balearics: Majorca, Minorca, Ibiza and Formentera* (Jonathan Cape, 1979)

LANGUAGE

Get by in Spanish: A Quick Beginners' Course for Holidaymakers and Business People (BBC, 1977)

Ellis, D L & Ellis, R, *Travellers' Spanish* (Pan Books, 1981)

Oliva, Salvador, & Buxton, Angela. *Diccionari Català-Angles* (Barcelona, 1985)

LISTING OF CICERONE GUIDES

BRITISH ISLES CHALLENGES, COLLECTIONS AND ACTIVITIES
The End to End Trail
The Mountains of England and Wales
  Vol 1: Wales
  Vol 2: England
The National Trails
The Relative Hills of Britain
The Ridges of England, Wales and Ireland
The UK Trailwalker's Handbook
Three Peaks, Ten Tors
Unjustifiable Risk? A social history of climbing
World Mountain Ranges: Scotland

NORTHERN ENGLAND TRAILS
A Northern Coast to Coast Walk
Backpacker's Britain: Northern England
Hadrian's Wall Path
The Dales Way
The Pennine Way
The Spirit of Hadrian's Wall

LAKE DISTRICT
An Atlas of the English Lakes
Coniston Copper Mines
Great Mountain Days in the Lake District
Lake District Winter Climbs
Roads and Tracks of the Lake District
Rocky Rambler's Wild Walks
Scrambles in the Lake District North & South
Short Walks in Lakeland
  Book 1: South Lakeland
  Book 2: North Lakeland
  Book 3: West Lakeland
The Central Fells
The Cumbria Coastal Way
The Cumbria Way and the Allerdale Ramble
The Lake District Anglers' Guide
The Mid-Western Fells
The Near Eastern Fells
The Southern Fells
The Tarns of Lakeland
  Vol 1: West
  Vol 2: East
Tour of the Lake District

NORTH WEST ENGLAND AND THE ISLE OF MAN
A Walker's Guide to the Lancaster Canal
Historic Walks in Cheshire
Isle of Man Coastal Path
The Isle of Man
The Ribble Way
Walking in Lancashire
Walking in the Forest of Bowland and Pendle
Walking on the West Pennine Moors
Walks in Lancashire Witch Country
Walks in Ribble Country
Walks in Silverdale and Arnside
Walks in The Forest of Bowland

NORTH EAST ENGLAND, YORKSHIRE DALES AND PENNINES
Historic Walks in North Yorkshire
South Pennine Walks
The Cleveland Way and the Yorkshire Wolds Way
The North York Moors
The Reivers Way
The Teesdale Way
The Yorkshire Dales Angler's Guide
The Yorkshire Dales:
  North and East
  South and West
Walking in County Durham
Walking in Northumberland
Walking in the North Pennines
Walking in the Wolds
Walks in Dales Country
Walks in the Yorkshire Dales
Walks on the North York Moors
  Books 1 & 2

DERBYSHIRE, PEAK DISTRICT AND MIDLANDS
High Peak Walks
Historic Walks in Derbyshire
The Star Family Walks
Walking in Derbyshire
White Peak Walks:
  The Northern Dales
  The Southern Dales

SOUTHERN ENGLAND
A Walker's Guide to the Isle of Wight
London: The Definitive Walking Guide
The Cotswold Way
The Greater Ridgeway
The Lea Valley Walk
The North Downs Way
The South Downs Way
The South West Coast Path
The Thames Path
Walking in Bedfordshire
Walking in Berkshire
Walking in Buckinghamshire
Walking in Kent
Walking in Sussex
Walking in the Isles of Scilly
Walking in the Thames Valley
Walking on Dartmoor

WALES AND WELSH BORDERS
Backpacker's Britain: Wales
Glyndwr's Way
Great Mountain Days in Snowdonia
Hillwalking in Snowdonia
Hillwalking in Wales
  Vols 1 & 2
Offa's Dyke Path
Ridges of Snowdonia
Scrambles in Snowdonia
The Ascent of Snowdon
The Lleyn Peninsula Coastal Path
The Pembrokeshire Coastal Path
The Shropshire Hills
The Spirit Paths of Wales
Walking in Pembrokeshire
Walking on the Brecon Beacons
Welsh Winter Climbs

SCOTLAND
Backpacker's Britain:
  Central and Southern Scottish Highlands
  Northern Scotland
Ben Nevis and Glen Coe
Border Pubs and Inns
North to the Cape
Not the West Highland Way
Scotland's Best Small Mountains